The Feminist Standpoint Revisited
and Other Essays

FEMINIST THEORY AND POLITICS

Virginia Held and Alison Jaggar, Series Editors

The Feminist Standpoint Revisited and Other Essays,
Nancy C.M. Hartsock

Feminists Rethink the Self,
edited by Diana Tietjens Meyers

*Revisioning the Political: Feminist Reconstructions
of Traditional Concepts in Western Political Theory,*
edited by Nancy J. Hirschmann and Christine Di Stephano

Care, Autonomy, and Justice: Feminism and the Ethic of Care,
Grace Clement

A Mind of One's Own: Feminist Essays on Reason and Objectivity,
edited by Louise M. Antony and Charlotte Witt

The Feminist Standpoint Revisited and Other Essays

Nancy C.M. Hartsock

Westview Press
A Member of Perseus Books, L.L.C.

For Genevieve and Ruth

Grateful acknowledgment for allowing us to quote Nancy Hirschmann on the cover is made to *Women and Politics* 18(3), 1997 (Binghampton, N.Y.: The Haworth Press, Inc.), p. 73.

Published in 1998 in the United States of America by Westview Press, 5500 Central Avenue, Boulder, Colorado 80301-2877, and in the United Kingdom by Westview Press, 12 Hid's Copse Road, Cumnor Hill, Oxford OX2 9JJ

Library of Congress Cataloging-in-Publication Data
Hartsock, Nancy C.M.
    The feminist standpoint revisited and other essays / Nancy C.M. Hartsock.
        p. cm.
    Includes index.
    ISBN 0-8133-1557-3
    1. Feminist theory. I. Title.
HQ1190.H374 1998
305.42'01—dc21   98-11317
                                                                                                              CIP

The paper used in this publication meets the requirements of the American National Standard for Permanence of Paper for Printed Library Materials Z39.48-1984.

10   9   8   7   6   5   4   3   2   1

Contents

Acknowledgments   ix

Introduction   1

written 1974-1980, in political activism

PART ONE: Political Movements and Political Theories   9

1 Political Change: Two Perspectives on Power   *Quest*   15

Power, Change, and Social Science, 15
Other Approaches to Political Change, 18
The Personal and the Political, 18
Organization and Leadership, 20
Patriarchy, Capitalism, and White Supremacy, 22
Ideas and History, 25
Conclusions, 28
Notes, 29

2 Fundamental Feminism: Process and Perspective *Quest*   32

Patriarchal Socialism and Socialist Feminism, 33
Feminism as a Mode of Analysis, 35
Integrating Personal and Political Change, 36
Recognizing Process and Interaction, 37
Appropriation, Necessity, and Revolution, 38
Feminist Theory and Practice, 38
New Directions, 39
Organizations and Strategies, 40
Conclusion, 41
Notes, 42

3 Staying Alive   *Quest*   44

Estranged Labor, 45
Work: The Central Human Activity, 47
Alternatives to Estranged Labor, 48
Power and Political Change, 49
Mental and Manual Labor, 51
The Development of a Feminist Workplace, 51

Collectives and Cooperatives Work, 52
Conclusions: The Fragility of Alternatives, 54
Notes, 54

4 **Difference and Domination in the Women's Movement:
   The Dialectic of Theory and Practice**   56

The Denial of Difference, 58
Difference as Domination in Feminist Practice, 59
Transforming Difference into Specificity, 62
Empowerment and Difference, 63
Difference and Domination: Breaking the Links, 64
Difference and Creativity: Toward a New Understanding
   of Power, 67
Conclusion, 70
Notes, 70

PART TWO: Reoccupying Marxism as Feminism   73

5 **Objectivity and Revolution: The Unity of Observation
   and Outrage in Marxist Theory**   85

Human Activity as Ontology, 87
The Unity of Outrage and Observation in
   Marxist Analysis, 91
Objectivity, 94
Knowledge as Appropriation, 98
Objectivity and Revolution, 100
Notes, 101

6 **The Feminist Standpoint: Developing the Ground
   for a Specifically Feminist Historical Materialism**   105

The Nature of a Standpoint, 107
The Sexual Division of Labor, 113
Abstract Masculinity and the Feminist Standpoint, 117
Conclusion, 125
Notes, 127

7 **Louis Althusser's Structuralist Marxism:
   Political Clarity and Theoretical Distortions**   133

Althusser's Marxism, 136
The Last Instance, 137
Theoretical Antihumanism, 148
The Production of Knowledge: Theoretical Practice and
   Political Practice, 152

Althusserian Politics, 159
Notes, 162
References, 164

PART THREE: Structuralism, Poststructuralism, and Politics   167

8 The Kinship Abstraction in Feminist Theory   171

Language, Symbols, and Values, 173
The Exchange of Women as Social Contract, 178
Lévi-Strauss's Marxism, 184
Notes, 186

**9 Gayle Rubin: The Abstract Determinism
of the Kinship System   192**

Rubin's Reading of Lévi-Strauss, 194
Capitalist Production from the Perspective of
   the Exchange Abstraction, 196
The Kinship System and the Production of Gender, 198
Conclusion, 201
Notes, 202

10 Postmodernism and Political Change   205

The Enlightenment Tradition, 206
The Construction of the Colonized Other, 207
Richard Rorty's Conversational Alternative, 211
Foucault's Resistance and Refusal, 215
Foucault's Perspective, 217
The Evanescence of Power, 219
Toward Liberatory Theories, 221
Notes, 223

11 The Feminist Standpoint Revisited   227

My Project, 228
Some Responses, 230
Reformulations, 239
Notes, 245

Afterword   249

Notes, 252

Index   254

Acknowledgments

I have for many years believed that feminist theory must be understood as a fundamentally collective enterprise. Despite the fact that these essays appear under my name, I view them as not simply indebted to others but as a representation of the work of many who are involved in dense webs of communities—both inside and outside the university. It is of course impossible to acknowledge all the people and institutions who have contributed to these essays. I have been very fortunate in being given opportunities to have conversations in many contexts. I would like to thank the many colleges, universities, and institutes that provided me with both audiences and temporary colleagues.

These essays are marked as well by several important contexts. And as I attempted to put together a list of some of those who helped through comments, intellectual challenges, dinners, or working together in organizations, I was struck by the fact that many of those I encountered first in one context resurfaced in others—some activists became academics, some academics left the university, and so on. First, I want to thank the women who worked on *Quest: A Feminist Quarterly* for introducing me to the possibilities, joys, and sorrows of doing feminist theory in the context of a feminist organization. The original staff included Charlotte Bunch, Jane Dolkart, Beverly Fisher-Manick, Alexa Freeman, Karen Kollias, and Mary-Helen Mautner. At the same time as I was working on the journal, I was involved in a very fruitful feminist theory discussion group, which met at Johns Hopkins University. At different times, it included Sarah Begus, Annette Bickel, Toby Ditz, Donna Haraway, Sandra Harding, Nancy Hirschmann, Emily Martin, and Harriet Whitehead. I also benefited from ongoing discussions with my colleagues Richard Flathman and J.G.A. Pocock. My ideas were influenced as well by my work with the Women's Union of Baltimore.

My students and colleagues at the University of Washington have also been willing to engage with me on these issues. Special thanks to Carolyn Allen, Judy Aks, Christine di Stefano, Judy Howard, Hyun Mee Kim, Thiven Reddy, Carol Reed, Karen Stuhldreher, and Kathi Weeks.

Many others influenced these essays by reading my work, engaging me in (sometimes) long distance conversations, or sharing their own work. Thanks to Martha Ackelsberg, Sandra Bartky, Nancie Caraway, Spencer

Carr, Sue Carroll, Robin Dennis, Irene Diamond, Zillah Eisenstein, Ann Ferguson, Kathy Ferguson, Jane Flax, Nancy Folbre, Ruth Frankenberg, Nancy Fraser, Heidi Hartmann, Frigga Haug, David Harvey, Val Hartouni, Susan Hekman, Virginia Held, Alison Jaggar, Fredric Jameson, Abdul Jan Mohamed, Rita Mae Kelly, Sally Kenney, Ynestra King, Stephanie Koontz, Sonia Kruks, Eva Kreisky, Jane Mansbridge, Bertell Ollman, Carole Pateman, V. Spike Peterson, Shane Phelan, Sarah Ruddick, Chela Sandoval, Dorothy Smith, Judith Stiehm, Barbara Schaeffer-Hegel, Roberta Spalter-Roth, Barrie Thorne, and Iris Young. Special thanks to Stephen Rose for his companionship and support during the writing of many of these essays.

Nancy C.M. Hartsock

Introduction

I never set out to become a feminist theorist. Indeed, when I set out to become a political theorist, such a choice was impossible because feminist theory in anything like its present form did not exist. Nor did I set out to become (in whatever sense I have become) a Marxist, since in terms of my graduate education, that possibility too did not exist. In looking over the essays that I have chosen to reprint I find myself asking how it happened. Each of these essays grew out of and responded to questions that arose from the social contexts in which I found myself. I am reminded of Jane Flax's thought on her own history: It "was pure luck from my individual point of view that the women's movement emerged when it did. What would have happened had I been ten years older?"[1] There are many "what ifs" involved in the writing of these essays.

As I reflect on these essays, which span a period of twenty years, I am struck with the extent to which they are autobiographical in that they respond to issues I found urgent at different times. In this regard, my work is no different than that of other political theorists: Every social context poses questions for those who inhabit it, construct it, and are in turn constructed by it. Could Machiavelli have written *The Prince* or *The Discourses* in a context where the Roman Republic was not held up as the best possible society, in contrast to the world in which he lived? But I think it is important to remember not only the ways the content and concerns of political theorists express/reflect the questions of the historical moments in which they were written. These essays were written in the context of a series of feminist communities concerned with both reading and writing about issues such as these and using what we were learning to bring about change—in fact, massive social change. These pieces are of course my own, and their limitations are mine as well. Still, in writing them I was responding to the concerns of many women of my generation who, like myself, were committed to feminist goals. As a result, I see feminist theory as a collective political practice. As the communities that they were written both among and for changed over the years, so did the questions. For example, as feminist theory moved solidly into the academy, questions rooted in academic disciplines became more prominent.

1

So how did the concerns elaborated here come to be? The roots of my activism were in social gospel Methodism but with an unusual twist. I grew up in a lower-middle-class family in Ogden, Utah, a town where almost everyone else was Mormon, and in which not only Protestants and Catholics but even Jews were considered to be "gentiles." My family experienced life in a theocracy in which our religion had important effects on every aspect of our social life—work, friendships, possibilities for advancement on the job, and even possibilities of getting a job. As a teenager, I remember that those of us who were gentiles developed a code to identify each other: When we were unsure of others in a group, we always ordered coffee, a stimulant proscribed by Mormonism. I think it was that experience that led me to question choices about grounds for exclusion and to puzzle over why and how the selected grounds were made into such powerful social forces.

I attended an elite women's college (Wellesley) in the early sixties. That experience also raised a number of questions for me, in some cases questions that I was only able to formulate years later, questions about both class and about expectations for (middle- and upper-class) women. During my years there, I knew only that I was profoundly uncomfortable. My questions at the time took very specific forms: Why should scholarship students, who mostly hadn't had the advantages of a private school education, be required to work for the college for several hours a week, when they needed the time to study in order to catch up to the nonscholarship students? (Many scholarship students also had jobs for wages at the college.) What did it say about a concern for the school's reputation but not necessarily student safety that an overnight stay in Boston required a separate parental letter for each stay, whereas a stay outside a certain radius would be permitted on the basis of one annual letter, appropriately named a "blanket permission"? Why should a women's college sponsor almost-annual, highly publicized debates about why and whether a woman should receive a higher education? Why did we have to bring high heels to a required gym class and practice walking across the gym floor to sit gracefully in an armchair brought in for the exercise? What did our class motto, "gracious living," mean? Why were all the Black students on campus for "Junior Year in the North" given single rooms? Clearly these questions had a great deal to do with intersections of class and gender and the state of white racism in the "enlightened" North.

At the same time, the civil rights movement was in full organizing swing in the South and some of us in the North were attempting to lend it support. I became involved with (and later cochaired) the Wellesley Civil Rights Group. We engaged in a number of activities such as tutoring children in Boston and trying to raise money to send to those working in the South. The rhetoric and actions of the civil rights movement in the South during this period and the theories that were developing out of it were part of a crucial series of transitions for me. What movement activists were saying about segregation resonated with what I had experienced growing up. (I certainly do not mean to compare my experience to that of a southern Black child during that period, but rather to mark the beginnings of a point of contact and support.)[2]

I went to graduate school in political science (my undergraduate major) at the University of Chicago and soon became involved with electoral politics and efforts to work against the Daley Machine. Chicago politics then was almost completely controlled by the Machine, and many city workers were in reality patronage employees whose main purpose was to deliver votes on election day (buying them with cash if necessary) and to punish those who voted against the Machine candidates. Abner Mikva, a White House counsel in the mid-nineties, was running for Congress against the Machine in 1966. He was the first on what became a long list of losing candidates I worked for and supported. In the process, I learned a great deal about how democratic forms can be subverted and how power can maintain itself both by using and strategically ignoring these forms.

During the summer of 1966, Martin Luther King, Jr. brought the Southern Christian Leadership Conference (SCLC) to Chicago to show that prejudice was not just a Southern problem, and Chicago and its suburbs proved him right. I participated in the marches to demonstrate against segregation in housing and against the redlining of areas so that Black Chicagoans were unable to buy or rent housing. By this time, the student movement and the antiwar movement were also beginning. My involvement in these movements raised a variety of questions for me about how committed I could and would be to social justice. The civil rights and antiwar marches were often frightening; in the former, people were attacked by local residents, and in the latter, by federal agents and local police. Moreover, we were often confronting those who had not only legitimate authority in society but also vastly more resources than we had. The question of what I would or could risk for what I believed to be right emerged for me during this period and remains with me to this day.

It is interesting and disturbing to remember that while I was involved in these marches, the student movement, and the antiwar movement, nothing in my formal studies at a university located on the South Side of Chicago, an area with a large Black population (most of them poor), addressed these issues. There were debates about whether political science was a science like physics or whether social sciences were inherently inferior. In terms of political theory, my Straussian teachers argued that the classic works of political thought were accessible only to those who were able to read between the lines to find the concealed messages only there for exceptional thinkers.

My time in Chicago as an activist and a graduate student taught me
several things. It gave me a sense of the extent to which politics and government can matter in people's everyday lives. For example, during the
years in which I volunteered one afternoon a week for the Fifth Ward alderman, the only non-Machine alderman in the city during those years, I
learned that snowplowing was a political, rather than a maintenance, issue. The aldermen played an important role in this, as constituents rou-
tinely called to request service. But the pattern which emerged in the Fifth
Ward (which was obviously not at the top of the priority list for snow-
plows) was one in which the middle-class people of Hyde Park called
right away for plowing, whereas the building supervisors for the poor
and working-class people in Woodlawn called only when coal supplies
had become dangerously low. The juxtaposition of Hyde Park and Woodlawn not only made class and race issues prominent, but it also illustrated
on the ground how entangled these two are in the United States. Class
has far too often been coded as race, and discussions of racial differences
have assumed that all people of color are poor or working class. This has
impeded both systematic efforts to discuss the role of class divisions and
efforts to disentangle and reentangle the complex connections between
race and class. One can see some of the results in arenas such as the public
discussions of the Anita Hill–Clarence Thomas hearings, or the recent debates about how to abolish welfare as we know it.

I tried to combine my academic work with my political interests in my
dissertation, *Politics, Ideology, and Ordinary Language: The Political Thought
of Black Community Leaders*. I was fortunate not only to have a job at the
National Opinion Research Center on a large study of school desegrega-
tion in 95 Northern cities but also to be able to insert questions into an at-
titude/ideology questionnaire that would go to over 450 Black community leaders who had worked on desegregating the schools. I wanted to
explore a fairly traditional issue in political theory—the concept of obligation, specifically, obligations between citizens and states. But perhaps
more important, I wanted to demonstrate that these Black community
leaders were practical political theorists whose concerns echoed those of
Hobbes, Locke, Rousseau, and Mill and were therefore people who
should be taken more seriously as political thinkers, not dismissed as
street-corner orators.

During all this time, I had no formal education in either feminist theory
or Marxist theory. No formal education in feminist theory between 1965
and 1970 is perhaps understandable, since at that time the work of previous generations had been very successfully suppressed or lost. Most of us
did not know who our predecessors were or what they had written. More
surprisingly, perhaps, Marxist theory was not taught, despite its importance as a world-wide social movement that had made a large number of

theoretically sophisticated contributions. My only classroom encounter with Marxist theory was contained in one week of a course on the history of political thought.

Between 1969 and 1970, feminism began to emerge both on campus and off. Three friends and I began our own consciousness-raising group; the Women's Radical Action Project began at the University of Chicago; WITCH (Women's International Terrorist Conspiracy from Hell) performed several hexes; and the Chicago Women's Liberation Union came into existence. I was job hunting and only peripherally involved with the latter three groups. I was successful in finding a job but suffered the misfortune of being the first woman hired by the University of Michigan political science department.

In 1970, the political science department at the University of Michigan was already very large, made up of over fifty white men—some welcoming, others with no idea of how to deal with a female colleague—one Sri Lankan man, and me.[3] The next year the department hired two American Black men. The four of us, along with one white man, began to think about a program in political science that would be responsive to the needs and interests of Black graduate students and women graduate students. We wanted a new subfield called political economy. And we wanted an entering graduate class that would be half Black and half women (25 percent of each group), and thus made up of only 25 percent white men. Needless to say, the department was resistant. The next two years were spent struggling to make this a reality. Because of cooperation between the Black Matters Committee and the Women's Caucus, we came very close to meeting our goals for the new graduate class. Curricular matters were difficult, and it became evident to some of us that we would not be allowed to remain at the University of Michigan. During this period, I was also involved with the faculty committee to begin Women's Studies at the university but was too constrained by time-consuming departmental politics to be very much involved in the exciting things that were happening in Women's Studies there in 1972 and 1973.

I learned many negative things about the academic world in this period. In an institution with the stated goal of a search for knowledge, those who wanted to explore new or different ideas were penalized, sometimes to the point of having careers destroyed. Those who wanted to change the boundaries of the fields of inquiry inherited from the nineteenth century were told that their questions were not "real" questions of knowledge that belonged in the university. And those who wanted to make the possibilities of the life of the mind available to some for whom this had not been a possibility because of race or gender were given the message by Kingman Brewster, president of Yale at the time, who said so eloquently that Yale had the responsibility to educate 1,000 (white) male leaders a year.

I spent the summer of 1973 and the following academic year on leave thinking about whether I wanted to continue as an academic. I spent the summer in Paris with many pounds of reading material—most of it Marxist literature I had begun to read. I lived on a street that was a center for prostitution and that served the truckers of the wholesale market, Les Halles (since torn down). Besides the prostitutes, there were the several alcoholics who worked in the box factory on the first floor of my apartment building. From my apartment, I could see through the windows of the apartment building across the narrow street into the crowded dormitory rooms of Algerian guest workers. I went to the Bibliothèque Nationale and read the first volume of *Capital.* I found I could not put it down. It fit not only some of my own experiences but also what I walked through on a daily basis. And then I began to read the rest—or at least some of the rest: *The Economic and Philosophical Manuscripts of 1844, The German Ideology*, several volumes from the Frankfurt School, and more.

Since I had been close to the male Left and the Marxist Left in the United States, I had previously run into interpretations of these and other texts. I had found these interpretations at the least unhelpful and at the most simply bizarre. When I had tried to figure out how Stalin's *Historical and Dialectical Materialism* could possibly make sense with a group of others, under the direction of someone who was supposed to know, it was not a helpful exercise in creative thinking—or perhaps it should be seen as an exercise in very creative thinking. But reading alone, without a specific direction, I was able to find sections of Marx's own writing that spoke to me. This is not to say that I found Marx totally satisfactory. Despite his recognition of the difficulties women have faced, the heart of his theory excludes women in favor of examining the male worker and his life with an assumed-to-be wife.[4]

While on leave, I moved to Washington, D.C., clear that I had had enough of midwestern winters and unclear about my future as an academic. I sat in on a feminist theory course taught by Charlotte Bunch through the Institute for Policy Studies. She had been active in women's liberation in Washington and subsequently was a member of the Furies, a lesbian-feminist separatist group. She had come to feel that her position was too isolating and was attempting to reach a larger and more diverse audience. The sessions proved to be an excellent way for me to become involved in at least one segment of what was then a badly split feminist movement in the city; they also introduced me to the theoretical ideas of lesbian feminism as developed by the Furies, in the wake of the "Woman Identified Woman" statement by Radicalesbians. The experience also led to my involvement with the group of women who came together to start *Quest: A Feminist Quarterly*. We wanted to address ideas from a variety of feminist perspectives and to explore questions of power and leadership in the context of divisions by class, race, and sexuality. We were movement activists who wanted to connect theory with our activism and who saw theory as an important tool for developing better strategies. And so began what has now become my career as a feminist theorist.

In the introductions to the three parts of this book, I say more about the specifics of writing the essays I have chosen to reproduce here. But as I reflect on the collection as a whole, it is evident that there are two central convictions that have motivated these essays over the years. The first is that theory plays an important part in political action for social change. The second is that political theorists must respond to and concentrate their energies on problems of political action, most fruitfully as these problems emerge in the context of efforts for social change. The essays gathered here take up two interlocking themes: power and epistemology. The importance of issues of power for activists committed to social change cannot be exaggerated. We need to know how relations of domination are constructed, how we participate in these relations, how we resist, and how we might transform them. Given the history of the feminist movement, with its initial distrust of leadership and fear of power, it is an especially important topic for feminist theory to address. In the contemporary context, with attention focused on multiplicity, interlocking and crosscutting patterns on the one hand, and the complete triumph of market ideology on the other, attention to issues of systematic relations of power becomes both more difficult to sustain and more crucial. The focus on multiplicity and the articulation of a variety of subject positions can lead us away from sustained attention to systematic axes of domination. It can dilute theorizing and make it instead into complex descriptions that are not only local but also unique and therefore less useful in setting broad outlines of strategies for change. The triumph of the ideology of the market obscures issues of power in a different way: In theory, when we enter the market, we arrive in an environment populated by free and equal individuals who have chosen to come together for their mutual benefit, none with power over any others. Moreover, it is often claimed that the market can act as a school for democracy and a tool for encouraging democracy. I, however, see the market as a mechanism for increasing inequality both globally and locally. And at the same time, it obscures systematic power relations and the structure of global capitalism.

Questions of epistemology are a second concern that has animated these essays. Efforts to understand the workings of power necessarily lead to larger questions. Different theorizations of power rest on differing assumptions about both the content of existence and the ways we come to know it. There are now, of course, many questions about whether such knowledge is possible, but this too is an epistemological stance.[5] Thus, my interest in systematic power relations led me to questions involving the appropriate methods for research, alternative epistemologies and ontologies, and the relation of theories of knowledge to human activity. Although these issues may not at first seem closely connected to questions about power relations, I have found them essential to my efforts at understanding more about how we both construct and are constructed by social relations. These essays reflect the juxtaposition of these two themes.

NOTES

1. Jane Flax, *Disputed Subjects* (New York: Routledge, 1993), p. 8.

2. See the moving account by Anne Moody, *Coming of Age in Mississippi* (New York: Dell, 1968).

3. For the sake of historical accuracy I should report that I was not in fact the first woman hired by the University of Michigan political science department. Nellie Varner, a Black woman with a Ph.D. from that department had been hired a year earlier, but she went directly into administration. Thus I was the first woman to occupy the halls of the department on a daily basis.

4. I laid out a number of my differences with Marx in the Introduction to Part 2 of my book *Money, Sex, and Power* (New York: Longman, 1983; Boston: Northeastern University Press, 1984).

5. My point here is similar to W. B. Gallie's point that power is an "essentially contested" concept. Gallie, however, seems not to have recognized the epistemological implications of his position. See W. B. Gallie, "Essentially Contested Concepts," *Proceedings of the Aristotelian Society* 56 (1955–1956), 167–198.

Part One

Political Movements and Political Theories

Over the course of 1973, a group of feminists in Washington, D.C., came together to try to overcome some of the fragmentation of the D.C. women's movement after a bitter split between lesbian and heterosexual women. By the time I arrived in Washington and became involved with the group in the fall of 1973, that group had decided to begin publication of a journal that was to be more than a journal, really an organizing tool. As Charlotte Bunch put it, the story of *Quest*'s early years consists of several stories:[1] It is a story of feminist theory and its evolution in the women's movement, of tensions between theory and action and between intellectual and activist demands. It is the story of a feminist group determined to create a nonauthoritarian work process based on feminist principles of cooperation and sharing of skills, a process that would also meet the rigorous demands of publishing. Finally, it is a story about the effort to build a feminist institution with an independent economic base controlled by women. We saw producing the journal not as an end in itself but as one part of a series of strategies. Most important, we saw the journal as a way to debate issues and develop ideas that could be the basis for a new national organization or (with the ambition characteristic of the 1970s) a new political party.

As Karen Kollias wrote in the introduction to the first issue:

> Our goal is to promote a continuing, active search for ideologies and strategies that will bring about the most comprehensive change by the most effective and humane methods. . . . *Quest* wishes to explore differences and similarities in ideologies and strategies among the various segments of the women's movement. We are about strategies. *Quest* wishes to contribute to the evolution of better strategy and tactics, to be a process for evaluating previous theory and practice. . . . We are about change. We assume that the women's movement, and those involved in it, consider complete and funda-

mental change as a primary goal. We are about ideology, . . . The time has come to expand feminist ideology. Differences in geographical location, race, class, sex preference, religion, age and other factors must be included for a broader, more realistic ideology that moves toward a workable base for unity.[2]

We shared the conviction that political action relied on political theory and that political theory was central to the success of activism. We aimed our journal at activists and worked hard to get activists to write about their experiences, their ideas for the future, and what they had learned about successful and unsuccessful strategies. *Quest*, as both an organization and a journal, was attempting to be politically relevant to current issues *and* intellectually rigorous in developing the long-term implications of theory. We saw questions of class, race, and sexual oppression as central to our movement. Many of us had worked in the civil rights movement, and others had been active in the D.C. Statehood Party.

Our living in a majority Black city made race a prominent and unavoidable issue for us. Issues of class in the women's movement were usually not addressed but had been raised by the Furies, and that group had done some of the most fruitful thinking and writing about class at the time. The Furies was a lesbian-feminist separatist collective that split from the rest of the D.C. women's liberation movement in 1971. Its members decided that they would not only work together but also live together. In a matter of days, class issues became a difficult problem. The group, however, avoided further splits and began a series of analyses of how class functioned in the women's movement.

Several of the *Quest* staff members had been part of the Furies and others had been close to that group.[3] This background was important in the kinds of issues and analyses *Quest* sought out and published. The focus on class was also a result of the fact that over half of the original staff grew up in lower- or working-class circumstances, and most of the staff had experienced the strains that class differences had produced in the women's movement. This too became an important concern in the kinds of analyses *Quest* sought out and published. The issue of oppression on the basis of sexuality was also an issue that had roots in the activist histories of a number of staff members. *Quest* came to articulate the position that lesbian feminism was not a matter of identity but a useful political perspective that could guide feminist analysis, whether produced by lesbians or not.[4] This represented an important early critique of identity politics.

In the manner of many feminist groups, we wanted to use our organization to prefigure the society we wanted. Therefore, we thought carefully about how to organize our work, how to assign responsibility, how to allow for power differences, and so on. *Quest* for some years was run out of Charlotte Bunch's office while she was a fellow at the Institute for Policy Studies, a Left think tank in Washington, D.C. We usually had three full-time staff people, who sometimes had to exist on unemployment insurance, and ten or so part-time staff people, and later we developed other kinds of relationships to the journal/organization, depending on the time and effort people could contribute. We were very conscious that we needed to recognize the specific work that staff members did and not to insist that we were all equal or all, in a sense, alike. We wanted to recognize and develop our different skills. Unlike *Off Our Backs,* the other national feminist publication that came out of Washington, D.C. (and is still publishing), we did not all do layout. Indeed, after my own first (lengthy) attempt to add a letter to a laid-out page, I was banned from all further layout activities and became instead the subscription department.

All this sounds very simple and easy from the perspective of 1997, but in fact none of it was. We were inventing our politics, our organizations, and ourselves, all at the same time. During my first years of working on and with *Quest,* I sometimes found my situation problematic: I was the only academic (an assistant professor at Johns Hopkins University) and, perhaps more important, the only practicing heterosexual in a group and in a city that had very recently experienced one of the more bitter "gay-straight" splits.

Developing our ideas about political change took first priority, and we made it a point to have dinner before our regular weekly meetings where we planned special issues, decided on new directions, and worked through the politics of the articles we were going to publish or wanted to find. The editing process was very much a part of what I now refer to as collective writing. The group as a whole discussed each piece and the political directions we believed it was important to stress. Then the work was assigned to a committee of two that aggressively edited the work. Although some authors from outside the group were able to keep their own article titles, titles were more often than not collectively invented during our weekly meetings. The products, especially those written by group members, could not be attributed in any clear way to the original author. The questions we wanted to address were very large ones. How involved should we be in the efforts to gain statehood for D.C.? What should we say about prostitution? Where should we look for money to publish? How should we relate to the United Nations Decade of Women? What kind of society do we want? How do we get what we want?

This is the general context in which the essays in this section were written. Chapter 1, "Political Change: Two Perspectives on Power," originally published in summer 1974, was my first effort to write about feminism in a theoretical way. As it happened, the "famous feminist" we had asked to write an essay on political change was too busy. And so I volunteered to do it. Until I wrote this essay, I had seen my feminism as separate from my academic work. But I began to see how some of what I had learned in graduate school could be of use in the nonacademic, political work I was doing. This piece, published in the first volume of *Quest: A Feminist Quarterly*, as we were learning how to write, edit, and publish, went through many drafts and many editors. I recall seeing one with corrections and changes in three different colors of pencil, from three different staff members.[5]

"Fundamental Feminism: Process and Perspective" (Chapter 2) proved to be a similar experience. It was very much a product of a group discussion about what we wanted to say as a journal and a political entity about the 1975 Socialist Feminist Conference. Those of us on the staff who had attended found ourselves profoundly dissatisfied with and angered by the speakers' tone and the agenda of the conference. We agreed on the points to be made, but I was the only one of us with a background in Marxist theory, as opposed to our shared backgrounds in Left and feminist activism. And so after a group discussion I wrote the article "Staying Alive" (Chapter 3—almost the only thing I have ever written without a colon in the title), which was a part of our special issue, titled *Work, Work, Work*, published in winter 1976–1977. This issue was a natural topic of concern for me, given the centrality of work in the Marxist theory, which has so influenced my own work. In this essay, as well as in "Fundamental Feminism," the freedom I had as an academic to explore different theories, the time to read, and to teach what I was reading contributed in a significant way to what I was able to bring to *Quest*.

By 1979–1980, it had become evident to a number of us that without institutional support of entities like IPS the demands of publishing a journal with few resources other than our subscription income precluded work on our more activist goals, and it was also becoming evident that our hopes for a national organization with more radical goals than NOW (the National Organization for Women) were futile. A number of us moved in different directions. I had by then divorced and moved closer to my job in Baltimore, and I became a part of a group of women who wanted to revive and expand the Women's Union of Baltimore, one of the socialist feminist organizations established in a number of cities in the seventies. We had a series of discussions about how socialist feminists in particular could contribute to feminist politics more generally, and about which issues might allow for more-inclusive feminist politics. We decided on a focus of violence against women and developed a series of speakouts and workshops for community organizations.

By this time, of course, women's studies was a presence on many other campuses. Chapter 4, "Difference and Domination in the Women's Movement," began as a contribution to a conference on scholarship and feminism held at Barnard in 1980. Taken together, these writings represent for me the kind of work that can be done in the context of a movement: The essays were part of a series of ongoing and almost daily discussions about how work should be organized, how to make political change, and how to understand what we were doing on an everyday basis.

I should also stress, however, that despite the number of notes, neither I nor my political science colleagues at Johns Hopkins saw these articles as academic work. Although women's studies had begun in some places as early as 1969 or 1970, the program was inaugurated at Johns Hopkins only in 1988. In fact, when I began to teach there in 1974, the graduating class was the first ever to include women and the student body was 65 percent male. Feminist theory was for me then clearly something I could not do in my "day job." These essays bear the marks of the time in which they were written, and I have, with the exception of putting back some material edited out of the published version of "Difference and Domination in the Women's Movement," left them in their published forms. They carry the sense of very large goals and the sense of hope and possibility that was then available. They also represent a kind of melding of the works of scholarship and political activism that may have been unique to the time but may also suggest some new possibilities for exchanges and common activities among academics and activists.

NOTES

1. The account of *Quest*'s history is from Charlotte Bunch's Introduction in *Building Feminist Theory: Essays from Quest: A Feminist Quarterly* (New York: Longman, 1981). She wrote the introduction to the collection of essays, which was then collectively edited (probably far more than she would have wished) by the other editors of the volume: Jane Flax, Alexa Freeman, Mary-Helen Mautner, and me. With the author's permission, I have reproduced much of pp. xv–xviii. See also Charlotte Bunch, Introduction, *Passionate Politics* (New York: St. Martin's Press, 1987).

2. Karen Kollias, "Spiral of Change: Introduction to *Quest*," *Quest: A Feminist Quarterly* 1, 1 (Summer 1974), 7–9.

3. This section significantly draws on the rest of Bunch's Introduction. The initial organizing group for *Quest* included Dolores Bargowski, Rita Mae Brown, Charlotte Bunch, Jane Dolkart, Beverly Fisher-Manick, Alexa Freeman, Nancy Hartsock, Karen Kollias, Mary-Helen Mautner, Emily Medvec, Gerry Traina, and Juanita Weaver.

4. See Charlotte Bunch, "Not for Lesbians Only," *Building Feminist Theory*, pp. 67–73. (Originally a speech she delivered to the first socialist feminist conference in Yellow Springs, Ohio, Summer 1975, it was reprinted in *Passionate Politics*, pp. 174–181). It should be read as a companion piece to my "Fundamental Feminism:

Process and Perspective," Chapter 2 in this volume. Both pieces represent instances of what I will call "collective writing." As Bunch noted in her Introduction, many of the articles grew out of discussions among the staff and with other movement organizers who were interviewed, cajoled, and encouraged to put their insights on paper (p. xviii).

5. This was all precomputer, so we tried to keep retyping to a minimum.

one

Political Change: Two Perspectives on Power

Feminists agree that the political change we seek means an end to sexism in all its forms, but political change involves more specific and more controversial goals as well. While most of us would agree that free, 24-hour, client-controlled child care and proper health care for women are goals whose achievement would both result from and represent major political change, agreement is not widespread about many other issues, such as the Equal Rights Amendment or campaigns to integrate women into police forces. Does the women's movement see the last two as demands for political change? Some women argue that they are not, while others see them as important and central political changes. In order to work effectively, we must understand what political change means from a feminist perspective and work out criteria for developing and evaluating strategies for change.

Power, Change, and Social Science

Power

Politics is about power—that much is generally agreed upon by practitioners and students of the political—and discussions of politics have included power as a fundamental concern. Most social scientists have based their

In *Building Feminist Theory: Essays from Quest* (New York: Longman, 1981). Originally published in *Quest: A Feminist Quarterly* 1, 1 (Summer 1974).

trad ⇒ power = power over
def.

discussions of power on definitions of power as the ability to compel obedience, or as control and domination. They link this definition with Bertrand
Russell's statement that power is the production of intended effects, and
add that power must be power over someone—something possessed, a
property of an actor such that he* can alter the will or actions of others in a
way that produces results in conformity with his own will.[1] Effects on the
actions of others are fundamental to this understanding of power.

Social theorists have argued that power, like money, is something possessed by an actor which has value in itself and which is useful as well for
obtaining other valued things. In an article on the concept of power, Talcott Parsons, the most influential of these theorists, states that he regards
power as "a circulating medium, analogous to money, within what is
called the political system," and suggests that we can best understand
power by looking at "the relevant properties of money as such a medium
in the economy."[2]

Parsons argues that money itself has no value in use but acts as a measure of value. He adds that modern monetary systems require an institutionalized confidence in the system as a whole, and argues that money
only works as a medium of exchange within networks of market relationships. By analogy, power "is generalized capacity to secure the perfor-
mance of binding obligations by units in a system of collective organization."[3] Both kinds of transactions require a system within which they can
be managed as symbols.

That Parsons and others compare the uses of power with the uses of
money in a capitalist market society indicates their acceptance of that society's assumptions about the nature of market transactions, and their expansion of these patterns to cover essentially all human interactions.
Their analogy of the uses of money and power supports Marx's claim that
the development of the importance of money (or, as Marx designated the
broader category, exchange value) leads to the transformation of all human activities into patterns modeled on monetary transactions.[4]

Money functions as a universal commodity, since it is defined as the exchange value of other commodities and at the same time has an independent existence. The parallel properties of power are apparent in the distinction between power as a value in itself and the other values one can
obtain if one has power.

Marx stressed the historical importance of exchange value in creating a
society in which power functions like money when he pointed out that
"the influence of exchange over all production relationships can only develop fully and ever more completely in bourgeois society."[5] Only in a so-

---

*Note on gender: "He" and men" are not generic terms in this article, but refer specifi-
cally to men and not women. Here, "she" is the more generic pronoun.

ciety based on the market, in which human interdependence is not personal but based on exchange value, can power come to be sought as a value in itself, and domination of others—or the use of power to "purchase" certain behavior—become the almost exclusive measure of power.

The idea that power refers to something possessed by individuals (a commodity) and means domination over others can be found in philosophical writing of the seventeenth century where it served as a justification for the ways society was managed and controlled by the marketplace.

Thomas Hobbes, one of the earliest and most influential theorists in this tradition, conceived of society as the structured relations of exchange between proprietors, and of political society as a "device for the protection of this property and for the maintenance of an orderly relation of exchange."[6] In order to form the state, Hobbes argued, each individual gave up "the right of protecting and defending himself by his own power," and turned to the sovereign for protection. "Without that security, there is no reason for a man to deprive himself of his own advantages, and make himself a prey to others."[7] It is not surprising that Marx could say of such a society that we carry both our power over society and our association with it in our pockets.[8] Similar formulations have persisted, all of them based on the assumption that individuals are isolated, in competition, and without community.[9]

These definitions of power aid us in discussing male supremacy. Berenice Carroll notes Bertrand de Jouvenel's statement that "a man feels himself more of a man when imposing himself and making others the instrument of his will," and adds that "it is no accident that the subject of this assertion is 'a man.' The associative links between ideas of manliness and virility on the one hand, and domination, conquest and power on the other hand, are strong and pervasive in Western culture."[10]

Change

Social scientists' discussions of change are based on the same assumptions as their discussions of political power. *Webster's Third International Dictionary* defines the verb *change* as "to make different," and then distinguishes variation, alteration, and modification from transformation. Social science treatments of change have focused on either societal change or individual change, but have frequently ignored the process or dynamic of change itself.[11]

One major textbook on methodology, *The Language of Social Research*, treats only change in individuals. It presents three methods for measuring individual change.[12] These methods for measuring change assume that change is variance and make little attempt to separate variance from the concepts of modification or transformation. Any difference uncovered in what is measured over time is labeled "change." These methods do not distinguish superficial differences from fundamental social change.

Other social scientists, such as Lasswell and Kaplan in *Power and Society*, understand that political change can involve a transformation. But Lasswell and Kaplan still conceptualize revolution as a change of elites: "the counter-elite cannot attain power without the instrumentality of the mass, but the instrument is a threat to its own position as well as to that of the elite it seeks to supplant." Moreover, "the course of a revolution is sought to be limited by each participant group to the attainment of a favorable power position for itself."[13] Lasswell and Kaplan clearly regard human beings, both individual and groups, as competitors in a hostile world.

In summary, social scientific discussions of political change give little attention to the process of change itself, and the assumption that the basic units of society are competitive, hostile, and isolated individuals leads to an overemphasis on people taking power for their own advantage and an underemphasis on the importance of change in the institutions and structures of society.

Other Approaches to Political Change

A feminist redefinition of the concept of political change requires an understanding of the women's movement's concern for the relationships of the personal and the political; a perspective on the struggles within the movement over the nature and uses of power, leadership, and organization; sensitivity to the importance of process and interaction in social change; and finally, recognition of the fundamental links between economics and social relationships. Feminists regard change as a process that takes place on several levels: the personal, the group or organizational, and the level of social institutions. Political change, then, involves redefining the self, building different kinds of political organizations, gaining economic power for women, and most important, a sense of how each of these arenas for change relates to the interlocking structures of patriarchy, white supremacy, and capitalism. Finally, change at each of these levels must be understood as important not only as a facet of political change in itself but as a precondition for further change, which can take place in several of these structures at once.

The Personal and the Political

If what we change does not change us we are playing with blocks.
—**Marge Piercy**

Small-group consciousness raising at the beginning of the contemporary women's movement—with its stress on clarifying the links between the personal and the political—led women to conclude that change in consciousness and in the social relations of the individual is one of the most important components of political change. Women talked to each other to understand and share experiences and to set out a firsthand account of women's oppression.

But a great deal of unexpected energy and method came out of these groups. We learned that it was important to build an analysis of sexual politics from the ground up—from our own experiences. The idea that the personal lives of women should be analyzed in political terms both grew out of the experience of women in these groups and served as a focus for continued small-group activity. We drew connections between personal experience and political generalities about the oppression of women: we took up our experience and transformed it through reflection. This transformation of experience by reflection and the subsequent alterations in women's lives laid the groundwork for the idea that liberation must pervade aspects of life not considered politically important in the past. While many of the questions addressed by the small groups were not new, the methodology differed from the practice of most social movements, particularly those in Western capitalist countries.

Stressing the links between the personal and the political led women to conclude that first, a fundamental redefinition of the self was an integral part of action for political change; and second, that the changed consciousness and changed definition of the self could occur only in conjunction with a restructuring of the social relationships in which each person was involved.

In the process of developing a new sense of self, we made many advances. We took good points too far, however, and created new kinds of problems. Charlotte Bunch notes four of them: women have turned oppression into a source of identity but have also made it an excuse for inaction; we have relied on the women's movement to provide a ready-made identity; we have fixed on ideals that we require of all women without attention to what each woman can do well; and we have built identity and respect not on our own strength but on our relationships with other women.[14] Each of these can become a way to avoid creating an independent and responsible self. At the same time, each of these problems represents a successful attempt to create change, and each provides us with one element of a feminist definition of change: change is the process of creating new problems out of our solutions to earlier problems.

Developing an independent sense of self necessarily calls other areas of our lives into question. We must ask how our relationships with other persons can foster self-definition rather than dependence and accommodate our new strengths. What is the role of consciousness in creating change? What kinds of organizational structures contribute to the process of changing our self-concept? How does our sense of self relate to economic issues, to class within capitalism, heterosexuality within patriarchy? Finally, our efforts to develop new selves focus our attention on process and interaction. We constantly confront new situations in which we act out of our changed awareness of the world and experience the changed reactions of others. As Georg Lukacs summarized it, "to posit oneself, to produce and reproduce oneself—that is *reality*."[15] By working out the links between the personal and the political, the women's movement has begun to understand existence as a social process, the product of human activity. The realization that the social world is a human creation and that through our own activity we have already changed important aspects of that world leads to a sense of our own power and provides a source of energy for further changes.

Organization and Leadership

Independent and strong selves at the personal level must be expressed and reinforced by organizations. Discussion has centered on the kinds of organizations that can both express and develop women's strengths, and power within women's organizations has come to be an important issue. While leadership and power are not the only issues important in working out questions of organizational structure, they bear on the central issues of political power, and consideration of those problems is useful.

Reaction against leadership was often a reaction to the earlier experience of some women in male-dominated organizations, but soon it became an issue within the women's movement as well. Women who had been active in male-dominated organizations associated power with "loudmouthed, pushy, ego-centered men,"[16] who advocated a "macho" style of violence and sometimes listed women among the objects to be readily available after the revolution. The predominance in the movement of middle-class women, who lacked the tradition of women's strength and independence more frequent among working-class and rural women, also contributed to the identification of leadership and power as oppressive male characteristics.

"Informal" leaders developed, and some were recognized by the media and transformed into stars, at both national and local levels. Women who had argued for the abolition of leadership and power found that some women were far more influential than others. It is useful to examine this issue as one concerning what kinds of power are legitimate in the women's movement. Women were rightly dissatisfied with the idea of power as money (a value in itself and a possession which enables one to obtain other things) in the male Left. There are alternative definitions of power that do not require domination of others.

Berenice Carroll points out that in *Webster's International Dictionary* (1933), power is first defined as "ability, whether physical, mental or moral, to act; the faculty of doing or performing something," and is synonymous with "strength, vigor, energy, force, and ability." The words "control" and "domination" do not appear as synonyms.[17] Although this concept of power does appear in contemporary social science, it has not been as important as ideas of power as a form of domination. Christian Bay cites one such definition of power as "any activity where there is accomplishment, satisfaction of needs, mutual attainment of goals not distorted by . . . thwarting . . . experience."[18] Carroll, too, cites arguments about power as the need for activity and achievement, the drive to "interact effectively with" the environment. She also notes that the work of A. Kardiner on the "development of the effective ego" presents a similar view.[19]

Significantly, these understandings of power do not require the domination of others; energy and accomplishment are understood to be satisfying in themselves. This kind of power is much closer to what the women's movement has sought, yet this aspect of power is denied to all but a few women; the common female experience of being treated as though we were invisible can scarcely be characterized as effective interaction with the environment.

One source of the difficulties in the women's movement about leadership, strength, and achievement has been our lack of clarity about the differences between the two concepts of power. A letter of resignation from the women's movement, used by two different women in different cities, expresses some of these problems. They complain of being attacked by their sisters for having achieved something, and of being "labelled a thrill seeking opportunist, a ruthless mercenary, out to make her fame and fortune over the dead bodies of selfless sisters."[20] The letter argues that leadership qualities should not be confused with the desire to be a leader, and, similarly, that achievement or productivity should not be confused with the desire to be a leader (by implication, to dominate others). These statements indicate that women have not recognized that power understood as energy, strength, and effective interaction need not be the same as power that requires the domination of others in the movement.

But we must nevertheless recognize and confront the world of traditional politics in which money and power function in similar ways. Thus, creating political change involves setting up organizations based on power as energy and strength, groups that are structured and not tied to the personality of one individual, groups whose structures do not permit the use of power as a tool for domination of others in the group. At the same time, our organizations must deal with the society in which we live on its own terms—that is, terms of power as control, power as a means of making others do what they do not wish to do.

Recognition of the two faces of power, and of the necessity for working on both levels, means that our organizations must be structured and ongoing. With few exceptions, the radical wing of the women's movement has fragmented into small groups that are difficult to find and join. We cannot create political change until we structure our own organizations to deal with power as domination in the institutions of society. As our sense of self develops, we should be able to experiment more with different forms of organization and to understand how changes in organizational structure increase our ability to control the structures which now control us. Thus, while political change is about changes in power relationships, we are not talking about women simply participating in power relationships as they are at present constituted, but rather using our methods of organization as strategies for the redefinition of political power itself. The organizations we build are an integral part of the process of creating political change, and in the long term can perhaps serve as the groundwork for new societal institutions.

The process is not as easy as it sounds. History provides many confirmations of Lord Acton's famous dictum that power corrupts and absolute power corrupts absolutely. We have seen organizations in the male-dominated Left mirror some of the worst evils of the capitalist structures they said they wanted to replace. We must constantly ask: To what extent must we build organizations that mirror the institutions we are trying to destroy? Can organizations based on power as energy and initiative be effective tools for changing sexist, heterosexist, racist, and classist institutions such as the media, the health industry, and the like? To what extent will both we and our organizations be transformed by the struggle for power (domination)? Can our organizations serve as tools for taking power for women and still lay the groundwork for new nonsexist, nonracist, nonclassist societal institutions? While there are no easy answers to these questions, we must continue to ask them as we work to create political change.

Patriarchy, Capitalism, and White Supremacy

The transformation of our sense of self and the creation of organizations which express our new ideas cannot take place in a vacuum. We change ourselves and our organizations for the purpose of changing the interlocking structures which control our lives. The economic position of women is fundamental to the political change we seek. Moreover, when we look closely at the economic roles of women we see the ways capitalism, patriarchy,* and white supremacy reinforce one another and how the

---

*Institutionalized heterosexuality is an important element of patriarchy, and my references to patriarchy in the text include it. The discussion of the importance of the family should be read with this in mind.

ideology of individualism provides a philosophical justification for these structures. When we understand that the economic condition of women is maintained and structured by several institutions rather than only one, it becomes clear that the change we are working for cannot succeed in the economic sphere merely by providing paid work for every woman.

Women are exploited as wage laborers just as men are, but our position differs from theirs in three major ways: first, women are heavily concentrated in service and clerical jobs; second, we are paid less than men who do comparable work; and finally, all women, along with minority-group men, are used as a reserve labor force. In sum, we are viewed as supplementary workers to be brought into the money economy when needed and removed when no longer necessary. That more than half the population can be regarded as supplementary workers indicates the strength of the institution of patriarchy and the roles it forces on women.

Western capitalist society presents the middle-class family as the ideal, a unit in which the man has both economic and psychological power over its other members. Family relationships structured in "acceptable" ways act as a stabilizing force for the economic system as a whole. Economic dependence of several people on one wage earner (male or female) and wages so low that both parents must work to support their children are useful resources for capitalism. As one manufacturer pointedly remarked, he prefers married women, "especially those who have families at home dependent on them for support; they are attentive, docile, more so than unmarried females, and are compelled to use their utmost exertions to procure the necessities of life."[21]

The ideology of the family performs other services as well. The proper role of woman is supporter and reconstructor of the male ego after the workplace has damaged it. The male worker's position of domination in the family reverses his own domination by his boss at work and enables him to transfer tensions developed at the workplace to the family, thus lowering the probability that he will focus anger on the workplace.

Patriarchy considers work for wages improper for women and imposes the myth of "woman's place" on working women. Many women believe they are temporary or supplemental wage earners. Patriarchal ideas are also used by the employer to question the motives of women who complain about their jobs. If they are older and single, he dismisses their protests as the neuroses of spinsters; if the women are young, he dismisses their protests as those of temporary workers who will leave when they marry or get pregnant; if they have husbands, they are regarded as both supplementary and temporary; and the problems of women with children to support alone are simply not recognized. That the reality of women's lives often runs counter to these myths does not significantly lessen their impact.

Capitalism makes a place for the economically dependent woman through consumption. According to Friedan, advertising consultants know that finding "bargains" has come to be a housewife's major contribution to the economy of the family, just as the husband's contribution consists of bringing home a paycheck.[22] The upgrading of consumption assumes that every family has at least a middle-class income; contains a woman, a man, and several children; and is supported by the paid labor of one (male) worker. While many women's lives contradict the myth, the ideas it expresses affect us all. Women working for wages can be led to buy things for their families out of guilt for spending time away from home. The woman who must support others is in a double bind: she is blamed for leaving her children and her wages are often so low that she is unable to purchase many of the goods every family "needs."

Women's services in the home are the source of another link between patriarchy and capitalism. The work of housewives increases the real wages of families with two adults[23] and thereby enables them to purchase commodities they could not otherwise afford. At the same time, women employed outside the home still produce a portion of this value in the home. The employment of married women living with their husbands thus provides a measure of expansion in the market for goods and services in boom times. Firing women at other times provides a cushion against the full consequences of recession, since the women's increased home production will partially make up for their lost salaries.

Capitalism and patriarchy in the United States are also linked with white supremacy. The popularization of the myth that black matriarchy is responsible for the problems of the black community is one of the most obvious and vicious links between patriarchy and white supremacy. The efforts by both blacks and whites to make the black family mirror the white middle-class patriarchal family, and efforts to push black women into supportive roles, not only oppress black women but also decrease the energy available for the struggle against white domination. The creation of divisions and hostilities between black women and men is useful to the ruling class to defuse effective attacks on racism.[24]

Second, capitalism requires marginal work forces, and white supremacy as well as patriarchy are convenient instruments for this purpose. Racial and ethnic minorities are used as marginal labor in most advanced industrial countries—Southern Europeans in Germany, North Africans in France. Racial minorities are used by capitalism in other ways as well:

> The extent to which the capitalist class is able to isolate segments of the working class from each other strengthens its position. . . . If one group of workers is able to command higher pay, to exclude others from work, and if

the other group or groups of workers are limited in their employment opportunities to the worst jobs and lowest pay, then a marginal working class has been created which benefits the labor aristocracy and to an even greater extent the capitalist class.[25]

Third, minority-group men provide a more varied reserve labor force than women, who are confined to a few types of work. Finally, the idea that the problems of minority-group workers can be traced to "discrimination" alone is an important tool for capitalist control. One writer has argued that ending discrimination as such would make only a small difference in the economic role of minorities.[26] Yet the concept of discrimination, based on an understanding of the individual as a person who carries both her power over society and her association with it in her pocket, helps maintain the belief that employers buy some products (workers) rather than others for reasons as innocuous as preference or taste. They can argue that those of us who object are inconsistent:

> We do not regard it as "discrimination"—or at least not in the same invidious sense—if an individual is willing to pay a higher price to listen to one singer than another, although we do if he is willing to pay a higher price to have services rendered to him by a person of one color rather than by a person of another.[27]

The idea that persons are products whose value is measured by their price, the stress on freedom of "contract" between equals, the assumption that each individual goes to the market with the ability and willingness to pay certain prices to achieve some preferences—all these are implied by the concept of discrimination.

While we have discussed only a few of the links among capitalism, patriarchy, and white supremacy, it is obvious that we cannot end any woman's economic oppression and dependency without at the same time destroying those structures. Power as domination is fundamental to the three; taking power as domination appears to be the only way to take over and transform them.

Ideas and History

It is difficult to refer to the concept of the individual as a structure in the same sense as capitalism, patriarchy, or white supremacy. Nevertheless, these structures could not be maintained without a set of assumptions about what human beings are and what they might become. We cannot work effectively for change without understanding the importance of ideas and recognizing the reciprocal effects of consciousness on actions and organizations.

The content of the intellectual and emotional life of a society is bound up with the way it reproduces its material life. Ideas play the role of justifying, legitimating, and then stabilizing economic changes. As Marx stated, when

> each new class . . . puts itself in the place of one ruling before it, (it) is compelled, merely in order to carry through its aim, to represent its interest as the common interest of all the members of society, that is expressed in ideal form; it has to give its ideas the form of universality and represent them as the only rational, universally valid ones.[28]

Thus, bourgeois philosophers, political economists, and others developed the ideas capitalist society required for its survival and growth, and saw their assumptions as universal and eternal truths about humankind.[29]

Earlier I argued that contemporary definitions of power as domination were based on assumptions of possessive individualism and the requirements of capitalist society. In addition to power, the possessive individual is concerned with the myth of equality and the compartmentalization of life.

The idea of equality as presented by Hobbes begins from a world that in its state of nature is populated by "human calculating machines,"[30] each one basically equal to all the others. Marx argued that the idea of self-interested and fundamentally equal beings was important because capitalism required interchangeable laboring units. Once human equality had become accepted as a universal truth, the argument could be made that since all persons are in fact equal—that is, have "equality of opportunity"—then those who are unable to get as much money as others are solely responsible for their own state.

Nineteenth-century employers consistently objected to labor legislation as interference with freedom of contract. They argued that such legislation encouraged "the workman to look to the law for the protection which he ought to secure for himself by voluntary contract"; the legislation "limits a *man's* power of doing what *he* will with what *he* considers *his* own."[31]

This argument relies on the assumption that the employer and employee are in equal positions of power with respect to each other. This assumption is not accurate, since the laborer cannot survive without selling her labor power; yet it has been widely accepted by those who suffer from it as well as those who benefit. The practice of blaming the victim for her plight is a powerful obstacle to the creation of political change, since it suggests that if those involved were "worth" equality of treatment, they would in fact be accorded equality.

We know from our efforts to break free of them that these are powerful ideas. The idea of the isolated individual who protects and expands his own position allows the ruling classes to justify and expand their positions of dominance as the just reward for having the strength to act on their own interests. Those of us who are not so successful are kept from looking beyond ourselves by our shame at failing to expand our power (domination).

The compartmentalization or fragmentation of life is a second corollary of possessive individualism.[32] The system of purchasing labor by the day or hour rather than by lifetimes of loyalty is compatible with the idea that in different spheres one behaves according to different rules. An important separation in industrial society has been between modes of behavior appropriate for the family and behavior appropriate for the workplace or public life.[33] The women's movement has been particularly concerned with the separation of the personal from the political, but this distinction is simply one of many compartmentalizations that divide the world into disparate spheres: the public is separated from the private; professional judgments from human ones; the world of facts (reason) from that of values (emotion).

Anais Nin has commented on this phenomenon from a woman's perspective:

> I have always been tormented by the image of a multiplicity of selves.... My first concept of people about me was that all of them were coordinated into a whole, whereas I was made up of a multitude of selves, of fragments. ... There were always, in me, two women at least, one woman desperate and bewildered, who felt she was drowning, and another who only wanted to bring beauty, grace, an aliveness to people, and who would leap into a scene, as upon a stage, conceal her true emotions because they were weaknesses, helplessness, despair, and present to the world only a smile, an eagerness, curiosity, enthusiasm, interest.[34]

Compartmentalization is a way of separating us from ourselves, but it is also a technique of survival: if we have only the self who is drowning, we die.

W. E. B. DuBois comments on a similar phenomenon among blacks:

> It is a peculiar sensation, this double-consciousness, this sense of always looking at one's self through the eyes of others, of measuring one's soul by the tape of a world that looks on in amused contempt and pity. One ever feels his two-ness—an American and a Negro.... [35]

The compartmentalization of the world leads to a fragmentation of the self among working- and lower-class people as well. "Dividing the self defends against the pain a person would otherwise feel, if he had to submit the whole of himself to a society which makes his position a vulnerable and anxiety-laden one."[36]

fragmentation & multiplicity

After passing through the prisms of capitalism, white supremacy, and patriarchy, the compartmentalization of the world takes different forms for middle- and upper-class white women, for minority women and men, and among white working- and lower-class people. But in each, the fragmentation of the self is a mechanism for survival, a way (however damaging to us) of getting by in an oppressive world, a way of coping with the all-too-frequent failures in one or more areas of our lives. Yet the fragmentation of the self maintains our oppression. By compartmentalizing our lives we implicitly accept individual responsibility for the failures that grow out of our collective oppression and absorb into ourselves the impact of these failures. As long as we fail to challenge the structures controlling our lives, the fragmentation of ourselves is necessary for survival. By contrast, the process of directly challenging patriarchy, white supremacy, and capitalism both creates and requires a sense of ourselves as wholes rather than fragments.

Conclusions

We have returned to the importance of our sense of self, but now we can see it as a part of our efforts for political change. Since our sense of self is bound up with the structures of social control, we cannot allow our work for political change to stagnate at the level of personal change. At the same time, we must recognize that change takes place in several areas and both affects and is affected by changes in other areas. We have seen that patriarchy, capitalism, and white supremacy have pervasive effects on all aspects of our lives. Thus, efforts for change in any area should lead us to examine the obstacles to change created by the existence of the other structures as well.

Political change is a process of transforming not only ourselves but also our most basic assumptions about humanity and our sense of human possibility. Political change means restructuring our organizations to reflect our constantly changing understanding of the possible and to meet the new needs and new problems we create. Political change requires strategies that attack the interlocking structures of control at all levels. At bottom, political change is a process of changing power relationships so that the meaning of power itself is transformed.

Our strategies for change must grow out of the tension between using our organizations as instruments for taking and transforming power in a society structured by power understood only as domination, and using our organizations to build models for a new society based on power understood as energy and initiative. Thus, in evaluating a particular strategy we must ask: 1) how it will affect women's sense of self, and sense of our own collective power; 2) how it will make women aware of problems beyond questions of identity—that is, how it will politicize women; 3) how the strategy will work to build organizations that will increase both our strength and competence, and will give women power to use (like money) to weaken the control and domination of capitalism, patriarchy, and white supremacy; and 4) how the strategy will weaken the links between these institutions.

As Juliet Mitchell pointed out, a change in one of several interlocking structures can be offset by changes in the others.[37] This is a particularly difficult question, since weakening the structures that oppress us depends heavily on how the strategy is conceived, followed through, and expanded. How, for example, can support for the Equal Rights Amendment lead to women taking power in such a way that the structures of social relations as they are at present constituted cannot survive?

Finally, we must examine every strategy for change in terms of the understanding of process and interaction it contains: does the strategy contain at least the seeds of its own supersession, or is it a way of forever doing the same things for the same people?

These criteria for evaluating strategies for political change grow out of the four concerns I listed at the beginning of the discussion: the importance of the relationship between the personal and the political; questions of power and leadership in feminist organizations; the importance of process and interaction; and the problems posed by the interlocking nature of capitalism, patriarchy, and white supremacy. Political change can occur only if each of these concerns is an important and continuing element of our thought. They call our attention to the fact that what we mean by political change is structural change.

NOTES

1. See Bertrand Russell, *Power, A New Social Analysis* (n.p., 1936), p. 35, cited by Anthony de Crespigny and Alan Wertheimer, *Contemporary Political Theory* (New York: Atherton Press, 1970), p. 22; Harold Lasswell and Abraham Kaplan, *Power and Society* (New Haven: Yale University Press, 1950), p. 76; and Howard Warrender, *The Political Philosophy of Hobbes* (Oxford: Clarendon Press, 1957), p. 312.

2. Talcott Parsons, "On the Concept of Political Power," in *Political Power*, ed. Roderick Bell, David V. Edwards, and R. Harrison Wagner (New York: Free Press, 1969), p. 256.

3. Ibid., p. 257.

4. Karl Marx, *The Grundrisse*, ed. David McLellan (New York: Harper & Row, 1971), p. 65. The development of credit, in which all that one has or is or does can be translated into a measure of one's exchange value, provides an example of how the transformation takes place. See David McLellan, *Marx Before Marxism* (New York: Harper & Row, 1971), p. 176.

5. *Grundrisse,* p. 65.

6. C. B. MacPherson, *The Political Theory of Possessive Individualism* (London: Oxford University Press, 1962), p. 3.

7. Thomas Hobbes, *De Corpore Politico, English Works,* Molesworth ed., 4:128–29, quoted by Warrender, *The Political Philosophy of Hobbes,* pp. 112–13.

8. Marx, *Grundrisse,* p. 66.

9. Christian Bay, *The Structure of Freedom* (New York: Atheneum, 1968), p. 250, and Kate Millett, *Sexual Politics* (Garden City, N.Y.: Doubleday, 1970), p. 23, cite a number of these discussions.

10. Berenice Carroll, "Peace Research: The Cult of Power" (paper presented to the American Sociological Association in Denver, Colorado, September 1971), p. 6. She takes de Jouvenel's statement from Hannah Arendt, "Reflections on Violence," *Journal of International Affairs,* 23, no. 1 (1969): 12.

11. J. A. Ponsioen, in *The Analysis of Social Change Reconsidered* (The Hague: Mouton, 1965), discusses a number of writers.

12. Paul Lazarsfeld and Morris Rosenberg, *The Language of Social Research* (Glencoe, Ill.: Free Press, 1955), pp. 203–81.

13. Lasswell and Kaplan, *Power and Society,* pp. 268–78.

14. Charlotte Bunch, "Perseverance Furthers: Women's Sense of Self," *The Furies,* February 1973, pp. 3–4.

15. Georg Lukacs, *History and Class Consciousness* (Cambridge, Mass.: MIT Press, 1971), pp. 15–16.

16. Rita Mae Brown, "Leadership vs. Stardom," *The Furies,* February 1972, p. 20.

17. Carroll, "Peace Research," p. 7. The author is indebted to her paper for the scholarly sources discussing power as energy.

18. Bay, *The Structure of Freedom,* p. 248, cited by Carroll, p. 8.

19. Robert White, "Motivation Reconsidered: The Concept of Competence," *Psychological Review* 66 (1959): 297, 310, 318, cited by Carroll, pp. 9–10.

20. Anselma dell-Olio and Joreen, printed in *Chicago Women's Liberation Union Newsletter,* July 1970.

21. Karl Marx, *Capital* (New York: International Publishers, 1967), 1:402.

22. Betty Friedan, *The Feminine Mystique* (New York: Dell, 1963), pp. 214–15.

23. Chong Soo Pyun, "The Monetary Value of a Housewife," in *Woman in a Manmade World,* ed. Non Glazer-Malbin and Helen Youngelson Waehrer (New York: Rand McNally, 1972), p. 192.

24. See Robert Staples, "The Myth of the Black Matriarchy," *Black Scholar,* January–February 1970, p. 15.

25. William K. Tabb, "Capitalism, Colonialism, and Racism," in *Institutions, Policies, and Goals: A Reader in American Politics,* ed. Kenneth M. Dolbeare and Murray J. Edelman, with Patricia Dolbeare (Lexington, Mass.: D. C. Heath, 1973), p. 174.

26. Ibid., p. 175.

27. Ibid., p. 167.

28. Karl Marx and Friedrich Engels, *The German Ideology,* ed. C. J. Arthur (New York: International Publishers, 1970), pp. 65–66. They also point out that "the ideas of the ruling class are in every epoch the ruling ideas, i.e., the class which is the ruling *material* force of society is at the same time its ruling *intellectual* force."

29. MacPherson, *Possessive Individualism,* has documented the role of these assumptions in political philosophy.

30. Ibid., p. 92.

31. T. H. Green, *The Political Theory of T. H. Green,* ed. John R. Rodman (New York: Appleton-Century-Crofts, 1964), pp. 43–44. Italics mine.

32. From the vantage point of the nineties and the influence of postmodernism, this seems a very prescient observation.

33. On this point see Eli Zaretsky, "Capitalism, the Family, and Personal Life: Part 2," *Socialist Revolution,* 3, no. 3 (May–June 1973).

34. Anais Nin, *Diary, 1931–34* (New York: Harcourt, Brace, and World, 1966), quoted by Meredith Tax, "Woman and Her Mind: The Story of Everyday Life," in *Notes from the Second Year* (1970), p. 15.

35. W. E. B. DuBois, *The Souls of Black Folk* (New York: Fawcett World Library, 1968), p. 16 in Joyce Ladner, *Tomorrow's Tomorrow* (New York: Anchor Books, 1971), pp. 273–74.

36. Richard Sennett and Jonathan Cobb, *The Hidden Injuries of Class* (New York: Random House, 1972), p. 208.

37. Juliet Mitchell, *Women's Estate* (New York: Pantheon, 1971), p. 120.

two

Fundamental Feminism: Process and Perspective

Several of the *Quest* staff went to the Socialist Feminist Conference in Yellow Springs, Ohio, in July, 1975. We went because we thought of ourselves as feminists who were socialists, but we discovered that despite the obvious disagreements among the speakers, most of the views expressed from the speakers' platform were in conflict with our politics. This article began, then, from a discussion among the five of us who went, and represents our attempts to respond constructively to the conference. We do not intend the article to be primarily a criticism of the conference, but rather an attempt to set out our own concerns as they emerged through our experience in Yellow Springs.

We found ourselves in opposition not to the stated goals of the conference—the destruction of capitalism, imperialism, and patriarchy* but rather to the framework of analysis in which these concerns were presented. Since the framework was defined by the white, male-dominated Left in the United States (hereafter referred to simply as the male Left), it is clear that, as such, it can only lead a socialist feminist movement to the same paralysis that has immobilized the male Left.

In *Building Feminist Theory: Essays from Quest* (New York: Longman, 1981). Originally published in *Quest: A Feminist Quarterly* 2, 2 (Fall 1975).
    *Although we would not include the destruction of white supremacy under the heading of destroying imperialism, that seemed to be a frequent interpretation at the conference.

Patriarchal Socialism and Socialist Feminism

The role of the male Left in defining the terms on which socialist feminism is to develop was clear. For example, the speaker who opened the conference stated that its concern was with the ways racism, class, and imperialism affect women; she did not say that the conference was concerned with the ways patriarchy affects women. She added that socialist feminism as a movement was concerned with transforming the Left. In response to such positions, the Lesbian Caucus was driven to state that it is legitimate to struggle against sexism "whether or not it is the direct result of capitalism and imperialism."[1]

The conference in general assumed that feminism is a culture, while socialism is a politics. A comparison of the statements of the tasks of two workshops—one relating to the autonomous women's movement and one working with mixed leftist and anti-imperialist groups—highlights this assumption. In discussing the relation of socialist feminism to the autonomous women's movement, the session description stressed the need for "politicization (infusing our politics into other groups)."[2] In contrast, sessions on working with mixed leftist groups were to discuss ways to build the Left and "ensure that our analysis is heard in our joint work— the *integration* of sex, class, race, and lesbianism."[3] The difference between infusing politics into an apolitical group and integrating or making one's voice heard in a more powerful political group makes it clear that the conference looked to the male Left to define what is political.

But male Left politics lead to problems in the way we do political work and think about politics—problems resulting from their mode of analysis. And these problems of method lead in turn to difficulties in dealing with substantive areas of concern—how to organize against class society, racism, and imperialism—not to speak of sexism.

The history of the male Left demonstrates that it has no concept of process. As a result, it has been unable to understand the fundamental unity of theory and practice. This separation of theory and practice surfaced in a very traditional form at the conference. "Theory" meant reading and studying a few sacred texts that are frequently recited but seldom connected with reality. "Practice," in contrast, meant organizing other people (never one's self) by applying textbook teachings to their situations. The male Left has forgotten that "it is essential to educate the educator himself. [Their] doctrine must, therefore, divide society into two parts, one of which is superior to society."[4]

The separation of theory from lived reality leads the male Left to adopt the elitist assumptions of capitalist society. Their unexamined and unresisted classism surfaces most clearly in the assumption that the "working class" is incapable of working out its own future; that it needs a vanguard party to lead it to freedom; and that the core of the vanguard party will be made up of a group of people who have memorized the sacred texts and are thus equipped to organize the world. The clear assumption is that the male Left will come to the oppressed masses with Truth, and will make for them a revolution they cannot make for themselves.

The separation of theory and practice and the unconscious classism that accompanies it result in the notion that we work for revolution, not for ourselves and out of necessity, but for others, out of an idealistic commitment. The refusal to recognize that revolution begins in our own lives first and that it concerns our own identities as human beings took many forms at the conference. For example, the subsumption of racism under the more impersonal heading "imperialism" makes it possible to avoid the racism we participate in and practice. The inclusion of a workshop on lesbian organizing among a number of sessions on community organizing lets us avoid the tensions between lesbians and straight women and the problems created by heterosexual privilege. To see questions in this way means that we accept the terms of capitalist society in which politics has to do with "public" life, and in which our personal lives can be kept at a distance from our politics.

The separation of theory from practice leads the male Left to mechanically apply Marx's paradigm of capitalist society as made up of two classes—the bourgeoisie and the proletariat. Many conference speakers gave the impression that once this had been said, the analysis was complete. That the analysis is not complete was obvious in the confusion of so many speakers about the reality of class itself. The reiteration that we are almost all working class (because 90 percent of the United States population has nothing to sell but labor power), and the repeated expression of concern that most of the women at the conference were white and middle class, indicate the difficulties of mechanically applying the two-class formula to concrete reality.[5]

The divisions among those who are not part of the bourgeoisie were not seen as fundamentally important. Problems of sexism,* racism, and other barriers between people were seen only as worth noticing because they prevented united action, not because they represent important social forces in themselves. Thus, the kind of tokenism that has occurred at male Left conferences, where women's concerns are often relegated to a single session, was directed at Third World women and lesbians. Rather than integrate their concerns into all the panels as aspects of the issues taken up by each session, conference organizers asked that Third World women and lesbians share a single morning. The implication of this kind of scheduling

---

*And heterosexism is an essential part of sexism.

is that such concerns are special interests and are fundamentally irrelevant to the "real" questions raised by monopoly capitalism.

A final, profoundly disturbing aspect of the Socialist Feminist Conference was its lack of feminism. Very few of the speakers had any concept of patriarchy or saw patriarchy as an important and autonomous social force. Rather, the conference focused almost exclusively on the problems and needs of an ill-defined but unitary "workers' movement." The conference provided little aid in analyzing how the forces of white supremacy, patriarchy, capitalism, and imperialism interact in a specific setting; yet if we do not understand how we are divided from each other in everyday life, how can we work against the forces that divide us?

While we cannot define ourselves as socialist feminists in the terms used at the conference, we feel that the conference itself was very useful in asking what we mean by a feminism that includes a socialist analysis. The exploration of feminism that follows should make it clear that if those who call themselves socialist feminists read and understand Karl Marx, they should develop a better understanding of feminism. As Georg Lukacs has pointed out, orthodox Marxism is not the uncritical acceptance of Marx's results: "On the contrary, orthodoxy refers exclusively to *method*."[6]

Feminism as a Mode of Analysis

Women who call themselves feminists disagree on many things. Many are not socialists at all. One would be hard pressed to find a set of beliefs or principles, or even a list of demands, that could safely be applied to all feminists. Still, when we look at the contemporary feminist movement in all its variety, we find that while many of the questions we addressed were not new, there is a methodology common among feminists that differs from the practice of most social movements, particularly from those in advanced capitalist countries. At bottom, feminism is a mode of analysis, a method of approaching life and politics, rather than a set of political conclusions about the oppression of women.

The practice of small-group consciousness raising, with its stress on examining and understanding experience and on connecting personal experience to the structures that define our lives, is the clearest example of the method basic to feminism. Through this practice, we learned that it is important to build an analysis of patriarchy from the ground up—beginning with our own experience. We examined our lives not only intellectually but with all our senses.[7] We drew connections between our personal experiences and political generalities about the oppression of women; in fact, we used our personal experience to develop political generalities. We came to understand our experience, our past, in a way that transforms both our experiences and ourselves.

The power of a feminist method grows out of the fact that it enables us to connect everyday life with an analysis of the social institutions which shape that life. Application of a feminist method means that the institutions of capitalism (including its imperialist aspect), patriarchy, and white supremacy cease to be abstractions we read about. Through their impact on us they become lived, real aspects of daily experience and activity. In this way, feminism provides us with a way to understand our anger and direct our anger and energy toward change.

Integrating Personal and Political Change

Feminism as a mode of analysis relies on the idea that we come to know the world, to change it and be changed by it, through our everyday activity. The focusing on daily life and experience makes it clear not only that we are active in creating and changing our lives but that reality itself consists of "sensuous human activity, practice."[8] We ourselves produce our existence as a response to specific problems posed for us by reality. As feminists, we cannot avoid the realization that we experience patriarchy on a daily basis and that we must oppose the institutions of male supremacy daily as well, in every area of our lives.

Feminism as a method makes us recognize that human activity is also self-changing.[9] A fundamental redefinition of the self is an integral part of action for political change. But our selves are social phenomena, and take their meaning from the social whole of which we are a part.[10] We do not act in a vacuum to produce and reproduce our lives; changed consciousness and changed definitions of self can occur only in conjunction with restructuring the social (societal and personal) relationships in which each of us is involved. Thus, feminism leads us to oppose the institutions of capitalism, white supremacy, and patriarchy.

A feminist mode of analysis makes it clear that patriarchy, capitalism, white supremacy, certain forms of social interaction, and language all exist for us as historic "givens." While they are not unalterable, the historical structures that mold our lives pose the questions to which we must respond, and define the immediate possibilities for change.[11] Thus, although we recognize that human activity *is* the structure of the social world, this structure is imposed not by individuals but by masses of people, building on the work of those who came before. The shape of social life at any point depends on needs already developed as well as embryonic needs—needs whose production, formation, and satisfaction are historical processes. Developing new selves, then, requires that we recognize the importance of large-scale forces for change and recognize as well that the fully developed individuals we are trying to become can only be products of history and struggle.[12] We can transform ourselves only by simultaneously struggling to transform the social relations that define us: self-changing and changed social institutions are simply two aspects of the same process.

Thus, although we found that many socialists at the conference believe that beginning with personal experience is invalid, a cultural if not even bourgeois enterprise, we have come to think that "the coincidence of the changing of circumstances and of human activity or self-changing can be conceived and rationally understood only as *revolutionary practice.*"[13]

Recognizing Process and Interaction

By beginning with everyday life and experience, feminism has developed a politics that incorporates an understanding of process and of the importance of appropriating our past as an essential element of political action. We find that we constantly confront new situations in which we act out of our changed awareness of the world and ourselves and experience the changed reactions of others. What patriarchal socialism sees as static, feminism sees as structures of relations in process—a reality constantly in evolution.

Feminist reasoning "regards every historically developed social form as in fluid movement, and therefore takes into account its transient nature no less than its momentary existence."[14]

Each of the interlocking institutions of capitalism, patriarchy, and white supremacy conditions the others, but each can also be understood as a different expression of the same relationships.[15] This mode of understanding allows us to see the many ways processes are related and provides a way to understand a world in which events take their significance from the set of relationships which come to focus in them.

Since each phenomenon changes form constantly as the social relations of which it is composed take on different meanings and forms, the possibility of understanding processes as they change depends on our grasp of their role in the social whole.[16] For example, in order to understand increased wage work by women in the United States, we need to understand the relation of this work to the needs of capitalism. But we must also look at the conditions of work and the kind of work prescribed for women by patriarchy and white supremacy as *different* aspects of the same social system. In this context, production, consumption, distribution, and exchange are not identical but are different aspects of a unity; a mutual interaction occurs between these various elements.

Feminists cannot separate workplace organizing from community organizing from building a movement. We begin from the perspective that possibilities for change in any area are tied to change in other areas. The precise forms of human activity as it appears in the family, the workplace, or elsewhere are intelligible only in the context of the whole society—including both its past and its future.

When patriarchal socialists separate workplace from community organizing, they demonstrate that they have forgotten that the significance of any form of human activity depends on its relation to the whole.[17] They have forgotten that both capitalism and socialism are more than economic systems, and that capitalism does not just reproduce the physical existence of individuals: "rather it is a definite form of activity of these individuals, a definite form of expressing their life, a definite *mode of life* on their part . . . [and this coincides with] both *what* they produce and *how* they produce."[18] A mode of life is not divisible. It does not consist of a public part and a private part, a part at the workplace and a part in the community—each of which makes up a certain fraction, and all of which total 100 percent. A mode of life, and all the aspects of that mode of life, take meaning from the totality of which they are parts.

Appropriation, Necessity, and Revolution

The feminist method of analyzing experience is a way of appropriating reality. Appropriation (or constructive incorporation) means the incorporation of experience in such a way that our life experience becomes a part of our humanity itself. Clearly, appropriation of things or experiences does not mean simple possession or gratification. Our knowledge of ourselves and our world is an aspect of our appropriation of that world, just as the incorporation of our knowledge into who we are as people changes our world. Appropriation, then, refers to the expansion of human powers and potentialities through the transforming impact of experience.

By appropriating our experience and incorporating it into our selves, we transform what might have been a politics of idealism into a politics of necessity. By appropriating our collective experience, we are creating people who recognize that we cannot be ourselves in a society based on hierarchy, domination, and private property. We are acquiring a consciousness that forces us "by an ineluctable, irremediable and imperious *distress*—by practical *necessity*—to revolt against this inhumanity."[19] Incorporating, making part of ourselves what we learn, is essential to the method of feminism. It is a way of making both our past and our future belong to us.

Feminist Theory and Practice

The feminist mode of analysis has important results for questions of theory and practice. For feminists, theory is the articulation of what our practical activity has already appropriated in reality. In theorizing, we examine what we find within ourselves; we attempt to clarify for ourselves and others what we already, at some level, know.

Theory itself, then, can be seen as an aspect of appropriation, a way of taking up and building on our experience. This is not to say that feminists reject all knowledge that is not firsthand, that we can learn nothing from books or from history. But rather than read a number of sacred texts, we make the practical questions posed for us in life the basis for our study. Feminism recognizes that political philosophy and political action do not take place in separate realms. On the contrary, the concepts with which we understand the social world emerge from and are defined by human activity. We agree with Antonio Gramsci that the philosophy of each person "is contained in its entirety in [her] political action."[20]

For feminists, the unity of theory and practice refers to the use of theory to make coherent the problems and principles expressed in our practical activity. Feminists argue that the role of theory is to take seriously the idea that all of us are theorists since we "engage in practical activity and in [our] guiding lines of conduct there is implicitly contained a conception of the world, a philosophy."[21] The role of theory, then, is to articulate for us what we know from our practical activity, to bring out and make conscious the philosophy embedded in our lives. Feminists are in fact creating social theory through our political action. We need to conceptualize, to take up and specify what we have already done, in order to make the next steps clear.[22]

New Directions

Because feminists begin from our own experience in a specific advanced capitalist society, we recognize that the lived realities of different segments of a society are varied. While it is true that most people have only their labor power to sell (for wages or not), there are real differences in power, privilege, ability to control our lives, and even in our survival chances. We cannot ignore these divisions. Only by recognizing our different situations in their complexity can we use our anger constructively. Feminists have begun to learn about the meaning of class and race by looking at the impact of these divisions on everyday life. We are beginning to understand that our class is not defined by our relationship to the mode of production in the simple sense that if we sell our labor power (for a day or a lifetime), or are part of the family of someone (presumably male) who does, we are working-class. Being working-class is a mode of life, a way of living life based on, but not exclusively defined by, the simple fact that we must sell our labor power to stay alive.

Class distinctions in capitalist society are part of a totality, a mode of life structured as well by sexism and racism. Class distinctions in the

United States affect the everyday lives of women and men, whites or black or Third World people, in different ways. Feminism leads us to ask questions about the nature of class distinctions and what they mean in the lives of people every day. It compels questions that recognize that we already know a great deal about class, but need to appropriate what we know—to make it into theory.

The method of feminism means as well that we need to look at the ways patriarchy and white supremacy interlock with capitalism. Our experience provides us with many examples of the ways patriarchy, capitalism, and white supremacy interlock.[23] The myth of black matriarchy, women's role as houseworkers, their functions as part of a reserve labor force, and the participation of women and minorities in a separate and secondary labor market—all these fulfill specific functions for capitalism but would be impossible without the institutions of white supremacy and patriarchy. We need to know more about the nature of these relationships. What are the processes that define them? How are they changing? What are they becoming?

Feminism as a mode of analysis leads us to respect experience and differences, to respect people enough to believe that they are in the best position to make their own revolution. Thus we cannot support the elitism implicit in the concept of a vanguard party. Patriarchal socialists have forgotten that the Leninist model of a vanguard party was developed to "replace a part of the historical process by conscious intervention,"[24] that is, it was developed to create a vehicle that could function in the *absence of* the kind of political education that grows from the experience of capitalist society.

Luxemburg argued that even in nineteenth-century Russia, the vanguard party was inappropriate, since there is no "ready made, pre-established, detailed set of tactics which a central committee can teach its membership as if they were army recruits."[25] In general, the tactics of a mass party cannot be invented. They are "the product of a progressive series of great creative acts in the often rudimentary experiments of the class struggle. Here too, the unconscious comes before the conscious. . . . "[26]

Organizations and Strategies

Feminism, while it does not prescribe an organizational form, leads to a set of questions about organizational priorities. First, a feminist mode of analysis suggests that we need organizations that include theory building as the appropriation of experience, as a part of the work of the organization itself. We need to systematically analyze what we learn as we work in organizations. Too often, we have left analysis of our experience to small groups and have limited ourselves to understanding the relationship between personal experience and social institutions. While this is valuable, we need to develop ways to appropriate our organizational experience and to use it to transform our organizations themselves. Some feminist organizations are beginning to raise questions about the process of meetings or about the way work is and should be done. But because so many of us reacted to our experience of the male Left organizations by refusing to build any organizational structures at all, we have only begun to think about the way we should work in organizations with some structure, as opposed to the way we should work in small groups.

We need to build the latitude for change and growth into our organizations rather than rely on small groups for these forces. This means we need to systematically teach and respect different skills, and allow our organizations to change and grow in new directions. We need to use our organizations as places where we begin to redefine the social relations of work, where we begin to live as whole people. We can begin now to create new ways of working that do not follow the patterns of domination and hierarchy set by the mode of production as a whole.

In terms of strategies, we can begin to make coalitions with other groups that share our approach to politics. We will not go into places where we do not work to pass out leaflets, or try to bring people who do not share our experience into our organizations without changing those organizations to take account of and respect their differences. We cannot work in coalitions with people who refuse to face their responsibility for everyday life, with people who will not use their own experience as a fundamental basis for knowledge, with people who refuse to take an active part in their own existence. We cannot work with those who treat theory as a set of conclusions to be pasted onto reality, and who, out of their own moral commitment, make a revolution for the benefit of their "inferiors."

As feminists, we must work on issues that are real for us, which have real impact on daily life. These issues can vary—housing, public transportation, inflation, food prices, and shortages, to name a few. We can work on these issues either with women only, or in coalitions including men. So long as others in the coalition share our method, and so long as those we work with are working for change out of necessity (because they, like us, have no alternative), there is a real basis for coalition.

As we work on particular issues, we must continually ask how we can use these issues to build our collective power. We must ask how our work will help to educate ourselves and others to see the connections and interactions among social institutions. Finally, we must ask how work in a particular area weakens the institutions that structure our lives and how our work uses the processes that define our society to change it.[27]

Conclusion

Feminism makes us recognize that struggle itself must be seen as a process. We must avoid, on the one hand, developing a narrow sectarian outlook, and on the other, abandoning our goal of revolution. We must continue to base our work on the necessity for change in our lives. Our political theorizing can grow only out of appropriating the work we have done. While the answers to our questions can only come slowly and with difficulty, we must remember that we are involved in a continuous process of learning what kind of world we want to create as we work for change.

NOTES

1. "Lesbianism and Socialist Feminism" (paper read at the Socialist Feminist Conference, Yellow Springs, Ohio, July 1975), p. 1. (Mimeographed.)

2. "Building Our Movement and Relating to the Autonomous Women's Movement" (paper read at the Socialist Feminist Conference, Yellow Springs, Ohio, July 1975), p. 2. (Mimeographed.)

3. "Alphabet Soup: Or, Working With Mixed Left and Anti-Imperialist Groups" (paper read at the Socialist Feminist Conference, Yellow Springs, Ohio, July 1975), p. 1. (Mimeographed.) Italics mine.

4. Karl Marx, "Theses on Feuerbach," in Karl Marx and Frederick Engels, *The German Ideology*, ed. C. J. Arthur (New York: International Publishers, 1970), p. 121.

5. On the inaccuracy of this account of Marx's theory, see Georg Lukacs, "What Is Orthodox Marxism," *History and Class Consciousness* (Cambridge, Mass.: MIT Press, 1971), p. 8.

6. Ibid., p. 1.

7. On this point, compare Karl Marx, *Economic and Philosophic Manuscripts of 1844*, ed. Dirk Struik (New York: International Publishers, 1964), p. 140, and Antonio Gramsci, *Selections From the Prison Notebooks*, tr. Quinton Hoare and Geoffrey Nowell Smith (New York: International Publishers, 1971), p. 324.

8. Marx, "Theses on Feuerbach," p. 121.

9. Ibid., passim. See also Gramsci, *Selections*, p. 360.

10. See ibid., p. 352, on this point.

11. Marx and Engels, *German Ideology*, p. 59.

12. Marx, *1844 Manuscripts*, p. 141. See also Karl Marx, *Grundrisse*, tr. Martin Nicholaus (Middlesex, England: Penguin, 1973), p. 162.

13. Marx, "Theses on Feuerbach," p. 121.

14. Karl Marx, *Capital* (Moscow: Foreign Language Publishing House, 1954), 1:20.

15. Marx, *1844 Manuscripts*, p. 119.

16. See Lukacs, "Orthodox Marxism," p. 13.

17. Ibid.

18. Marx and Engels, *German Ideology*, p. 114.

19. Karl Marx, *Selected Writings in Sociology and Social Philosophy*, tr. T. B. Bottomore (New York: McGraw-Hill, 1956), p. 232.

20. Gramsci, *Selections*, p. 326.

21. Ibid., p. 344.

22. On this point, compare Marx, "Theses on Feuerbach," p. 122.

23. I have described this at greater length in Nancy Hartsock, "Political Change: Two Perspectives on Power," *Quest: A Feminist Quarterly* 1, no. 1 (Summer 1974): 10–25.

24. Rosa Luxemburg, "Organizational Questions of Russian Social Democracy," in *Selected Writings of Rosa Luxemburg,* ed. Dick Howard (New York: Monthly Review Press), p. 285.

25. Ibid., p. 289.

26. Ibid., p. 293.

27. Criteria for choosing strategies are discussed more extensively in Charlotte Bunch, "The Reform Tool Kit," and Hartsock, "Political Change," *Quest: A Feminist Quarterly* 1, no. 1 (Summer 1974).

three

Staying Alive

Gray is the color of work without purpose or end, and the cancer of hopelessness creeping through the gut.

—**Marge Piercy,** *To Be of Use*

You're there just to filter people and filter telephone calls. . . . You're treated like a piece of equipment, like the telephone. You come in at nine, you open the door, you look at the piece of machinery, you plug in the headpiece. That's how my day begins. You tremble when you hear the first ring. After that, it's sort of downhill. . . .

I don't have much contact with people. You can't see them. You don't know if they're laughing, if they're being satirical or being kind. So your conversations become very abrupt. I notice that in talking to people. My conversations would be very short and clipped, in short sentences, the way I talk to people all day on the telephone. . . . When I'm talking to someone at work, the telephone rings and the conversation is interrupted. So I never bother finishing sentences or finishing thoughts. I always have this feeling of interruption. . . . There isn't a ten minute break in the whole day that's quiet. . . . You can't think, you can't even finish a letter. So you do quickie things, like read a chapter in a short story. It has to be short term stuff. . . . I always dream I'm alone and things are quiet. I call it the land of no-phone, where there isn't any machine telling me where I have to be every minute. The machine dictates. This crummy little machine with buttons on it—you've got to be there to hear it, but it pulls you. You

In *Building Feminist Theory: Essays from Quest* (New York: Longman, 1981). Originally published in *Quest: A Feminist Quarterly* 3, 3 (Winter 1976-1977).

know you're not doing anything, not doing a hell of a lot for anyone. Your job doesn't mean anything. Because you're just a little machine. A monkey could do what I do. It's really unfair to ask someone to do that.

I don't know what I'd like to do. That's what hurts the most. That's why I can't quit the job. I really don't know what talents I may have. And I don't know where to go to find out. I've been fostered so long at school and I didn't have time to think about it.

—**Studs Terkel,** *Working*

Whether we work for wages or not, most of us have come to accept that we work because we must. We know that the time we spend on things important to us must somehow be found outside the time we work to stay alive. We have forgotten that work is in fact fundamental to our development as human beings, that it is a source of our sense of accomplishment, and an important aspect of our sense of self.

Work is an especially important question for feminists since in our capitalist and patriarchal society the work that women do goes unrecognized, whether it is done for wages or not. Housework is not defined as work at all, but rather as a "natural" activity, or an expression of love. Only in the last few years have women as a group demanded that housework be recognized as important work. Women who work for wages simply have two jobs—the one, though unimportant and temporary, recognized as work, and the other, completely unrecognized.

The liberation of women—and all human beings—depends on understanding that work is essential to our development as individuals and on creating new places in our lives for our work. We must develop a new conception of work itself. To begin this process, we must clarify what is wrong with the capitalist and patriarchal organization of work and define the requirements of *human* work. We must critically evaluate the ways we are structuring work in feminist organizations, where we can experiment, and invent ways to use our work for our development as human beings.

Estranged Labor

The receptionist has described the way most of us feel about our work—that it is not important and that the pace is often set by machines or by people who are not involved in the work itself. Work is something we must do, however painful. In our society, work is, almost by definition, something we cannot enjoy. Time at work is time we do not have for ourselves—time when creativity is cut off, time when our activity is structured by rules set down by others. The increasing use of unskilled labor (or more precisely, the skills everyone is taught in public schools), and the increasing application of scientific management techniques in manufacturing, the office, and even the home (as home economics) all contribute to the feeling that many jobs could be done by machines and that people should not have to do them. In these respects, housework does not differ fundamentally from women's wage work. Housewives too experience the isolation described by the receptionist, while the phrase "just a housewife" expresses the cultural devaluation of housework.

The work most of us do has been described by Marx as estranged labor—time and activity taken from us and used against us. Work that should be used for our growth as well-rounded human beings is used instead to diminish us, to make us feel like machines. Estranged labor distorts our lives in a number of ways, most of them illustrated by the receptionist's description of her work.* She expresses what Marx described as our separation from our own activity at work when she says, "the machine dictates. This crummy little machine with buttons on it," so that "you can't think."[1] We are not in control of our actions during the time we work; our time belongs to those who have the money to buy our time. Women's time in particular is not our own but is almost always controlled by men. Our time is not our own even away from work. The rhythms of estranged labor infect our leisure time as well; our work exhausts us, and we need time to recover from it. As a result we spend much of our leisure time in passive activities—watching television, listening to the radio, or sleeping.

In addition, Marx pointed out that our work separates us from others, preventing real communication with our fellow workers. Often our work separates us physically from others. Some manufacturers deliberately put working stations too far apart for conversation among employees. But just as often, we are kept from real contact with others not by actual physical barriers but by roles, status differences, and hierarchies. The receptionist points out that although she is surrounded by people, she has little contact with them. Competition on the job also separates us from others. We are forced into situations in which our own promotion or raise means that someone else cannot advance, situations where we can benefit only by another's loss.

Patriarchy, too, in giving men more power over women, separates us from real contact with other human beings. And here, too, the patterns of our lives at work invade our leisure as well. The receptionist says, "I never

---

*All this is more true for working- and lower-class women than for middle-class professional women. Women who are lawyers, for example, have much more control over their work, but the patterns that are so clear for most women (whether we work for wages or not) also structure and limit the ability of any woman to control her own work.

answer the phone at home. It carries over. The way I talk to people has changed. Even when my mother calls, I don't talk to her very long. I want to *see* people to talk to them. But now, when I see them, I talk to them like I was talking on the telephone. . . . I don't know what's happened."[2]

Finally, estranged labor prevents us from developing as well-rounded people and keeps us from participating in the life of the community as a whole. Marx argued that rather than participating in community work for joint purposes, our survival as individuals becomes primary for us, and prevents us from recognizing our common interests.[3] Our own activity, especially our actions in our work, separates us from other people and from the people we ourselves could become. We work only because we must earn enough money to satisfy our physical needs. Yet by working only to survive, we are participating in our own destruction as real, social individuals. Worst of all, even though we recognize the dehumanization our work forces on us, we are powerless as individuals to do anything about it. Patriarchy and capitalism work together to define "women's work" as suited only to creatures of limited talent and ambition; the sex segregation of the labor market ensures that women's work will be especially dehumanizing. The receptionist speaks for most of us when she says she doesn't know what she wants to do. We all have talents we are not developing but we don't really know what they are. As she says, we haven't really had the chance to find out.

Work: The Central Human Activity

Because of the perverted shape of work in a patriarchal, capitalist society, we have forgotten that work is a central human activity, the activity through which the self-creation of human beings is accomplished.[4] Work is a definition of what it is to be human—a striving first to meet physical needs and later to realize all our human potentialities. Marx argues that our practical activity, or work in the largest sense, is so fundamental that social reality itself is made up of human activity (work).[5]

Our work produces both our material existence and our consciousness. Both consciousness and material life grow out of our efforts to satisfy physical needs, a process that leads to the production of new needs. These efforts, however, are more than the simple production of physical existence. They make up a "definite mode of life." "As individuals express their life, so they are. What they are, therefore, coincides with their production, both with *what* they produce and with *how* they produce. The nature of individuals thus depends on the material conditions determining their production."[6] Here individuality must be understood as a social phenomenon, that human existence in all its forms must be seen as the product of human activity—that is, activity and consciousness "both in their content and in their *mode of existence,* are *social: social* activity and *social* mind."[7]

Finally, Marx argued that the realization of all human potential is possible only as and when human beings as a group develop their powers and that these powers can be realized only through the cooperative action of all people over time.[8] Thus, although it is human work that structures the social world, the structure is imposed not by individuals but by generations, each building on the work of those who came before. Fully developed individuals, then, are products of human work over the course of history.[9]

As we saw, however, capitalism perverted human work, has distorted the self-creation of real individuals. The fact that a few use the time of a majority for their own profit or their own pleasure makes work into a means to life rather than life itself. The work we do has become estranged labor; and as a result, our humanity itself is diminished. Our work has become a barrier to our self-creation, to the expansion and realization of our potential as human beings. Work in a capitalist and patriarchal society means that in our work and in our leisure we do not affirm but deny ourselves; we are not content but unhappy; we do not develop our own capacities, but destroy our bodies and ruin our minds.[10]

By contrast, creative work could be understood as play, and as an expression of ourselves. "In creative work as well as genuine play, exhaustion is not deadening. . . . When one selects the object of work, determines its method, and creates its configuration, the consciousness of time tends to disappear. While clock-watching is a characteristic disease of those burdened with alienated labor, [when we work creatively], we lose ourselves, and cease to measure our activities in so many units of minutes and hours. . . . "[11]

Alternatives to Estranged Labor

The perversion of our work, then, is the perversion of our lives as a whole. Thus our liberation requires that we recapture our work. Ultimately we can do this only by reordering society as a whole and directing it away from domination, competition, and the isolation of women from each other. What would work be like in such a society? What models can we look to for guidance about ways to reorganize work?

We know that a feminist restructuring of work must avoid the monotonous jobs with little possibility of becoming more creative and the fragmentation of people through the organization of work into repetitive and unskilled tasks. Although we have some ideas about what such a reorganization of work would look like, the real redefinition of work can occur only in practice. While our alternative institutions cannot fully succeed so long as we live in a society based on private profit rather than public good—a society in which work and human development are polar opposites—feminist organizations provide a framework within which to experiment. The organizations we build are an integral part of the process of creating political change and, in the long run, can perhaps serve as proving grounds for new institutions.

Some examples of alternatives to estranged labor occur in science fiction. There are worlds, for example, in which high status relieves one from the necessity to consume and provides a chance to work. To move up in that world means to move from a life of high consumption to a life of low consumption and work. In *The Female Man*, Joanna Russ describes a world where no one works more than three hours at a time on any one job except in emergencies, and the workweek is only sixteen hours. Yet, she says, Whilewayans work all the time. Marge Piercy, in *Woman on the Edge of Time*, shows us a future in which all the work is done by machines, and women no longer bear children. The high level of technology makes it possible for people to work at things that satisfy them, and spend only a small part of their time on supervising and overseeing the production.[12]

There are, however, contemporary alternatives. The Chinese restructuring of work does not depend on changes in technology but rather operates on two assumptions: first, creativity is an aspect of all kinds of labor, and ordinary women and men on ordinary jobs can make innovations and contributions to society that deserve honor and reward; second, all work that helps build a new society should be treated with the new significance previously accorded only to mental labor. The Chinese, too, have been concerned with avoiding the star mentality, and have argued instead that those who are capable of helping others should make that, rather than their own advancement, a priority. Thus, in China, to lead means to be at the *center* of a group rather than in front of others.[13]

These examples of alternatives to estranged labor draw our attention to the organization of the labor process itself. Feminists, in developing new organizational forms, have been concerned with two related factors that structure the estranged labor process in our society—the use of power as domination, both in the workplace and elsewhere, and the separation of mental from manual work. By understanding the ways these two aspects of estranged labor mold the labor process as a whole, we can correct some of the mistakes we have made as a movement and avoid making others in the future.

Power and Political Change

In an article on power, I argued that social theorists have generally conceptualized power as "the ability to compel obedience, or as control and domination."[14] Power must be power over someone—something possessed, a property of an actor such that he* can alter the will or actions of others in a way which produces results in conformity with his own will.[15] Social theorists have argued that power, like money, is something possessed by an actor that has value in itself as well as being useful for obtaining other valued things.

That power can be compared with money in capitalist society supports Marx's claim that the importance of the market leads to the transformation of all human activity into patterns modeled on monetary transactions.[16] In this society, where human interdependence is fundamentally structured by markets and the exchange of money, power as domination of others (or the use of power to "purchase" certain behavior, which diminishes rather than develops us), is what most of us confront in our work.

There are other definitions of power. Berenice Carroll points out that in *Webster's International Dictionary* (1933), power is first defined as "ability, whether physical, mental, or moral, to act; the faculty of doing or performing something," and is synonymous with "strength, vigor, energy, force, and ability." The words "control" and "domination" do not appear as synonyms.[17] In this definition of power, energy and accomplishment are understood to be satisfying in themselves. This understanding of power is much closer to what the women's movement has sought, and this aspect of power is denied to all but a few women; the experience described by the receptionist can scarcely be characterized as effective interaction with the environment.

Feminists have rightly rejected the use of power as domination and as a property analogous to money, but in practice our lack of clarity about the differences between the two concepts of power has led to difficulties about leadership, strength, and achievement. In general, feminists have not recognized that power understood as energy, strength, and effectiveness need not be the same as power that requires the domination of others.

We must, however, recognize and confront the world of traditional politics in which money and power function in similar ways. For those of us who work in "straight" jobs (whether paid or not) and work part time in feminist organizations, the confrontation occurs daily. Those of us who work full time for feminist organizations confront power as domination most often when our organizations try to make changes in the world. Creating political change requires that we set up organizations based on power defined as energy and strength, groups that are structured, not tied to the personality of a single individual, and whose structures do not permit the use of power to dominate others in the group. At the same

---

*"He" and "men" here refer specifically to men and not women.

time, our organizations must be effective in a society in which power is a means of making others do what they do not wish to do.

Mental and Manual Labor

One of the characteristics of advanced capitalist society is the separation of the conception of work from its execution.[18] This division between mental and manual labor—which also shapes the process of estranged labor—is an expression of the power relations between the rulers and the ruled, and is closely related to the concept of power as domination. Having power and dominating others is commonly associated with conceptual or mental work; subordination, with execution, or with manual (routine) work. Women form a disproportionate number of those who do routine work and rarely are insiders in capitalist rituals and symbols of know-how.

As the Chinese have recognized, subordination and lack of creativity are not features of routine work itself but rather are aspects of the socialist relations within which the work takes place. A feminist restructuring of work requires creating a situation in which thinking and doing, planning and routine work, are parts of the work each of us does; it requires creating a work situation in which we can both develop ourselves and transform the external world. Our work itself would provide us with satisfaction and with the knowledge that we were learning and growing. It would be an expression of our own individuality and power in the world.

The Development of a Feminist Workplace

Specific questions about how to restructure the labor process can be grouped under the two general headings of problems of power and problems about the division between mental and manual labor. Attention to these two factors can provide several specific guidelines. First, overcoming the domination of a few over the majority of workers in an organization requires that we have control over our own time and activity. Second, we need to develop possibilities for cooperative rather than competitive and isolated work; we need to develop ways for people to work together on problems rather than for one (perhaps more experienced) person to give orders to another.

We need to recognize the importance of enabling people to become fully developed rather than one-sided. We need to make sure that women can learn new skills well enough to innovate and improve on what they have been taught. We need to make space for changes in interests and skills over time. We need to include elements of both mental and manual work, both planning and routine execution, in every job we create. Finally, we must recognize the importance of responsibility as a source of power (energy) for individual members of feminist organizations. To have responsibility for a project means to have the respect of others in the group, and usually means as well that we must develop our capacities to fulfill that responsibility. The lines of responsibility must be clear, and unless the organization is large, they will often end with a single individual. Having responsibility for some parts of the work done by a group allows us not only to see our own accomplishments but also to expand ourselves by sharing in the accomplishments of others.[19] We are not superwomen, able to do everything. Only by sharing in the different accomplishments of others can we participate in the activities of all women.

Collectives and Cooperatives Work

Given these general guidelines, how should we evaluate one of the most common forms of the organization of work—the collective? Here I am concerned about one type of collective—a group that insists that the work done by each member should be fundamentally the same. This kind of organization is widespread in the women's movement, although not all groups that call themselves collectives function in this way. For example, the Olivia Records collective maintains all lines of individual responsibility for different areas of work.[20]

Just as the women's movement erred in its almost universal condemnation of leaders—and its mistaken identification of women who achieved with those who wanted to dominate—we have, through working in collectives, many times simply reacted against the separation of conception from execution. Collective work is our answer to the isolation, competitiveness, and the monotony of the routine work forced on us in capitalist workplaces. But collectives can at the same time reproduce some of the worst features of estranged labor—the separation of the worker from her own activity, the loss of control over her work, and the separation from real cooperative work—that is, work *with* rather than simply beside others. It can cut us off from real growth as individuals. This happens when collectives reproduce power as domination of others and at the same time reintroduce the division between conception and execution.

Informal rather than formal domination of some members of the collective by others often results from the attempt to avoid hierarchal domination by avoiding formal structure altogether. What is in theory the control of the entire group over its work becomes in fact the domination of some members of the group by others. Some members of the group lose control over their work to those who are more aggressive, although perhaps not more skilled. Also, informal decision making, which assumes that every collective member has the same amount to contribute in every area, can result in reducing opportunities for cooperative work, work that recognizes, combines and uses the differing skills and interests of members of the group to create something none could do alone.

In the attempt to make sure that every task is done by every member of the group, those who were less involved in setting up particular tasks are deprived of a sense of accomplishment—a sense that their activity is an individual and unique expression of who they are, a contribution to the group from which the group as a whole can benefit. By rotating all members through the various tasks of the group, and by insisting that every member of a collective do every activity that the group as a whole is engaged in, the collective, in practice, treats its members as interchangeable and equivalent parts. It reproduces the assembly line of the modern factory, but instead of running the work past the people, people are run past the work.

We are not all equally capable of planning and doing every task of the groups in which we are involved, although we may have some special skills in a particular area. For example, while I am incapable of doing layout or paste-up for *Quest*, I am a competent editor. If much of the work done by one member of the collective has been designed and planned by someone else, the accomplishment and creativity involved in designing a system for doing routine work is not possible. Instead, the tasks are already planned and one learns new operations, planned by someone else. The separation between conception and execution has not been overcome.

One reply to this criticism is that learning skills is important and that collectives provide a place to learn new skills. While we can agree that women very much need to learn new skills, it takes time to reach the point where we can be creative with a new skill. We need to *learn* skills rather than simply try out new things. One of the best ways to learn a skill completely is to be entrusted with full responsibility for one or more aspects of the operation.

In sum, my criticism of this form of collective work is that it is simply a reaction against being forced by the capitalist, patriarchal organization of work to do a single task over and over again. Requiring each of us to do everything is not a creative response and cannot provide a real alternative to estranged labor. A creative response allowing us to move toward unalienated labor requires that we examine the root causes rather than the surface appearances of estranged labor in our society. We should recognize, for example, that learning skills by working for long periods of time on one aspect of the activities of a group does not necessarily produce the estranged labor of capitalist society. If we recognize that the problem is not simply doing one kind of work for a long period of time but rather results from the social relations that surround the work process—power as domination of others, and the separation of conception from execution in our work—we can respond to the real problems of work in feminist organizations. Thus, learning skills means not only learning the physical operations involved in a particular kind of work but learning how to organize and set up that work in the best way—from the perspectives both of efficiency and of self-development.

Conclusions: The Fragility of Alternatives

Even if we correctly identify the factors that structure the labor process in our society, the alternatives we construct can be only very tenuous. Work in feminist organizations will exist in the tension between reformism and conformity on the one hand and simple reaction to work in our society on the other. Our strategies for change and the internal organization of work must grow out of the tension between using our organizations as instruments for both taking and transforming power in a society structured by power understood only as domination and using our organizations to build models for a society based on power understood as energy and initiative. Work in feminist organizations must be a way of expressing and sharing with others who we are and what we can do, a means of developing ourselves, as well as a place to contribute to the struggle for liberation. There are real pressures to reproduce the patterns of estranged labor in the interests of efficiency and taking power. At the same time, there are pressures to oppose estranged labor by insisting that each of us do every job. We can develop correct strategies only by critically examining the practical work we have done as we attempt to maintain organizations in which power is recognized as energy and in which we work to overcome the divisions between mental and manual labor.

NOTES

1. Studs Terkel, *Working* (New York: Pantheon, 1972), p. 30.

2. Ibid.

3. Karl Marx, *Economic and Philosophic Manuscripts of 1844*, ed. Dirk Struik (New York: International Publishers, 1964), pp. 112–13. The account of alienation is taken from pp. 106–19.

4. Herbert Marcuse, *Studies in Critical Philosophy*, tr. Joris De Bres (Boston: Beacon Press, 1973), p. 14; Karl Marx, *1844 Manuscripts*, pp. 113, 188.

5. Karl Marx, *Capital* (New York: International Publishers, 1967), 1:183–84.

6. Karl Marx and Frederick Engels, *The German Ideology*, ed. C. J. Arthur (New York: International Publishers, 1970), pp. 42, 59.

7. Karl Marx, *1844 Manuscripts*, p. 137.

8. Ibid., p. 17.

9. Karl Marx, *The Grundrisse,* tr. Martin Nicolaus (Middlesex, England: Penguin, 1973), p. 162.

10. Marx, *1844 Manuscripts,* p. 110.

11. Stanley Aronowitz, *False Promises* (New York: McGraw-Hill, 1973), p. 62.

12. Respectively, Frederick Pohl, "The Midas Plague," in *The Science Fiction Hall of Fame,* ed. Ben Bova (New York: Avon, 1973); Joanna Russ, *The Female Man* (New York: Bantam, 1975), pp. 53–56; and Marge Piercy, *Woman on the Edge of Time* (New York: Knopf, 1976).

13. See Marilyn Young, "Introduction," *Signs* 2, no. 1 (Autumn 1976): 2, and Mary Sheridan, "Young Women Leaders," *Signs* 2, no. 1 (Autumn 1976): 66.

14. "Political Change: Two Perspectives on Power," *Quest* 1, no. 1 (Summer 1974): 10–25.

15. See Bertrand Russell, *Power, A New Social Analysis* (N.P., 1936), p. 35, cited by Anthony de Crespigny and Alan Wertheimer, *Contemporary Political Theory* (New York: Atherton Press, 1970), p. 22; Harold Lasswell and Abraham Kaplan, *Power and Society* (New Haven: Yale University Press, 1950), p. 76; Talcott Parsons, "On The Concept of Political Power," in *Political Power,* ed. Roderick Bell, David V. Edwards, and R. Harrison Wagner (New York: Free Press, 1969), p. 256.

16. Marx, *Grundrisse,* p. 65.

17. Berenice Carroll, "Peace Research: The Cult of Power" (paper presented to the American Sociological Association, Denver, Colorado, September 1971), pp. 6–7.

18. Harry Braverman, *Labor and Monopoly Capital* (New York: Monthly Review Press), especially pp. 70–121.

19. As Marx put it, "I would have been for you the mediator between you and the species and thus been acknowledged and felt by you as a completion of your own essence and a necessary part of yourself and have thus realized that I am confirmed both in your thought and in your love. In my expression of my life I would have fashioned your expression of your life, and thus in my own activity have realized my own essence, my human, communal essence." In David McLellan, *The Thought of Karl Marx* (New York: Viking, 1969), p. 32.

20. Ginny Berson, "Olivia: We Don't Just Process Records," *Sister* 7, no. 2 (December–January 1976): 8–9.

four

Difference and Domination in the Women's Movement: The Dialectic of Theory and Practice

As a movement, contemporary feminism has found issues of difference very difficult both to understand and to cope with. In part, this has occurred because of the close links in our society between difference and domination. Differences among people, and among women, have been systematically used both to create and to justify the domination of some by others. Feminist understandings of difference, as these are expressed in our practices, have gone through several phases as our movement has developed. We have moved from a denial of the importance of difference, through an avoidance of difference, to the beginnings of a recognition that the differences among us need not imply relations of domination. Each phase enabled us to learn something important about difference, domination, and the nature of social change. Yet much of what we have learned about difference in practice has not yet been articulated as theory.

Originally presented at the seventh annual Scholar and Feminist Conference, held at Barnard College, April 1980.

My purpose here is to review our practices in an attempt to clarify what we as a movement already know at some level. This task is particularly important now, when issues of power and difference are such important topics among feminists.

I will take up several interrelated questions that the nexus of power and difference pose for feminists. First, does power mean only power over others? And does difference always provide a ground, or justification, for domination? Second, what effects does the practice of separatism (an avoidance of difference) have on the theory and practice of power? Third, separatism seems to institutionalize differences. Can a strategy of institutionalizing differences, whether in the forms of separatism, the formation of caucuses in larger organizations, or the construction of coalitions, help to overcome differences that lead to or support hierarchy and domination? But if our organizations institutionalize differences along the lines of race, sexuality, or class, can these organizations then be able to prefigure the society we want? These are difficult questions, and I do not claim to be able to answer them here.

I believe we can gain more clarity about these difficult questions by drawing some conceptual distinctions within the concept of difference, based on the ways feminists have in fact dealt with differences. Clarifying our understanding of these distinctions can help us both to ask and to answer the new questions posed for us by the contemporary focus on issues of difference within the women's movement. I propose to distinguish differences both from Difference and from specificity. Differences can best be understood as empirical phenomena. We are, after all, not all alike: Feminists differ in terms of income, occupation, race, sexuality, height, hair color, and a host of other characteristics. It is only when these characteristics are given a particular social and even ontological meaning that they become the ground for what I would call Difference, or radical alterity, and thereby can be used as a basis for domination.

Ursula LeGuin provided an important clue to what our society has made of differences, a clue to the way differences have been used to construct Difference, when she suggested that there was an important relationship between the treatment of aliens in science fiction and the treatment of humans who were considered to be somehow different. She made clear the consequences of declaring that the alien was sexually, racially, culturally, or socially different, whether our fear of it took the form of either hatred or reverence:

> If you deny any affinity with another person or kind of person, if you declare it to be wholly different from yourself, as men have done to women, and class has done to class, and nation has done to nation, you may hate it or deify it, but in either case you have denied its spiritual equality and its human

reality. You have made it into a thing to which the only possible relationship is a power relationship and thus you have fatally impoverished your own reality.[1]

LeGuin was claiming that the logic by which Difference was constructed was a logic of domination, a logic that resulted in damage to both parties. The existence of differences, then, allows for the construction of Difference and, thereby, domination.

Yet feminist practice has demonstrated that this need not be the inevitable result of differences. Indeed, one of the most important activities of the women's movement in the seventies was the transformation of socially constructed Difference into specificity, or positive collective identity. Thus, whereas men have defined women as radically "other," feminists have gradually been able to give a series of specific contents to this "otherness." We have constructed a series of collective and positive and overlapping identities as feminists, as lesbians, as women of color, specificities that can no longer be reduced to "otherness," to "not men." As an Italian feminist has put it, "otherness" is socially constructed for us, and specificity is what we make for ourselves.[2] And whereas the logic of Difference leads to domination, I will argue that the logic of specificity supports the development of a definition of power as energy, as an ability to act.

The transformation of Difference into specificity, and of domination into energy and ability to act, important and essential as it has been, simply mirrored and reversed the relations of capitalist patriarchy. Feminists need to move beyond simple reaction and reversal toward more creative and encompassing responses.[3] As a movement, we are only now beginning to develop an understanding of difference, an understanding that can transcend both capitalist logic and its reverse. The current efforts to confront issues of differences of race, class, and sexuality in the women's movement represent something new and important. We are beginning to see our differences as potential grounds for creativity, connection, and complementarity.[4] And I will argue that if we analyze difference in new ways, given the intimate connections between difference and power, we should expect new theorizations of power. Let us look more closely, then, at the practices in which these insights about difference and power have taken form.

The Denial of Difference

The strategy of civil rights organizations in the late fifties and early sixties and in turn that of a number of early feminist groups can be seen as efforts to make the rhetoric and promises of bourgeois democracy real. These reform strategies implicitly embodied an acceptance of the ruling-class account of our society as fundamentally constituted by the freely given consent of free and equal individuals. This account was believed to conflict with reality only in minor ways, and thus strategies for change in the early and mid-sixties did not grow from questions about the fundamentals of the American way of life.

In the first stage of feminist reform efforts, which I date roughly from the founding of the National Organization for Women up to the beginnings of the Women's Liberation Movement (1964–1968), feminists implicitly held that the differences between women and men were not a sufficient base on which to construct Difference, that is, that differences of gender were superficial and insufficient grounds on which to construct radical alterity, or "Otherness." Thus, efforts to overcome discrimination against women took the form of attempts to create what could only be a false universality and a concomitant refusal to recognize the economic and social underpinnings of power differences.

In retrospect, the reform strategies of both the civil rights movement and the early women's movement were partly manifestations of a failure to see the ways differences were systematically transformed into Difference and used to dominate both women and men of color and white women. Moreover, partly because these reform strategies failed to recognize the importance of Difference, they failed as well to confront the basic issue of who holds power.[5] In turn, failure to recognize the impact of socially constructed Otherness led to a failure to recognize the ways in which relations of domination were perpetuated within movements committed to change. To take just one example, in view of the fact that it was white, middle-class women with access to media visibility who named the problems that should be of concern to all women, it is not surprising that few women of color were interested in participating in feminist activities.[6]

The Black movement discovered early that the assumption that everyone was equal in movements for social change represented an unworkable and false universalism, and Black leaders were the first to point out that differences (existed and) were manifested as power differences. It is no accident, then, that Black separatism and Black liberation initially took form through a call for Black power: The discovery of the significance of socially constructed radical alterity was directly connected to the discovery of the importance of power relations. The transition from civil rights movement to Black liberation movement marked a fundamental shift and significant advance in understandings of power and difference.

Difference as Domination in Feminist Practice

Feminists benefited a great deal from the insights of the Black liberation movement. As the women's movement followed the same directions as those taken by the Black movement, feminist practice, though not yet feminist theory, implicitly held that it was Difference that defined Black and third world oppression, and Difference that was fundamental to the segmented labor market, in which women received less than 60 percent of men's wages, and in which Black women, until the fifties, worked almost exclusively as domestics. It was the women's movement that pointed out that it was socially constructed Difference that defined women as "other" and led to their exclusion from decision making both in society as a whole and in movements for social change. Feminist recognition of the importance and use of Difference to construct domination took the form of a series of practical efforts to prevent the construction of Difference within the women's movement and, thereby, to prevent domination. The opposition to structured organization and leadership, advocacy of collective work, and the development of separatism should all be understood as attempts to prevent differences from becoming the ground for relations of domination.

Unstructured consciousness-raising (CR) groups provided the first feminist organizational forms, and many small groups of grassroots activists as well as many women's centers have functioned on the CR group model. Thus, many groups have in the past opposed structured organizations as places in which some individuals could hold power over others. Decisions about the work to be done in the following year were often taken in meetings where anyone who came just for that meeting had as much right to participate as those who had kept the center going during the previous year. The obvious problems posed by these strategies only underline the seriousness of feminist efforts to prevent the construction of Difference. Related to feminist emphasis on unstructured groups was the stress on process. Many feminists remember the emphasis on the importance of "the growing self," or the "evolving consciousness," the presentation of matters for discussion again and again until everyone present agreed to a policy. Or the frequent practice of remaking and rethinking decisions when a new woman showed up at a meeting and questioned the decisions a group had already taken. The great weight feminists have given to making certain that everyone was satisfied with decisions makes clear both our reluctance to use the power of the majority to dominate and the seriousness of feminist efforts to prevent the construction of Difference.

In addition, in the early seventies, feminists overwhelmingly opposed leadership, a strand of thinking that is still very strong. Although this opposition grew in part from the strong influence of anarchism among the New Left in the United States, it came more immediately from feminist desires to eliminate bureaucratic structures and elitist leadership. Some have argued that the opposition to leadership meant that any woman who appeared competent or who took responsibility for accomplishing things was likely to be "trashed" for being a leader.[7] Feminists were reacting in expectable ways to their experiences of leadership in the male-dominated Left. Because women had been oppressed by elitist and unresponsive male leaders in these radical Left groups, they reacted by refusing to designate any leaders at all. The point that emerges from these strategies is that feminists attempted to avoid appointing, electing, or selecting *anyone* who would be in a position to exercise power over them. We recognized in practice the important ways structural differentiation in positions could serve as a basis for domination and attempted to avoid those effects by refusing to build more than minimal structures.

Feminist insistence on working collectively was a third response/reaction to the problems posed by Difference. Although there are a variety of models for collectives, one of the most common forms requires that the work done by each member of a group be identical with that of every other—a way of avoiding the division of labor that has in the past taken the form of a division between mental and manual labor, with resulting elitism. (Although not all groups that call themselves collectives function in this way, many do. These latter are the objects of my concern here.)[8] There is an important statement about both power and Difference in this practice. By implication, collectives of this sort state through their practices that permitting any differences inevitably leads to the social construction of Difference and therefore to inequality and to relations of domination. These collectives, by insisting on the identity and interchangeability of members, represent another important way feminists have worked against the construction of Difference.

Separatism developed along with these strategies for avoiding the construction of Difference and therefore domination. The early seventies marked a very painful period of splitting and separatism within the women's movement. First, feminists responded to masculine domination by insisting that they could only work separately, and used the split between Blacks and whites in the civil rights movement as justification for this position. When the power of heterosexual women over lesbians' visible presence within the women's movement and the ability of upper- and middle-class women to define issues for working-class women in the movement became clear, the first response was to split into smaller units. Racial separation, whether in the form of separate organizations for women of color or their indifference or hostility to the feminist movement, has been a constant. These small units meant that no woman had to work politically with others who might be in a position—whether through class, race, or heterosexual privilege—to exercise power over her. Each of these actions (I hesitate to call them conscious tactics at this point) was a means of avoiding either the exercising of power or the experience of domination.

The creation of structureless groups, where there were no differences of gender, sexuality, class, or race, implicitly affirmed the theoretical position that differences inevitably provided a ground for the construction of Difference and therefore domination or even, perhaps, that Difference and differences were identical. In addition, these strategies for avoiding power and domination implicitly accepted the idea that power was the ability to compel obedience, that power must be power over someone—something possessed, a property of an actor that enables him to alter the will or actions of others in a way that produces results in conformity with his own will.[9] Power as domination of others or the use of power to "purchase" certain behavior is what most women confront. On this understanding, power is exercised in situations in which one person gets another to do something the latter is disinclined to do by threatening some consequences that the second person will dislike more than taking the required action.[10]

All this amounts to a feminist acceptance of the phallocratic logic of domination. First, we failed to go beyond the phallocratic understanding that power is to be equated with domination, and second, we failed to see that differences need not lead to Difference. Our organizational and individual practices demonstrated that we accepted the phallocratic logic of domination, which held that Difference and differences were identical. Rather than reexamine this logic, we tried to prevent the existence of difference and therefore Difference within our movement. In saying this, I must point out that this acceptance was both untheorized and inarticulate. In addition, I do not mean to suggest that these several strategies were wrong. Separatism in particular has proved very fruitful in some respects.

Transforming Difference into Specificity

Separatism must be assessed and understood not simply as a defensive reaction to the phallocratic use of Difference to construct and reinforce domination, but it must be seen as well as the means by which feminists transformed our socially defined "otherness" into a self-defined specificity. Separatism allowed the creation of women's communities, women's spaces, and women's culture. On the one hand, these have helped to overcome some of the differences among women; on the other hand, they represent a repetition and strengthening of the patterns of avoiding those who might have power over us. Feminists have created spaces in a capitalist and patriarchal society where we could be free of our oppression as women—a world of women's music, women's businesses, coffee shops, bars, living communities, and so on. Separatism was fundamental to the survival and sanity of feminists, both as individuals and as a movement. We needed to create "safe" spaces where we could grow and learn and experiment, and we continue to need places where we define the terms (as women, as lesbians, as women of color, as working-class women).

Yet separatism and the avoidance of difference had a larger significance. Although we initially formed groups on the basis of our socially defined "otherness," feminists discovered in these groups that strengths as well as oppressions were shared. Our efforts to prevent the construction of Difference within the women's movement did allow space for the development of new ways of thinking and organizing. Consciousness-raising, with its stress on examining and understanding our own experience and on connecting that experience to the structures that define our lives, allowed for a very different mode of theorizing than one finds among other movements for change. We began to see feminism as a new and different mode of analysis rather than a set of political conclusions about the oppression of women, a worldview that could structure our understanding of society as a whole.[11]

As we attempted to develop new, nonhierarchical ways of working, we developed new organizational forms and feminist workplaces as well. In addition, the reclaiming of lesbian identity in the early seventies, the creation of lesbian feminism in both theory and practice, was one of the most important ways in which by reexamining our experience and reappropriating it, we managed to transform both our pasts and ourselves. All these changes were important results of our reaction against and opposition to the use of differences to construct Difference and relations of domination.

Empowerment and Difference

The experience of separatism led, as it had previously in the Black movement, to a transformation of the understanding of the nature and consequences of the differences along which the movement had split. It led as well to a transformation of feminist understandings of power. Within the movement, power exercised in and by feminist groups began to be seen, not as domination, but as ability to act and capacity to perform. It came to be synonymous with strength, energy, force, and ability. Important in all these descriptions of power is a vision of power as part of a process of change, a process that can be moved forward and directed. In attempting to develop and describe this understanding of power, I argued some years ago that feminists had to recognize that "power understood as energy, strength, and effective interaction need not be the same as power which requires domination of others in the movement." At the same time, I argued that because we also confront the world of traditional politics, "creating political change involves setting up organizations based on power as energy and strength, groups which are structured and not tied to the personality of one individual, groups whose structures do not permit the use of power as a tool for domination of others in the group. At the same time, our organizations must deal with the society in which we live on its own terms, that is, in terms of power as control, power as a means of making others do what they do not wish to do."[12] I repeat this because I think that my views were widely shared, and that my arguments reflected many feminists' efforts to construct organizational forms that expressed our newly developed sense of our strengths and identity. Thus, this theorization of power as energy grew both from the feminist fight against domination and from the development and discovery of capabilities. It expressed the experience of empowerment that the various separatist strategies had made possible, and it marked a willingness to think more explicitly about issues of power. Perhaps, most important, it represented a break with phallocratic reductions of power to domination.

In retrospect, however, I believe this was an incomplete understanding. Having the ability to act, or energy, is not the same as actually acting in ways that change the world. The feminist theory of power as energy and ability is uncomfortably close to Adrienne Rich's description of one of the traditional ways women's power has been experienced—as energy looking for objects into which to pour itself, even sometimes a demonic possession.[13] It is power bottled up and contained. Although feminist theorists, myself included, argued for an understanding of power as energy and ability, we have been silent about what actions might actually represent such an exercise of power. Perhaps this failure to consider the exercise of power or the impact of our actions reflected the insularity, isolation, and containment inherent in the several separatist strategies we had adopted.

In sum, the theorization of power as energy should be credited as a break with phallocratic understandings of power: It began to formulate a feminist reunderstanding of power that rested on and expressed the practical transformation of Difference into specificity in the daily practices of the women's movement. At the same time we should recognize it as an incomplete reunderstanding of power that avoided the questions of action in a heterogeneous world.[14] There is a sense for which, just as Difference was transformed into specificity and just as "otherness" was transformed into self-constituted identity, so too domination was transformed into energy and ability to act. Despite the fact that these understandings were simply reversals of the social relations of the capitalist patriarchy, they paved the way for breaking at least some of the links between difference and domination.

Difference and Domination: Breaking the Links

The current concern about racism in the women's movement is an indication both of the continuing difficulties of dealing with issues of difference among women and a collective expression of feminist willingness to re-think their meanings and to learn to use differences as sources of new ideas and strategies.[15] We are only beginning to understand the practical and theoretical significance of treating racial differences as sources of cre-ative tension rather than justifications for domination. Yet we can learn something about both the necessity for doing so and about some of the creative possibilities such strategies would make available by looking at the experience of an early lesbian-feminist separatist group in Washing-ton, D.C., organized in 1971. The Furies refused to work politically with straight feminists, and yet their efforts to live and work with others who shared their politics and sexuality were deeply handicapped by issues of Difference.

Despite the prominence of arguments that the women's movement has always consisted of white middle-class women, the Furies, like many feminist organizations, had a number of members from poor and work-ing-class backgrounds. These women insisted that class differences be confronted and argued that "refusal to deal with class behavior in a les-bian/feminist movement is sheer self-indulgence and leads to the down-fall of our own struggle."[16] One response to the discovery of the Differ-ence constructed out of class differences might have been to create yet another split, but perhaps because of the extent to which Difference had already become specificity in the context of the women's movement, the Furies began to work on issues of difference and to develop ways to make it possible to work together despite their differences. The creative tension that differences and the discovery of the importance of class can produce is illustrated by the fact that the Furies produced some of the best feminist analyses of class differences and their workings *within* the women's movement. Some of what they learned is worth recounting here, since it remains pertinent. Much of their analysis is relevant to discussions of re-lations between white women and women of color, as well as for women of color analyzing class differences in their own communities.

The Furies learned the sense in which we are all taught to take for granted that the "middle-class way is *the right way*." Being middle class "means being able to control people and situations for your benefit. No one in our movement would *say* that she believes she is better than her working class sisters, yet her behavior says it over and over again. Class arrogance can be expressed by looking down on the "less articulate,"[17] or regarding with "scorn or pity . . . those whose emotions are not repressed or who can't rap out abstract theories in thirty seconds flat." Class su-premacy, the Furies found, could also be apparent in a kind of passivity often assumed by middle- and especially upper-middle-class women for whom things have come easily.[18] Advocating downward mobility too can be another form of middle-class arrogance.[19] What is critical about all this is that the Furies saw that class differences worked to allow middle-class women to set the standards of what is good and to act "more revolutionary than thou" toward those concerned about money and the future. Middle-class women retained control over approval.

It is not surprising that the Furies' discoveries about class can be characterized by bell hooks's point about racism: "The force that allows white authors to make no reference to racial identity in their books about 'women' that are in actuality about white women is the same one that would compel any author writing exclusively on Black women to refer explicitly to their racial identity." She continues that "it is the dominant race that reserves for itself the luxury of dismissing racial identity while the oppressed race is made daily aware of their racial identity. It is the dominant race that can make it seem that their experience is representative."[20] Much the same can be said of class, though since class difference has been so well excluded from public debate in the United States, there seems to be even less awareness of classist behavior than of racism.

The Furies' experience indicates the potential value of differences to the feminist movement. For example, one white middle-class woman stated, "I learned out of necessity what classism was and I changed more quickly than if I had not been in a group with women who had class consciousness. . . . Class oppression was no longer an abstract concept. . . . It was a part of my life which I could see and change. And, having seen the manifestations of class in myself, I better understood how class operated generally to divide people and keep them down."[21]

In addition, the Furies' experience indicates the potential value of differences to the feminist movement. For example, they made organizational efforts to construct new forms and to develop strategies that took account of the class differences among them, strategies for sharing of income and responsibility that paid attention to both past and present privilege. These organizational changes signaled that differences need not become Difference, and that differences among women need not lead to the construction of "otherness." Rather, these differences could be used to clarify the class nature of our social system and help us protect feminist organizations from the full impact of class oppression. The existence of class differences among women, then, served the double purpose of exposing the daily workings of capitalist patriarchy and of helping feminists learn to oppose it.

It is important to stress that these efforts to deal creatively with class differences required organizational changes. These changes may be required when women of color and white women work together. As one writer has put it, "It is easy for white women to think that a group has been integrated if third world women have been brought in, but maybe they will also have to change the structure of their organization. Otherwise, the only third world women who can 'succeed' are those who can integrate. So we need fundamental changes in structure."[22]

Developing ways to work together across differences of class, race, sexuality, and gender once again raises the double question of power and differences, a question feminists can confront with the benefit of having discovered that differences need not only be sources of domination but can also become sources for creativity and growth. At the same time, by beginning to deal with differences in a new way, the Furies' experience implicitly posed problems for the feminist definition of power as empowerment and ability rather than domination. The feminist view of power as energy and ability grew from a period in which some, though not all, of the most damaging differences among women were muted by separatisms of various sorts. By going beyond this understanding, working together across differences, acting in a world in which women's differences are acknowledged, the Furies may have helped us to go beyond an understanding of power as energy.

Difference and Creativity: Toward a New Understanding of Power

The current phase, in which many feminists are attempting to move beyond separatism, raises in urgent form the need to learn to use differences as sources of creative tension. The Furies' experience can provide a sense of both the importance of dealing with differences and the creative possibilities differences make available. These possibilities emerge very strongly as well in one of the recent collections of writing by women of color, *This Bridge Called My Back*. Audre Lorde's contribution was one of the most powerful statements of what might occur. She argued:

> Advocating the mere tolerance of difference between women is . . . a total denial of the creative function of difference in our lives. For difference must be not merely tolerated, but seen as a fund of necessary polarities between which our creativity can spark like a dialectic. Only then does the necessity for interdependency become unthreatening. Only within that interdependency of different strengths, acknowledged and equal, can the power to seek new ways to actively "be" in the world generate, as well as the courage and sustenance to act where there are not charters.[23]

Interestingly enough, there is a resonance between Lorde's understanding of the creative possibilities of difference and the understanding of the role of differences that emerges in Marx's vision of human interaction in communism. Work, or conscious, self-realizing human activity, taken in its most inclusive definition as creative activity rather than toil, forms the basis for Marx's conception of the nature of humanity itself. Marx's description of an unalienated work process makes clear the possibilities for mutual interdependence and creation of community on the basis of difference—in this case a difference that takes the form of a division of labor. In an extraordinary passage from *The Economic and Philosophic Manuscripts of 1844* Marx speculated about nonalienated production.

> If I had produced in a human manner, I would have (1) objectified in my production my individuality and its peculiarity . . . (and thus both in my activity enjoyed an individual expression of my life and also in looking at the object have had the individual pleasure of realizing that my personality was objective, visible to the senses and thus a power raised beyond all doubt). (2) In your enjoyment of use of my product I would have had the direct enjoyment of realizing that I had both satisfied a human need by my work and . . . (also objectified the human essence and therefore) fashioned for another human being the object that met his need. (3) I would have been for you the mediator between you and the species and thus been acknowledged and felt by you as a completion of your own essence . . . (and a necessary part of yourself and have thus realized that I am confirmed in both in your thought and in your love). (4) In my expression of my life I would have fashioned your expression of life, and thus in my own activity have realized my own essence, my human, my communal essence.[24]

In this passage, too, differences among people create the possibilities for complementarity and creativity. The passage suggests as well that power or agency in a world composed of different beings need not take the form of domination. This passage suggests as well some rudiments for a new understanding of power, that is, that power need not be understood as energy bottled up but can be expressed in ways that change the world to help or enrich others different from oneself. Indeed, power can only work this way when the others with whom one associates differ from oneself, since only then can they and we receive the unique gifts each of us has. I am not suggesting that this brief passage, the organizational experience of the Furies, or Lorde's argument for using differences articulates a new understanding of power that grows from a new understanding of differences. Such a new theory of power can only emerge in the future from years of practical struggle with differences in our movement. Rather, I like to read these statements as visions and perhaps guides that underline the variety of possibilities for community and interdependence made available by differences among people.

Feminists are only beginning to explore the possibilities of working together across differences. Because of a widespread and urgent sense that we need to work together, a deep-going exploration of differences among feminists seems profoundly important. We need to look more closely at the ways class, race, or differences of sexuality result in the same feminist demand's having very different effects on different groups of women.

Black women, to take only one of these examples, have often argued that feminists are irrelevant, since they want every woman to have a job, when Black women would enjoy the luxury of being housewives.

But if our needs and desires are so different, how can we work together? I contend that it is only possible at present by using, preserving, and enhancing our differences. Feminist communities must make sure there are spaces for women of color, closed to white women; lesbian spaces, closed to heterosexual women. We must build these spaces into our political organizations as well—whether in the form of caucuses or the construction of coalitions. The one thing that can never be allowed is a separate space for the dominant or privileged group. If we attempt to construct a unified movement with men, then there must be no separate organizational space for white, heterosexual, and class-privileged men. They have always had access to separate spaces. *Their* separate spaces, *their* separate organizations, *their* differences from us, have been sources of their power. We cannot allow them to continue.

A strategy of preserving and institutionalizing our differences could respond to the twin problems posed by the fact that universalistic strategies that ignore differences do not work, and that separatist strategies fail to question the definition of differences as Difference (in part because Difference has been so central to the strategy of separatism itself). But this effort to institutionalize (our) differences in our movement raises yet another difficulty—one faced by any organization committed to social change, but not yet much faced by feminists—the contradiction between means and ends.

Many feminists have insisted that feminist organizations form a model for the society we want. But do we want a society in which differences of race, class, gender, or sexuality remain institutionalized? Are there important distinctions between "walling out" and "walling in"? Do we want a society in which all differences are individual differences? Or a society like the one Marge Piercy constructs in *Woman on the Edge of Time* in which ethnicities continue to exist but are disconnected from color? Is there something about our differences that is worth preserving?

I have worried about the extent to which both we and our organizations may be transformed by our struggle for power. I have wondered whether our organizations can serve as tools for taking power for women and still lay the groundwork for new nonsexist, nonracist, nonclassist societal institutions. Although I once thought our institutions could prefigure the society we want, now the question of means and ends, the issue of how our organizations are related to the world we want, seems permanently in flux. Perhaps it is time to abandon the notion that our organizations must prefigure the new society. It is important to experiment with new forms, but the history of the women's movement suggests that this is not always possible. We cannot expect feminist organizations to be small oases of universality and community in a patriarchal capitalist society. Nor can we develop a single organizational form appropriate to all parts of the movement. In the end, organizations can only be evaluated historically. What was right in the past will doubtless be wrong in the future.

The practice of the women's movement around the questions raised by differences suggests that political change is a process of transforming not only ourselves but also our most basic assumptions about humanity and our sense of human possibility, not just once but many times. Making change requires that we incorporate in our organizations both our constantly changing understandings of the possible and the needs of feminists involved in those organizations. At bottom, the change we seek requires transforming the meanings of both power and difference not once but many times.

Conclusion

The history of feminist understandings of difference and power makes it clear that different strategies are appropriate at different times, and that each strategy can make a contribution to our understanding of the significance of the differences among us. Each strategy contains an implicit analysis that needs to be "read out" of the practice and theorized in order to show us the new possibilities toward which it points. Our practice has demonstrated that differences need not be reduced to "otherness," and that the meaning of power is not exhausted by domination. We have been able to transform some of our socially defined "otherness" into self-defined specificity, and in so doing we were able to make important changes in our understandings of power. We have not, however, been able to avoid the differences among us. Our experience indicates that we are beginning to see that the links between differences and Difference can be broken in both theory and practice, and that our differences as feminists can instead be points of connection and creativity. Yet these new understandings will pose new problems for us—problems that center around questions of the relation of means and end, questions about the extent to which our organizations should be or can be expressions of the world we want, as opposed to the world in which we live. Perhaps the most fundamental question to be asked of every strategy for change is this: How does this strategy contain at least the seeds of its own supersession?

NOTES

The following people discussed this paper with me at a very early stage in its writing: Alexa Freeman, Sarah Begus, Annette Bickel, and Lucious Outlaw. In addition, I have been helped by comments from Sandra Harding, Amy Swerdlow, and Gerri Traina.

1. Ursula LeGuin, "American SF and the Other," *Science Fiction Studies* 1, 3 (November 1975), 208–209, cited in Pamela Sargent, Introduction, *More Women of Wonder* (New York: Vintage, 1976), xxxiv–xxxv.

2. This distinction was made by Erica Joy Mannucci, although she is not responsible for what I have made of it. See "Personal and Political Loyalty," mimeo available from Mannucci at University of Milan, Center for the Study of Women in Culture. (One can find a very similar distinction in Audre Lorde, "The Master's Tools Will Never Dismantle the Master's House," in Cherrie Moraga and Gloria Anzaldua, eds., *This Bridge Called My Back* (Watertown, Mass.: Persephone Press, 1981), p. 99.

3. This point is made in greater depth in Chapter 3 in this volume.

4. Audre Lorde is one of the best-known writers to make this claim and make it eloquently. See "The Master's Tools," p. 99.

5. I do not mean to condemn all reform strategies. For a discussion of the distinction between "reforms" and "reformism," see Charlotte Bunch, "The Reform Tool Kit," in *Passionate Politics* (New York: St. Martin's Press, 1987), pp. 103–117.

6. For example, see Judith Witherow, "Native American Mother," *Quest: A Feminist Quarterly* 3, 4 (Spring 1977); or bell hooks, *Ain't I a Woman?* (Boston: South End Press, 1981), p. 138.

7. See Charlotte Bunch and Beverly Fisher, "What Future for Leadership?" *Quest: A Feminist Quarterly* 3, 4 (Spring 1976), 2–14. See also the letter of resignation from the women's movement by Anselma dell'Olio, used also by Joreen, printed in *Chicago Women's Liberation Newsletter* (mimeographed), July 1970, p. 4.

8. See Ginny Berson, "Olivia: We Don't Just Process Records," *Sister* 7, 2 (December-January 1970), 8–9, for an analysis of a collective which does not work this way.

9. See, for example, Bertrand Russell, *Power: A New Social Analysis* (n.p.: 1936), cited by Anthony de Crespigny and Alan Wertheimer, *Contemporary Political Theory* (New York: Atherton Press, 1970), p. 22. See also Talcott Parsons, "On the Concept of Political Power," in Roderick Bell, David V. Edwards, and R. Harrison Wagner, eds., *Political Power* (New York: Free Press, 1969), p. 256.

10. See, for example, Harold Lasswell and Abraham Kaplan, *Power and Society* (New Haven: Yale University Press, 1950), p. 76.

11. Although I made this point in Chapter 2, "Fundamental Feminism: Process and Perspective," it was very much a widely shared view among the *Quest* staff. Several articles also made the point. I have been particularly impressed with Carol Gilligan, "Woman's Place in Man's Life Cycle," in *Harvard Educational Review* 49, 4 (November 1979); Sarah Ruddick, "Maternal Thinking," in *Feminist Studies* 6, 2 (Summer 1980); and Dorothy Smith, "A Sociology for Women," in Julia Sherman and Evelyn Beck, eds., *The Prism of Sex: Essays in the Sociology of Knowledge* (Madison: University of Wisconsin, 1979).

12. See Chapter 1, "Political Change: Two Perspectives on Power."

13. Adrienne Rich, *Of Woman Born* (New York: Norton, 1976), pp. 69, 101.

14. Interestingly enough, we simply recapitulated the ways a number of women, both feminists and nonfeminists, have thought about power. There are

important similarities with the views put forward by Hannah Arendt, or Dorothy Emmet, in this formulation. See Arendt, *On Violence* (New York: Harcourt, Brace, and World, 1967), and Emmet, "The Concept of Power," in *Proceedings of the Aristotelian Society* 54 (1953–1954).

15. This essay was written in 1981, but I believe that the term "current" is very telling about the continuing intractability of racism in 1998.

16. Nancy Myron, "Class Beginnings," *Furies* 1, 3 (March/April 1972), 3. See also Ginny Berson, "Only by Association," *Furies* 1, 5 (June/July, 1972), 5–7.

17. Charlotte Bunch and Coletta Reid, "Revolution Begins at Home," *Furies* 1, 4 (May 1972), 2–3. See also Delores Bargowski and Coletta Reid, "Garbage Among the Trash," *Furies* 1, 6 (August 1972), 8–9. Some of the essays from *Furies* are collected in Nancy Myron and Charlotte Bunch, eds., *Class and Feminism* (Baltimore: Diana Press, 1974).

18. Ibid.

19. This complaint has been echoed and made specific by Barbara Smith and Beverly Smith as it affects the lives of Black women. "An example I can think of and which drives me crazy is the arrogance some white women display about 'choosing' not to finish school, . . . downward mobility. . . . Race is a concept of having to be twice as qualified, twice as good to go half as far. . . . No way in Hell would I give up getting a degree or some piece of paper that would give me more economic leverage in this boys' system" (Smith and Smith, "Across the Kitchen Sink," in *This Bridge*, p. 113).

20. hooks, *Ain't I a Woman*, p. 138.

21. Ginny Berson, "Only by Association," *Furies* 1, 3 (March/April 1972), 3.

22. Remark attributed to Martha Quintanales at the December 1981 Women in Print conference. *Off Our Backs* 11, 11 (December 1981), 3.

23. Audre Lorde, "The Master's Tools," p. 99. It is interesting to note the extent to which the differences between the authors and their communities may have been responsible for some of the reflectiveness that appears in *This Bridge*. It is striking how many of the contributors in *This Bridge* note that they were different from other members of their community—looking white, being able to pass, being lesbian, going through puberty prematurely, being the lightest or the darkest of the family, and so on—a link with creativity?

24. Quoted in David McClellan, *Karl Marx* (New York: Viking, 1975), pp. 31–32.

Part Two

Reoccupying Marxism as Feminism

The title of this section, "Reoccupying Marxism as Feminism,"[1] means for me a literal reoccupation of the terrain defined by Marx in the nineteenth century. In his case, that terrain was occupied by the working class, with its historic mission of creating a more just society. For me, his work presented a mode of analysis that I believed could be profoundly useful to feminist theory. I recently ran across a review of an early essay of mine (a rejection letter) that said that all I was doing was taking over a methodology from Marx and calling it feminist. There is a sense in which that was true. As I have read critiques of my work, one of the central things that has impressed me is the ways my use of Marxism has been missed and misunderstood. I want the chapters in this section to help make clear the ways my own specific and somewhat idiosyncratic reading of Marx influenced my feminist work.

In 1970, when I began teaching at the University of Michigan, my partner began working for the National Lawyer's Guild in Detroit. Detroit was a city where the Old Left had a major presence, as did the New Left, and an important part of that presence was constituted as very politically involved lawyers, both white and Black. Some had been members of the CPUSA (Communist Party); others had worked to organize the CIO (Congress of Industrial Organizations) in the thirties; others had been targeted by McCarthy in the fifties. It was a very substantial exposure for me to the Marxism of the nineteenth century. The arguments I heard discounted the struggles of women and insisted that the only place to organize was at the point of production, where women, Blacks, and others could be organized as workers. It was not important to organize women as women, and certainly not in universities. I survived several weeks of an "educational" discussion conducted by the League of Revolutionary Black Workers in which the point was to figure out how Stalin's horrid little pamphlet, "Dialectical and Historical Materialism," made sense.[2] I came away from that experience with a conviction that textbook Marxism made no sense. Probably what persuaded me that I needed to read Marx myself was a combination of feeling that I needed to know more about the "point of production," a sense that my students and the political economy program needed more in-depth knowledge, and my having been intrigued by the little of Marx's own writings I had read. It was also partly a response to Heidi Hartman's essay "The Unhappy Marriage of Marxism and Feminism," which was at that time circulating in manuscript.[3] That essay was very clear on the theoretical status of feminism as opposed to Marxism: "The 'marriage' of Marxism and feminism has been like the marriage of husband and wife depicted in English common law: Marxism and feminism are one and that one is Marxism."[4]

This was indeed an accurate assessment of the state of feminist theory in the early seventies. Marxism was an important resource for feminist theory, as were the theories produced by civil rights/Black liberation movements. In both cases, feminist theory was indebted to and dependent on theories designed for and relevant to other collectivities—the working class in one case, and Black men in the other—but in both cases the specific situations of women (in those groups as well as others) were not addressed. Still, these were the bodies of thought generally held to represent legitimate accounts of exploitation and oppression by many on the Left.

The project of reading Marx was one undertaken by many activists during this period. We were not looking at Marx as a nineteenth-century thinker; rather, we wanted to mine the theory for what we could learn about contemporary issues. I have never been interested in working through what Marx really meant and how he fitted into the world of nineteenth-century socialist thinkers, among whom he became the most important.

All this led me to decide that I needed to read systematically. So I isolated myself for several months during the summer of 1973 to read Marx and Marxist literature. I had the luxury of choosing to do it in Paris. My partner and I rented an apartment from an anarchist on a street inhabited by a number of anarchists. It was also a street that was a center for prostitution. Moreover, it was home to a large number of North African immigrants. I could watch them as they watched me with my little manual typewriter across the narrow street. They were living six to a small room with bunk beds. Finally, the first floor of my building was occupied by a small box factory that seemed to employ only homeless alcoholics, one of whom—in a wheelchair—kept his bottle of wine in a pants leg made available by his amputated leg. It certainly provided me with a context conducive to thinking about the way the "free" market worked. As I left for the Bibliothèque

Nationale in the morning, I walked past prostitutes in short skirts and spike heels. When I came home for lunch, they were still there, and when I came back in the evening they were still there in their heels. They worked hard. As did the men and women in the box factory.

What does it mean to reoccupy Marxism as feminism? For me it came to mean to take up the methodological and epistemological advice and practices I found there and apply them in new directions, and to see dialectical thinking as applicable to many areas of social life. Although I found much of Marx's critique of capitalism and the increasing commodification of more and more areas of social life persuasive, the focus of my concern at that time was to understand the situation of women more specifically.[5] I was coming to believe that feminism was not a set of specific conclusions about the situation of women, but was instead a mode of analysis that could be usefully applied to studying, not simply women, but society as a whole.

I would like to suggest that aspects of the Marxist tradition represent important resources for insisting on the impossibility of neutrality and the necessity of engagement, for recognizing that the social relations in which we live structure (though do not determine) the ways we understand the world; and for providing tools that can allow us to trace the ways our concepts and categories both structure and express the ways we interact with the world. As Haraway so eloquently put it, "'Our' problem is how to have *simultaneously* an account of radical historical contingency of all knowledge claims and knowing subjects, a critical practice of recognizing our own 'semiotic technologies' for making meanings, *and* a nononsense commitment to faithful accounts of a 'real' world . . . friendly to earthwide projects of finite freedom."[6]

I have a number of problems with Marx's own theories—among them: (1) class understood centrally as a relation among men is the only division that counts; (2) the analysis is fundamentally masculinist in that workers' wives and their labor are presumed; (3) homosocial birth images mark the analysis in important ways; (4) women come and go in the analysis and are profoundly absent from his account of the extraction of surplus value—the heart of his analysis; (5) he is clearly a nineteenth-century Eurocentric writer who can pay little attention to contemporary concerns such as environmental issues and the rise of service industries.

But given this, why should I raise once again the importance of a nineteenth-century European patriarch for late-twentieth-century feminist theory? Why Marx? Why now? The fall of the Soviet state and the Berlin Wall have occasioned a global celebration of the market and of capitalism's successes. Frederic Jameson noted that for those who do not distinguish clearly between "Marxism itself as a mode of thought and analysis, socialism as a political and societal aim and vision, and Communism as a histor-

ical movement," Marxism can appear to be an embarrassing remnant of
the past.[7] And certainly Teresa Ebert was right when she suggested that
"under the pressure of the dominant discourses of Postmodernism, Marxism and historical materialism are becoming lost revolutionary knowledges for the current generation of feminists." Still, even figures such as
Derrida argue, regarding *The Communist Manifesto,* "I know of few texts in
the philosophical tradition, perhaps none, whose lesson seemed more urgent today."[8] I would add that in the context of a capitalism that has become truly global and in which ever more of life has become commodified, much of Marx's critique of capitalism remains very apt.[9]

I see Marx as an anti-Enlightenment figure on balance, although it must
be recognized that his relationship to the Enlightenment and the whole
tradition of Western political thought is that of both the inheriting son
and the rebellious son.[10] Thus, his account of the process of labor itself
can be seen in sexual/gendered terms: Marx theorized the relation of the
worker to his own activity as an alien activity not belonging to him: "activity as suffering, strength as weakness, *begetting as emasculating,* . . . self
estrangement."[11] Marx's account of estranged labor thus uses some of the
"second homosocial birth" images I have found problematic in many
other works in the history of Western political thought.[12] Thus, he argued,
the worker encounters himself in a world he has himself created, albeit in
a very negative form.

Feminist theory, too, exists in an ambivalent relation to the Enlightenment. On the one hand, feminist theorists sometimes argue for a "me too"
position to work for women's inclusion in a number of societal institutions.[13] On the other hand, women as women have never been the "subjects" of Enlightenment/Liberal theory, so women's insistence on speaking at all troubles those theories.[14] (It is certainly my suspicion that this,
along with decolonization and struggles for recognition by racial and ethnic groups, is one reason why Europeans and North American theorists
have lost hold of some of their certainties.)

My reading of Marx is one that some have suggested is itself postmodern. I am greatly indebted to Bertell Ollman's ideas about Marxist dialectics as based on an account of internal relations. I also share David Harvey's very similar understanding of dialectics.[15] Thus, I take from Marx
the idea that one must replace the idea that the world is composed of
"things" with that of the importance of processes. In addition, Marx's dialectical method holds that things do not "exist outside of or prior to the
processes, flows, and relations that create, sustain, or undermine them."[16]

I see my reading of Marx as making several important contributions to
my work in feminist theory. First, Marx's theories could enable an alternative to the Enlightenment account of what is to count as truth or knowledge. Second, Marx's work could provide a basis for a more nuanced and

socially embedded understanding of subjectivity. And third, his work could allow for a better understanding of the relation of knowledge and power, which could illuminate arguments for privileged knowledge. I will take up each of these points in turn.

In the modernist/Enlightenment version, truth has to do with discovering a preexisting external something that, if it meets some criteria, can be labeled as true. Moreover, it must be discovered from nowhere in particular so that truth can retain its pristine qualities. The definition of truth that I rely upon is more complex than this and is heavily indebted to my own reading of Marx. I want to refer to Marx in order to suggest in a shorthand way how my version of standpoint theory approaches the question of truth. In the "Theses on Feuerbach," he argued against an understanding of "things" as "objects," especially objects of contemplation, and made the following statement: "Man must prove the truth, i.e., the reality and power, the this-worldliness of his thinking in practice." Finally, there is Marx's famous conclusion: "The philosophers have only *interpreted* the world in various ways; the point is to *change* it."[17]

The Marxian project, then, changes the criteria for what is to count as knowledge: For Marx, to have knowledge includes seeing, tasting, feeling, and thinking. If truth is the reality and power of our ideas in action, then we must treat knowledge and truth in much more historically specific ways and devote attention to the social, historical, and ultimately conventional form of all definitions of truth. (And on this point one can be reminded of Foucault's claim that truth is simply error codified.) We are reminded that the search for knowledge is a *human* activity, structured by human requirements.

But here I become uncomfortable with the language of truth. The search for truth is not at all the way to understand Marx's project. Perhaps a better concept to use is that of certitude: a sense that one has credible knowledge, knowledge that is "good enough" to act on. The most fundamental point is to understand power relations; in his case, power relations centered on the development of capitalism and the commodification of human existence. But the point of understanding power relations is to change them. And to this end, Marx's categories move and flow, enacting the fluidity that many postmodernist theorists insist on. To give just a few examples, capital is described as "raw materials, instruments of labor, and means of subsistence of all kinds *which are utilized* to produce new raw materials, new instruments of labor, and new means of subsistence," as "accumulated labor," as "living labor serving accumulated labor," as "a bourgeois production relation, a social relation of production," as "an independent social power."[18] Capital is all these things at various moments and for various analytical purposes. Thus, for example, when Marx wanted to call attention to the specifics of the production process, he was likely to refer to capital as raw materials and instruments of labor. But when he wanted to point to the power of capital to structure society as a whole, he was more likely to refer to capital as an independent social power.

The result is a very complex idea of what constitutes "truth," which now becomes a difficult term to retain if one is to avoid falling back into Enlightenment categories of analysis. Susan Hekman was right to point to many similarities between Marx's claims about truth and a number of Foucault's positions. She stated tellingly that despite these similarities, Foucault would argue that the discourses of the oppressed are just that and are not closer to "reality." But she recognized that these discourses might, however, be closer to "a definition of a less repressive society."[19]

Marxist theories (and feminist standpoint theories) also remind us that the categories and criteria for judging truth that come most immediately to mind are likely to be those of dominant groups. Thus, Marx could argue that everything appears reversed in competition, and that the accumulation of wealth in capitalism is at the same time the accumulation of misery. Yet these categories and criteria are *made* true for all members of society. One can think of many examples such as this—compulsory heterosexuality enforced as a "truth"—not discovered but made real through a variety of practices.

To turn to the second issue—the nature of subjects—I found in Marx the kinds of social constructivist theories of the subject that others encountered only later in poststructuralism. But in contrast to the American tendency (certainly with the help of some European poststructuralists themselves) to interpret these theories in liberal-pluralist and, in some cases, libertarian terms, terms that rely only on accounts of the microprocesses of power, I found in Marxian thought an insistence on what some have called a "global," as opposed to a "totalizing," theory.[20] The focus is on the macroprocesses of power, which, although they may be played out in individual lives, can only be fully understood at the level of society as a whole. To claim that we can understand the totality of social relations from a single perspective is as futile an effort as was the claim that we could see everything from nowhere. But a focus on large-scale social forces highlights different aspects of subjectivity.

Thus, Marx can be read as providing a theory of the subject as subjected, as does Foucault. That is, one can read the essay on estranged labor, or the theory of surplus value in *Capital* (which I would argue are two versions of the same philosophical argument), as accounts of how men (and they are) constitute themselves as subjected and by pouring their lives into the objects that belong to others. Yet Marx's theory of subjects/subjection differs from Foucault's in its stress on potentials and possibilities for developing other forms of subjectivity.[21] In addition, the

Marxian theory of subjectivity is rightly classified as "theoretical anti-humanism," an idea developed under this heading by Althusser and passed on by him to Foucault and Derrida, his students. That is, the subjects who matter are not individual pre-existing subjects who are simply human beings, but subjects who are defined by their relation to larger, collective subjects, or groups. And these groups must be seen as defined by macroprocesses (whether languages, ideologies, or discourses) structuring societies as a whole.

At the same time, these groups must not be seen as formed unproblematically by their subjection, that is, by existing in a particular social location and therefore coming to (being forced to) see the world in a particular way. My effort to develop the idea of a feminist standpoint, in contrast to a "women's viewpoint," was an effort to appropriate this insight. Chela Sandoval's notion of the importance of strategic identity for women of color represented an important advance in understanding this process, as was her development of the notion of oppositional consciousness.[22]

Sandoval argued that U.S. third-world feminism could function as a model for oppositional political activity in the United States. She proposed that we view the world as a kind of "topography" that defines the points around which "individuals and groups seeking to transform oppressive powers *constitute themselves* as resistant and oppositional subjects."[23] She held that once the "subject positions" of the dominated were "self-consciously recognized by their inhabitants," they could be "transformed into more effective sites of resistance."[24] She discussed a "differential consciousness," which operated like the clutch of an automobile allowing the driver to engage gears in a "system for the transmission of power."[25]

Here, her views parallel those of Gramsci, who suggested that we re-think the nature of identity: "Our capacity to think and act on the world is dependent on other people who are themselves also both subjects and objects of history."[26] In addition, one must re-form the concept of individual to see it as a "series of active relationships, a process in which individuality, though perhaps the most important, is not the only element to be taken into account." Individuality, then, is to be understood as the "ensemble of these relations. . . . To create one's personality means to acquire consciousness of them and to modify one's own personality means to modify the ensemble of these relations."[27] Moreover, Gramsci held that each individual was the synthesis of these relations and also of the history of these relations, a "precis of the past."[28] The constitution of the subject, then, is the result of a complex interplay of "individuals" and larger-scale social forces. Groups are not to be understood, as Hekman seemed to do, as aggregates of individuals. Moreover, the constitution of the "collective subject" posited by standpoint theories requires an always contingent and fragile (re)construction/transformation of these complex subject positions. As Kathi Weeks has put it, "This project of transforming subject-positions into standpoints involves an active intervention, a conscious and concerted effort to reinterpret and restructure our lives. . . . A standpoint is a project, not an inheritance; it is achieved, not given."[29]

I shall turn now to my third point, the issue of privileged knowledge. Fundamentally, I argue that the criteria for privileging some knowledges over others are ethical and political as well as purely "epistemological." The quotation marks here are to indicate that I see ethical and political concepts such as that of power as involving epistemological claims on the one hand, and ideas of what is to count as knowledge involving profoundly important political and ethical stakes on the other. Marx made an important claim that knowledge that takes its starting point from the lives of those who have suffered from exploitation produces better accounts of the world than that starting from the lives of dominant groups. I want to expand this insight/argument and suggest that the view from the margins (defined in more heterogeneous terms) is clearer and better. The criteria Marx proposed provide important guidelines for contemporary theories: First, he argued that by adopting the standpoint of the working class, or, of production, one could understand the dynamics of capitalist society much more fully. That is, not just the supposedly neutral workings of the "free" market were taken into account, but the ways that production creates products, markets, and consumers became central to the analysis. In the essays in this section, I expand this argument and put it to feminist use.

Second, Marx argued for the privilege of some knowledges over others on the ground that they offer possibilities for envisioning more just social relations. There is a real need for a vision of utopia, a vision that seems particularly difficult to develop and retain in the final years of the twentieth century, with its unrelieved celebration of the market as the solution to all social problems.

There is a third aspect to the claim that some knowledges are "better" than others, and here I think Sandoval has elaborated the most important point of Marx's analysis: the self-conscious transformation of individuals into resistant, oppositional, and collective subjects.

The most important issue for me is the question of how we can use theoretical tools and insights to create theories of justice and social change that address the concerns of the present. Marx, for all of the difficulties with his theoretical work and the state of actually (non)existing socialism, called our attention to certain macrolevel issues to be addressed. In addition, one can find in the work of theorists such as Gramsci a much more useful and complex theorization of relations between "individuals" and society as a whole, one which opens up possibilities for both new knowledges and new collectivities.

These, then, represent the general concerns that structure the essays in this section. Each of them represents aspects of my encounter with Marx, and Marxist theory more generally. And each of these essays documents my efforts to develop analyses that can support the insights and struggles of those who have been exploited, marginalized, and oppressed.

Chapter 5, "Objectivity and Revolution," has not been previously published. I include it here because I believe it helps to clarify the ways I read Marx and how Marx's definitions and concepts differ from the usual social scientific categories. I treat both objectivity and science as less problematic concepts than they have come to be in the context of the contemporary "science wars." Many feminist theorists have argued that the idea of objectivity should be abandoned because it has served so many oppressive, exploitive, and imperialist purposes. I share the views of both Sandra Harding and Donna Haraway, who have argued against this strategy. Harding has argued for what she terms "strong objectivity." Strong objectivity for Harding requires that both the subjects and the objects of knowledge be placed on the same plane. I interpret that to mean that knowers and known are involved in a complex interactive process.[30] Haraway put the matter more colorfully but noted the congruence of Harding's concept of reflexivity to her own of diffraction: "The point is to make a difference in the world, to cast our lot for some ways of living and not others. To do that, one must be in the action, be finite and dirty, not transcendent and clean."[31] Along with Haraway and Harding, I believe that objectivity is too powerful and important a concept to give up. Rather, we need to struggle over its meanings and propose alternative accounts more friendly to feminist projects.

"The Feminist Standpoint: Developing the Grounds for a Feminist Historical Materialism" (Chapter 6) depends on my reading of Marx and is especially indebted to Lukacs's essay "Reification and the Standpoint of the Proletariat" as well as his argument that the core of Marx's theory was its method of analysis.[32] Lukacs, in his self-critical Introduction to *History and Class Consciousness*, made several points worth remembering. He noted that he had made three errors: first, his separation of the natural and social worlds, leading to his view of Marxism as a social philosophy, but not a theory of the natural world; second, following Hegel, his equating objectification with alienation; and third, perhaps most fundamental, his failure to ground his argument against the contemplative attitude of bourgeois thought in the activity of labor. He began, not with a consideration of work, but rather with the complicated structures of a commodified and reified economy. My reformulation of his project attempts to respond to each of the three self-criticisms he made. First, I try to stress the importance of nature as well as culture and to point to the ways in which they are mutually constitutive. Both Donna Haraway and David Harvey have very usefully taken on the artificiality of this distinction.[33] Here, I believe I am not only being faithful to Marx's intent (not a particular priority for me but perhaps a gesture of respect for the author) but also recognizing the ways that contemporary arguments rightfully stress the complexly social aspects of human embodiment. Second, in terms of the issue of whether or how objectification leads inevitably to alienation, Lukacs's self-criticism provides important advice: The objectification of human activity in the products of human work is the source of alienation in capitalist society but at the same time can be the basis for a utopian vision. By emphasizing only the former, Lukacs almost lost sight of the latter. Third, because of these consequences, in the chapters in this section, I stress the importance of work rather than reification. The two topics are of course profoundly interrelated, but attention to human activity, (here "reduced" to work) opens many avenues for envisioning potentials and possibilities for alternative forms of social organization.

With these provisos, I took Lukacs's concept of the standpoint of the proletariat and translated it into the concept of a feminist standpoint. I want to stress that I meant the notion of a feminist standpoint to differ from claims for either a standpoint of women or women's viewpoints.[34] But in keeping with Lukacs's project, I do want to emphasize that a standpoint does not refer to individual activities and perspectives: It can only be produced by a collective subject, or group. Moreover, the group must be a "marked" rather than an unmarked group, or, in Gramscian terms, a subaltern group.

In the essay on Althusser, Chapter 7, I turn to the effects of structuralism on/in Marxist theory. Althusser's work was important in the French context: It was an effort to move beyond Stalinist formulas and to respond to the powerful influence of structuralist thought in France. His work has been influential far beyond the Marxist tradition, in terms of his thinking on ideological state apparatuses and his influence on both Foucault and Derrida. I found his work troubling. The editors of *Rethinking Marxism* have aptly summarized my essay on Althusser in the following way: "Hartsock finds much that is 'correct' in Althusser's far-reaching reformulations, and though she admires his stated political aims, her detailed comments . . . [detect] in Althusser's work the blunt instruments of dualistic, idealist and relativist thinking that clumsily tear apart the more subtle, intricately woven fabric of Marx's own views of the unity of science and political practice."[35] I trace the appearance of these problems across the major themes that tie his works together: the notion of the last instance, theoretical antihumanism, and the process of production of knowledge.

NOTES

1. I am indebted to Kathi Weeks for this language and its meaning.

2. Joseph Stalin, "Dialectical and Historical Materialism," in Bruce Franklin, ed., *The Essential Stalin* (Garden City, N.Y.: Doubleday, 1972).

3. Amy Bridges was at that time the coauthor. The essay remained in manuscript until 1979 when it was published, not in the United States but in England, in the Conference of Socialist Economists' journal, *Capital and Class*. It is more accessible as the lead essay in Lydia Sargent, ed., *Women and Revolution* (Boston: South End Press, 1981).

4. Hartmann, "The Unhappy Marriage," in Sargent, *Women and Revolution*, p. 2.

5. Note that I write here of "women" with no effort to mark the category. I do so because that is faithful to my project of the time (and those of many other feminists as well).

6. Donna Haraway, "Situated Knowledges," *Simians, Cyborgs, and Women* (New York: Routledge, 1990), p. 187.

7. Fredric Jameson, "Actually Existing Marxism," in Saree Makdisi, Cesare Casarino, and Rebecca E. Karl, eds., *Marxism Beyond Marxism* (Routledge: New York, 1996), p. 14. See also Wendy Brown's statement in her *States of Injury* (Princeton: Princeton University Press, 1995), p. 4.

8. Jacques Derrida, *Spectres of Marx*, quoted in Teresa Ebert, *Ludic Feminism and After* (New York: Routledge, 1996), p. x.

9. See Donna Haraway's chapters on OncoMouse and vampire culture in *Modest_Witness@Second_Millennium: FemaleMan©Meets_OncoMouse™* (New York: Routledge, 1996).

10. E.g., Seyla Benhabib, "Epistemologies of Postmodernism," in Linda Nicholson, ed., *Feminism/Postmodernism* (New York: Routledge, 1990), p. 111.

11. See Robert Tucker, ed., *The Marx-Engels Reader* (New York: Norton, 1978), p. 76 (italics mine).

12. Achilles was one of the first to want to be born again in legend and song. He prayed that he would do some great thing first, before he died, so could live on.

13. See Kathy Ferguson's discussion in *The Man Question* (Berkeley: University of California Press, 1993).

14. See, for example, Zillah Eisenstein, *The Radical Future of Liberal Feminism* (New York: Longman, 1982).

15. See his discussion in David Harvey, *Justice, Nature, and the Geography of Difference* (New York: Blackwell, 1996), pp. 46–68. See also Bertell Ollman, *Alienation* (New York: Cambridge University Press, 1971).

16. Harvey, *Justice*, p. 49. See also Ollman's statement quoted by Harvey, p. 48: "Dialectics restructures our thinking about reality by replacing the common-sense notion of "thing," as something that *has* a history and *has* external connections to other things, with notions of "process" which *contains* its history and possible futures, and "relation," which *contains*, as a part of what it is, its ties with other relations." Bertell Ollman, *Dialectical Investigations* (New York: Routledge, 1993), p. 11.

17. *Marx-Engels Collected Works*, vol. 5 (New York: International Publishers, 1976), p. 3..

18. See *The Marx-Engels Reader* (2nd ed.), pp. 176, 207, 208, respectively.

19. Susan Hekman, "Truth and Method: Feminist Standpoint Theory Revisited," *Signs: Journal of Women in Culture and Society* 22, 2 (Winter 1997), 10.

20. See Rosemary Hennessey, *Materialist Feminism and the Politics of Discourse* (New York: Routledge, 1993).

21. As I would like to adapt Marx to the uses of contemporary feminism, I would like to change the potential of the proletariat, its "historic mission," to what bell hooks has described as a yearning for a different (and, I would argue, better) world. See bell hooks, *Yearning*, especially chapter 3, on "Postmodern Blackness" (Boston: South End Press, 1990).

22. She made an excellent point in her essay on the development of the category of "women of color" out of the consciousness-raising sessions at the 1981 NWSA (National Women's Studies Association) meetings. See "Feminism and Racism: A Report on the 1981 National Women's Studies Association Conference," in Gloria Anzaldua, ed., *Making Face, Making Soul/Haciendo Caras* (San Francisco: Aunt Lute Foundation, 1990). Much of what follows comes from Sandoval's article, "U.S. Third World Feminism: The Theory and Method of Oppositional Consciousness in the Postmodern World," *Genders*, no. 10 (Spring 1991).

23. Sandoval, "Oppositional Consciousness," p. 4 (italics mine).

24. Ibid.

25. Ibid., p. 14.

26. Antonio Gramsci, *Prison Notebooks*, ed. and trans. Quintin Hoare and Geoffrey Nowell Smith (New York: International Publishers, 1971), p. 346.

27. Ibid., p. 352.

28. Ibid., p. 353.

29. Kathi Weeks, "Subject for a Feminist Standpoint," in Makdisi, Casarino, and Karl, *Marxism Beyond Marxism*, p. 101.

30. See Sandra Harding, "Rethinking Standpoint Theory: What Is Strong Objectivity?" in Linda Alcoff and Elizabeth Potter, eds., *Feminist Epistemologies* (New York: Routledge, 1993).

31. Haraway, *Modest_Witness*, p. 36.

32. Georg Lukacs, *History and Class Consciousness* (Cambridge, Mass.: MIT Press, 1971).

33. See Haraway, *Simians, Cyborgs, and Women;* and David Harvey, *Justice, Nature, and the Geography of Difference* (New York: Blackwell, 1996).

34. For discussions of these concepts, see Alison Jaggar, *Feminist Politics and Human Nature* (Totowa, N.J.: Rowman and Allenheld, 1983); and Dorothy Smith, *The Everyday World as Problematic* (Boston: Northeastern University Press, 1987).

35. Editors, "In This Issue," *Rethinking Marxism* 4, no. 4 (Winter 1991), 1.

five

⚓

Objectivity and Revolution: The Unity of Observation and Outrage in Marxist Theory

Problems of objectivity are at the center of a number of important issues for social science—such as problems about the relation between facts and values in social research, questions about the relationship of "is" and "ought" in philosophy, issues of neutrality, detachment and commitment, of action and observation, and even of theory and practice. I will argue that Marx can give us an important new perspective on the current debate over the nature of social science, since his work is meant to be at once an objective and scientific analysis of capitalism and a call for revolution. As Lucio Colletti has put it:

> Marx—utilizing an aspect of *reality*—overthrows the arguments of the economists and points to the overthrow of capitalism itself. Marxism is therefore science. It is an analytical reconstruction of the way in which the mechanism of capitalist production works.

Written 1977–1978.

On the other hand, as well as being a science, Marxism is revolutionary ideology. It is the analysis of reality from the viewpoint of the working class. This in its turn means that the working class cannot constitute itself as a *class* without taking possession of the scientific analysis of *Capital*.[1]

In traditional empiricist terms, the terms of mainstream social science, a statement such as this misunderstands both science *and* revolution. Social scientists have often claimed that the student of politics needs some detachment from political activity and commitment. Many have argued that although values have a legitimate role in the selection of research problems, they play a less legitimate role in the identification of fact, in the assessment of evidence, and in the working out of conclusions. On this view, because there is no logical connection between facts and values, it should be at least in principle possible to eliminate the illegitimate effects of value positions, however difficult it may be to do so in practice.[2]

In the context of most social scientific discussions, being objective has come to mean that one is detached, impersonal, or indifferent. Terms such as these, as well as arguments for the use of measures that exclude possibilities for human interference, clearly separate thought, observation, and science on the one hand from action, participation, and politics on the other. These formulations are based on the view that knowledge is the discovery of externals: In Humean or perhaps Enlightenment terms more generally, we have impressions of objects, and by comparing our ideas (reflections, or imitations) of the objects, we work out their resemblances, identity, relations of time and place, proportion in quantity or number, degrees of quality, contrariety, and causation.[3] This discovery of externals may dissolve into probability, since in all cases depending on observation, human beings are fallible and may fall into error. One can only attempt to reduce these errors as much as possible. To do this, contemporary social science has attempted to develop more and more sophisticated observation and measurement techniques. In this context, truth is the verification of our impressions and the ideas (i.e., logic) we have formed from them. Since truth consists in an agreement of our ideas either with the real relations of ideas or with real and external matters of fact, those things not susceptible to this agreement (e.g., passions, volitions, and actions) cannot be said to be true or false.[4]

Thus, knowledge arises from data external to us, impinging on the senses and creating perceptions and impressions. Here, human activity may blur impressions that would otherwise be clear, since our fallibility may distort our perceptions.[5] Moreover, even knowledge of ourselves must take the form of knowledge of external "facts." On the view I have described, we can have only partial knowledge of ourselves. Our passions, wants, and needs cannot agree with external matters of fact and therefore cannot be the subject of knowledge. Only when we treat passions as external facts, states of being, or conditions one recognizes as an observer rather than participant can we have knowledge about them.

Marx's vision of science differed fundamentally from this. In his view, the sciences of economics and politics have become the basis for a theory of revolution, a revolution implied by Marx's own analysis and included in the analysis from the beginning. Marx escaped the duality of observation and action by beginning from a worldview founded on acting and feeling human beings. His stress on human activity (in the various forms of "praxis," "work," and "labor") as the core of human existence forms the basis for his unification of observation and outrage. We must begin our analysis with a brief account of Marx's concept of human activity and of the alienation of human activity through the alienation of labor in a capitalist mode of production. In this account, it will become apparent that Marx conceptualized the world in categories very different from those of empiricist social scientists. Mediation, the concept of totality, and the importance of history are important aspects of Marx's mode of understanding. For Marx, self-knowledge is *the* fundamental form of all human knowledge. In this context, objectivity takes on several meanings, all of which differ from the empiricist understanding of objectivity as a form of indifference or detachment, and all of which allow for the reestablishment of the integral relation between objectivity and revolution.

Human Activity as Ontology

Conscious, self-realizing human activity, or, for Marx, work, is at once both a statement about the ways we come to understand the world and the basis for his conception of the nature of humanity itself. That is to say, human activity has both an ontological and an epistemological status. Human feelings and activities are not "merely anthropological phenomena" but are "truly ontological affirmations of being."[6] Work is for Marx the real human life activity, the activity through which the human creation of human beings is accomplished.[7] Work is "human action with a view to the production of use-values, appropriation of natural substances to human requirements; it is the necessary condition for effecting exchange of matter between man and Nature; it is the everlasting Nature-imposed condition of human existence, and therefore is independent of every social phase of that existence, or rather, is common to every such phase."[8]

Marx restated the issue more generally when he asked, "What is life, but activity?"[9] The concept of praxis, or human work, is a definition of what it is to be human—a striving first to meet physical needs and later for the realization of all human potentialities.[10] The concept of praxis refers to the idea that one can only know and appropriate the world (change it and be changed by it) through practical activity. Marx argued not only that persons are active but also that reality itself consists of "sensuous human activity, practice."[11] Thus Marx could speak of products as crystallized or congealed human activity or work, of products as conscious human activity in another form. He could state that even plants, animals, light, and so on constitute theoretically a part of human consciousness and a part of human life and activity.[12] Nature itself, for Marx, appears as a form of human work, since we duplicate ourselves actively, in reality, and so come to contemplate the selves we have created in a world of our own making.[13]

Although human beings do not create the world from nothing, human activity does produce existence differentiated into individuals, species, and all the categories we take as given—categories and concepts that respond to specific problems posed for us by social life. At the same time, however, consciousness is itself a social product.[14] Human consciousness and the shape of human society depend on each other. What can be appropriated (constructively incorporated into human consciousness) varies with the practical forms of human activity. For example, some music can be appropriated only by a few, since it can only be an object for people whose senses can give it meaning.[15] The production of the linked processes of consciousness and material existence is directed by human attempts to satisfy physical needs, a process leading to the production of new needs. These efforts, however, are more than the simple production of physical existence. They form a "definite *mode of life.*"

> As individuals express their life, so they are. What they are, therefore, coincides with their production, both with *what* they produce and with *how* they produce. The nature of individuals thus depends on the material conditions determining their production.
>
>   This sum of productive forces, capital funds and social forms of intercourse . . . is the real basis of what the philosophers have conceived as "substance" and "essence of man."[16]

Marx was arguing that individuality must be understood as a social phenomenon, that human existence in whatever form it takes must be seen as the product of human activity—human activity rooted in, but not confined to, the process of production. Activity and consciousness "both their content and in their mode of existence, are *social: social* activity and *social* mind."[17]

History is also important to Marx's definition of what it is to be human. Marx argued that the realization of all human potential is only possible as the species as a whole develops its powers, and that these powers can be realized only through the cooperative action of all, as the result of history.[18] Thus, although it is human activity that gives structure to the world, the structure is not imposed by individuals, but by generations, each building on the work of those who came before. The precise shaping of material life at any point in time depends on needs already developed, as well as embryonic needs—needs whose production, shaping, and satisfaction is a historical process. Fully developed individuals are, then, not the products of nature but of history.[19] Thus, "hunger is hunger, but the hunger gratified by cooked meat eaten with a knife and fork is a different hunger from that which bolts down raw meat with the aid of hand, nail and tooth. Production thus produces not only the object but also the manner of consumption. . . . Production thus creates the consumer."[20]

Human activity, then, the human production of human life, is at the core of Marx's worldview. This production, however, must be understood to be social and historical, that is, formed and changed by the work of generations. Even activity not performed in community with others, not immediately including others, is social. Marx argued that his *"own* existence *is* social activity."[21] In addition, social activity is fundamentally historical; it is formed and changed by the work of generations. However, human work, the creation of real individuals, has been perverted. In capitalism, work has become a means to life, rather than life itself. It has become a barrier to self-creation, to the expansion and realization of our potential as human beings. That is, human work has become alienated labor; and as a result, because of the ontological character of activity, humanity itself is alienated.[22]

Alienation, or estrangement, is founded upon estranged activity. It is constituted first by the fact that in capitalism, labor is external to the worker, that it "does not belong to his essential being; that in his work, therefore, he does not affirm himself but denies himself, does not feel content but unhappy, does not develop freely his physical and mental energy but mortifies his body and ruins his mind."[23] Through this activity objects are produced. Because products are simply human activity in another (physical) form, and because the objects are expressions of our potential and actual species life itself, objects produced through alienated activity can only confront the worker as alien powers. The worker's relation to these objects represents the second aspect of alienation—the worker's relation "to the sensuous external world, to the objects of nature, as an alien world inimically opposed to him."[24] Third, alienation refers to a separation from the life of the human species. That is, estranged labor makes "the *life of the species* into a means of individual life. First it estranges the life of the species and individual life, and secondly it makes individual life in this abstract form the purpose of the life of the species, likewise in its abstract and estranged form."[25] Thus the life activity of workers separates them from their human potential; it makes them work only to satisfy

needs rather than for the pleasure of the work itself. Finally, estranged labor leads to a separation from other human beings. "What applies to a
man's relation to his work, to the product of his labor and to himself, also
holds of a man's relation to the other man's labor and object of labor."[26]
Thus, the workers' own production destroys what they could become,
separates each human being from others, and creates the domination of
the nonproducer over the product. Capitalism forces people to participate
in the separation of their life activity from themselves and makes them
confer that activity on strangers.

By starting from human activity, Marx came to see private property as
"the product, the result, the necessary consequence, of *alienated labor*, of
the external relation of the worker to nature and to himself."[27] As he
pointed out,

> though private property appears to be the source, the cause of alienated la-
> bor, it is rather its consequence, just as the gods are *originally* not the cause
> but the effect of man's intellectual confusion. Later this relationship becomes
> reciprocal.
>
> Only at the last culmination of the development of private property does
> this, its secret, appear again, namely, that on the one hand it is the *product* of
> alienated labor, and that on the other it is the means by which labor alienates
> itself, the *realization of this alienation*.[28]

Marx's writing in *Capital* must be understood, then, as an analysis of
private property. As such, it is at the same time a statement of the laws
governing the systematic perversion and theft of the worker's humanity.
The economy as "immediately perceptible private property is the material perceptible expression of *estranged human* life."[29] Communism, by contrast, is the positive transcendence of private property and human estrangement or alienation. It is "the real *appropriation of the human* essence
by and for man; communism therefore [is] the complete return of man to
himself as a *social* (i.e. human) being."[30] Given this analysis of alienation
and private property, Marx argued that "it is easy to see that the entire
revolutionary movement necessarily finds both its empirical and its theoretical basis in the movement of private property—more precisely in that
of the economy."[31]

This, in extremely brief outline, is the core of Marx's analysis. The centrality of human activity, or, for him, work, in his analysis is clear.[32] Alienation and private property are facts, but they are not simple facts that a
detached and impersonal social science might discover. The centrality of
human work, the perversion of this work, the fact that human labor has
been made to serve death rather than life—all this means that to represent
and analyze the alienation of the worker is at the same time to justify revolution.

The Unity of Outrage and Observation
in Marxist Analysis

We should now look more closely at this analysis in order to make clear the aspects of Marxist analysis it exemplifies and to provide a context for the outline of Marx's understanding of objectivity. The importance of totality and process, the role of history, and a dialectical understanding of mediation lead to a redefinition of knowledge as self-knowledge, a redefinition of knowledge as the appropriation of life itself. All of these are important to understanding the nature of science and objectivity in Marxist theory and to constituting the internal relation between objectivity and human liberation.[33]

Totality, Process, and the Importance of History

Lukacs's work makes it clear that Marxism is revolutionary, not simply because it espouses revolutionary ideas, but, more important, because of its method. As he put it, "*The primacy* of the category of totality is the bearer of the principle of revolution in science."[34] Although it may be possible to describe an event without understanding it as part of a historical process, Lukacs argued that the "intelligibility of objects develops in proportion as we grasp their function in the totality to which they belong."[35]

The philosophic importance of the whole in giving meaning to the parts calls attention to the links between the facts as they are given to us and their mediated meaning, or put in a different way, to the links between their isolated meanings and their social significance.[36] Indeed, it calls attention to their status as manifestations or expressions of the whole of social relations. It requires one to treat "things"—even simple commodities—not as objects but as manifestations of the social relations of a society. The term "capitalism," then, is one way of conceptualizing a totality of social relationships. Facts such as wage labor as opposed to wageless labor have a meaning and significance in capitalist society that they do not have, for example, in tribal societies.

The category of totality is important in a second way as well. In demanding that the significance of any aspect of social relations (that is, any "fact") must be comprehended from the perspective of social relations as a whole, Marx provided a contrast to the ideas of aggregation common among empiricists. No aggregation of individual characteristics will yield Marx's concept of class; the aggregation can only provide a theory of stratification based on individual possession of differing amounts of money, education, and so on. Sex and race are similar to class: No amount of data about the physical, psychological, or economic attributes of women or people of color will yield the concepts of patriarchy or white supremacy. Sex, race, and class understood as abstract, eternal categories are fundamentally useless concepts. In order to make use of the concept of class, Marx had to include in its meaning all the social relations that came to a focus under that heading and then was able to argue that one could, out of an analysis of class relations, uncover all of the social relations of contemporary global capitalism, including its development and the possibilities for its destruction. "Facts," then, are only manifestations or expressions, however telling, of the social relations of contemporary global capitalism, and without the concept of totality, or a sense of how the relations articulate, one cannot grasp those social relations.

Third, and closely related, because Marx focused not on objects as such but on the relations between them, he could understand reality as a social process and look at the processes defining individuals, rather than at the properties or attributes of the individuals themselves.[37] Since each phenomenon changes form constantly, as the relations of which it is composed take on different meanings and forms, the possibility of understanding processes as they change depends on one's grasp of their role in the social whole.[38] Thus, Lukacs argued that production, consumption, distribution, and exchange were not identical but were "members of one totality, different aspects of a unity. . . . A mutual interaction takes place between these various elements. This is the case with every organic body."[39] The precise forms of human activity and other phenomena are intelligible only in the context of the whole society, a context that includes both its past and its future. For example, one cannot understand money as a social relationship without putting money's metallic form in the context of the social relations determining its role. Similarly, the concept of class as a social relation refers to and is in turn defined by an ongoing interaction between capitalist and wage laborer. The focus is not on the individuals, but on the pattern and process of their activity. The relations among them and their interaction have been elevated to the same plane of reality as their physical existence.[40] Thus, the subject matter of historical materialism must be understood as itself literally invisible, manifested only in secondary ways as the physical movements of men and women.

The importance of the whole, coupled with the centrality of process, leads us to look for overarching historical tendencies. The whole for Marx does not refer to a single set of events or even to an entire social system at a single moment in time. The unity of the whole includes both its history and its future possibilities as well as its present configuration. The processes that structure life in capitalist society—the particular forms taken by production, consumption, and distribution—can only be what they are because of the previous modes of life, the language, and social rules developed out of a particular human history.[41] Even the simplest things are the result of the activity of a succession of generations, each building on or reacting to the work of the preceding one, each modifying its social system according to changed needs.[42] Science in this context cannot be the search for universally valid laws of human behavior. Knowledge can grow only out of an examination of historical tendencies, an analysis of their roots and their future possibilities as well as their present forms. For example, to understand the processes involved in the integration of third-world women workers into the wage labor force requires an overview of the long-term economic trends in capitalism—problems of imperialism, the expansion of assembly and service industries, the globalization of both capital and labor markets, changes in political ideologies, family structures, and so on. Each factor must be understood as a series of processes; these processes change form over time, each within itself and more complexly as they interact.

Dialectical Thinking

One cannot make these arguments without coming to appreciate how a dialectical method enabled Marx to conceptualize and come to grips with a reality created by human activity, a reality at the same time constitutive of humanity itself and constantly in the process of becoming something else. What empiricists have seen as static objects, Marx grasped as structures of relations in process. Thus, for Marx, production, taken together with the social relationships it both creates and requires, could be better understood as the interaction of production, distribution, exchange, and consumption. Each, he argued, *is* immediately the other, at the same time forms the others, and in the working out of its own logic "creates the other in completing itself, and creates itself as the other."[43] Each element conditions the others but each can also be understood as a different expression of the same relationships.[44] Dialectical reasoning, then, "regards every historically developed social form as in fluid movement, and therefore takes into account its transient nature not less than its momentary existence."[45] The dialectical mode of understanding provides a means for us to investigate the manifold ways social forces are related, a way to examine a world in which "objects" are defined by the relations coming to focus in them, and in which these objects are constantly changing in response to the changing weights of other factors.

Moreover, a dialectical understanding is essential to an understanding of reality in mediated as opposed to unmediated form. It calls attention to distinctions contained within the apparent (ideological, dominant) categories. Marx made it clear that in any society,

> the class which has the means of material production at its disposal, has control at the same time over the means of mental production, so that thereby,

generally speaking, the ideas of those who lack the means of mental production are subject to it. The ruling ideas are nothing more than the ideal expression of the dominant material relationships, the dominant material relationships grasped as ideas; hence of the relationships which make the one class the ruling one, therefore, the ideas of its dominance.[46]

If one understands that economic categories are the theoretical expressions of the social relations of production, it is clear that data present themselves immediately, that is, directly and obviously, in forms and categories that are in the strict sense capitalist. That is, they are expressions of social relations from the perspective of the ruling class. To accept the data in this form as falling within eternal and unalterable categories is to acquiesce in the reproduction of capitalist social relations in the realm of ideas.

Only a dialectical conception of reality can dissolve the reified forms in which facts immediately appear in the capitalist mode of production, and allow them to appear as illusions that are at the same time both real and necessary for the preservation of capital.[47] Marx's understanding of dialectical reasoning allowed him to see the laws of capitalist development, not simply as an account of the accumulation process, but at the same time as an account of the destruction of humanity. His understanding of the ways each process contains its opposite are so clear in the following statement that it is worth quoting at length. Marx argued that

> within the capitalist system all methods for raising the social productiveness of labour are brought about at the cost of the individual labourer; all means for the development of production *transform themselves* into means of domination over, and exploitation of, the producers; they mutilate the labourer into a fragment of a man, degrade him to the level of an appendage of a machine, destroy every remnant of charm in his work and turn it into a hated toil; . . . *But all methods for the production of surplus-value are at the same time methods of accumulation; and every extension of accumulation becomes again means for the development of those methods.* It follows therefore that in proportion as capital accumulates, the lot of the labourer, be his payment high or low, grows worse. . . . *Accumulation of wealth at one pole is, therefore, at the same time accumulation of misery, agony of toil, slavery, ignorance, brutality, mental degradation, at the opposite pole,* i.e., on the side of the class that produces its own product in the form of capital.[48]

Objectivity

In the context of Marx's understanding of human activity as the foundation of social life, and of his analysis of the perversion of that life, objectivity takes on several meanings. Obviously for Marx, objectivity does not mean indifference or detachment. Rather, it can be expressed first along the line of objectification (as the interactive existence of the material bodily world and our involvement in it); and second, along the line of the mediated understanding of the social world available from the perspective of the working class.

Objectivity as the Existence of the Material World

Perhaps the most straightforward sense of objectivity in Marxist theory is its affirmation of the existence of the material world. As Marx put it, "*to be* objective, natural and sensuous, and at the same time to have object, nature, and sense for a third party, is one and the same thing. *Hunger* is a natural *need;* it therefore needs a *nature* outside itself, an *object* outside itself, in order to satisfy itself, to be stilled." To take the simplest possible relation, and one that demonstrates the integration of natural and social science in his work, Marx suggested that "the sun is the *object* of the plant—an indispensable object to it, confirming its life—just as the plant is an object of the sun, being an *expression* of the life-awakening power of the sun, of the sun's objective essential power."[49]

Human beings need external objects in order to exist. It is significant that for Marx these are objects of needs rather than of senses or perceptions (here understood in a passive sense). Human beings must interact with these objects in an active way. When the objective world confirms essential human powers, all objects become the objective forms of ourselves, objectifications that "confirm and realize" individuality. We are then "affirmed in the objective world not only in the act of thinking, but with *all* [our] senses."[50] Not only are human powers affirmed and realized through the objective world, but the objective world becomes an extension of ourselves in both human and nonhuman forms. All objects come to be objects *for us,* with real relations to human needs, hopes, and possibilities.

Yet it is this very objective quality of the material world that allows for its perversion. Although those things that are objects for us can only be things essential to human life, things that can confirm and develop essential human powers, alienation can prevent people from interacting constructively with the objective world.[51] Producers are separated from their products because they have been separated from their activity. But they are as well separated from other human beings and from the fulfillment of their needs to develop themselves. They need to create themselves as whole human beings. Thus, alienation means that other people we are in contact with confront us as sometimes separate and overpowering things that act to prevent us from becoming fully developed individuals.[52] Alienation thus creates the division between each individual and the rest of the world. It is one source of the sense of an unbridgeable gulf between the observer and the external world or between observer and actor that contemporary social science refers to most frequently under the heading of objectivity. Alienation distorts objectivity so that rigid commodity forms become part of an overpowering and alien objective world.[53] It is this reified, alienated objectivity that must be transformed to create the objectivity of self-realizing human beings.

Objectivity as Involvement

Clearly, a Marxist worldview contains an understanding of objectivity that directly opposes the empiricist understanding that to be objective is to be detached and/or indifferent. One must recognize that any selection of facts implies a method or theory.[54] In addition, in a worldview that has at its center an active orientation to a world in constant change, questions about the intrusion of values into a world of facts given to our senses or facts "discovered" by our reason do not occur. For Marx, concepts grow out of the human activity creating both human subjectivity and the (natural and social) world. Language as well as the state of the physical environment is a result of human efforts to objectify and create themselves in the first sense discussed. Human practices and purposes are expressed in our conceptualizing activity itself. The valuative as well as descriptive purposes of such conceptual activity is apparent in concepts such as "exploitation," "oppression," "stable democracy," and "social mobility." Human purposes, however, are not whims. Nor, usually, are they unique to individuals. Here, too, history is important in developing some purposes rather than others, in developing some human needs (and the techniques to satisfy them) to a greater degree than others.

Because they are themselves aspects of the social relations they express and represent, concepts in their immediate form can manifest both our alienation and the possibilities for our achievement of a truly human world. Thus, Marx could argue that the categories that come most easily to mind express the requirements and categories of capitalist society. Concepts like those Marx used, which transcend the dualisms that society constructs between thought and action, or "is" and "ought," or nature and culture are more difficult to grasp. Yet understanding these concepts as both expressions of the dualities of human existence in class society, and as containing the potential for their supersession, is important for understanding a Marxist account of objectivity.[55] Objectivity in this sense refers to the involvement and entanglement of human beings with the world and calls attention to the different consequences of this involvement. If involvement takes the form of alienated activity, other human beings appear as fundamentally separate from oneself and as part of an overpowering and threatening world. Self-creative activity (or self-affirming work, taking that term in the most general sense), by contrast, allows one to recognize in others the importance of others in the expansion and extension of oneself.

Objectivity as Mediation

It is through mediation that Marx was able to lay the foundations for supersession of a reality based on alienated activity, indeed, a reality *constituted* by that activity. Marx refused to accept the data in their immediately given, or capitalist, form. His rejection of these forms goes so deep as to be rejection even of the language.[56] Objectivity in this sense consists in understanding phenomena in the context of the totality of social relations. To be objective in this sense means to use the vantage point of the realization of human powers to understand the world. Because in capitalist society this point of view is available to the proletariat, Lukacs could argue that "the self-understanding of the proletariat is therefore simultaneously the objective understanding of the nature of society."[57]

Marx's vision of human activity as ontology formed the source of his ability to take up the point of view of the process of production, or put differently, the standpoint of the proletariat. The vantage point provided by the process of production differs profoundly from liberal views that take the exchange of goods and services to be the prototypic human interaction. The standpoint of production requires a focus on process, change, and creation rather than on "eternal verities," on the results of cooperation rather than competition, on the links between the natural and human worlds (as natural objects become social goods) rather than on the gap between them. This change in standpoints allowed Marx to demonstrate that the categories that are expressions of the social relations of capitalism are illusory. He argued, for example, that "*everything appears reversed in competition.* The final pattern of economic relations as seen on the surface, in their real existence and consequently in the conceptions by which the bearers and agents of these relations seek to understand them, is very much different from, and indeed quite the reverse of, their inner but concealed ... pattern and the conception corresponding to it."[58]

These inner, but concealed, historical patterns become visible from the standpoint of the working class. This vantage point exposes the importance of the production process and makes clear the ways human relations to human beings have been made into relations between things, commodities. Because the life activity of the worker is a commodity in capitalism, the worker is led to the dual perspective of both a (self-conscious) commodity and a human subject denied her/his humanity, the perspective of a human being who embodies within her/himself the inhumanity of the social order. It is from this standpoint that the accumulation of capital becomes visible as its opposite—the accumulation of misery.

Because for Marx the working class is in a position to create a society free from all forms of domination and, therefore, has no need to ignore or conceal important aspects of social life, its position provides a vantage point, a standpoint, for bringing into view the totality of social relations—a mediated understanding. Thus, the forms of *immediacy* are the same for both the working class and the bourgeoisie, but the vantage point of the working class, that is, the standpoint from production, is such that it discloses a fundamentally different reality. Through mediation, "the proletariat is capable of the transformation of the immediately given into a truly understood (and not merely an immediately perceived) and *for that reason* really objective reality, . . . "[59]

Objectivity, or in other terms, science, in this sense consists in the discovery of a potential humanity that can be constructed only by going beyond the immediacy of (reified) capitalist relations. Although Marx began with the forms given him by capitalism, he recognized that these were not simply modes of thought but expressions of real social relations. For that reason to go beyond the immediacy of capitalist forms of thought requires at the same time "their *practical* abolition as the actual forms of social life."[60] Objectivity in this sense is the reality and power of our ideas in action. To strive for objectivity is to strive to appropriate our social life in a way that enables us to expand our human capacities and transform ourselves.

Knowledge as Appropriation

These redefinitions of objectivity require new definitions of both knowledge and science. Marx's premises require a redefinition of knowledge as awareness, as the appropriation of internals.[61] The concept of awareness here refers not simply to thoughtful introspection but more broadly to a kind of contemplation that proceeds from all the senses. (These included for Marx will, love, and other things beyond the operation of the five senses.) Appropriation in this context means the incorporation of experience in such a way that life experience becomes a part of what comes to be seen as human subjectivity itself. Appropriation refers to the expansion of human powers and potentialities through the transforming impact of experience; it is a truly human and therefore social relation to the world.

Marx argued that human beings appropriate their essence in a total manner, as whole persons. Appropriation means that in each of our relations to the world—"seeing, tasting, feeling, thinking, wanting, experiencing—all the organs of our individual beings are in their . . . *orientation to the object*, the appropriation of that object." Marx suggested that we have failed to understand appropriation because "private property has made us so stupid and one-sided that an object is only *ours* when we have it—when it exists for us as capital, or when it is directly possessed, eaten, drunk, worn, inhabited, etc.—in short, when it is *used* by us."[62]

Marx proposed a model for understanding social relations in which appropriating things or experiences does not mean simple possession or gratification, a model in which appropriation is human activity, a form of human self-realizing activity, or, for him, work, a form of subjectivity. In a society where truly human relations are possible, a society in which the transcendence of private property will appear as the appropriation of human life, "the senses and minds of other men [will] have become my *own* appropriation." In such a society, "activity in direct association with others, etc., [will have] become an organ for *expressing* my own *life*, and a mode of appropriating *human* life."[63]

Thus, for Marx, self-knowledge was the basis for his science of society, and the understanding made possible by taking up the standpoint of the working class was the objective understanding of society. This knowledge "begins with the knowledge of the present, with the self-knowledge of [the proletariat's] own social situation and with the elucidation of its necessity (i.e., its genesis)."[64] This self-knowledge is in the beginning the "self-consciousness of the commodity." But to appropriate this knowledge "brings about an objective structural change in the object of knowledge,"[65] or to put it in more contemporary terms, the self-construction of resistant subjects.

The recognition that knowledge takes the form of appropriation in Marxist theory means that social science must become the articulation of what human practical activity has already appropriated in reality. It should be an attempt to examine, clarify, and represent what people already, at some level, know from their practical activity. Theorizing should be seen as another aspect of appropriation.

The concept of internals, too, must be understood in Marx's terms. Because Marx included in (or perhaps saw implied in) the concept of humanity all human products and all human history as well as all human potential, he understood the social world as internal to humankind, as a configuration of human activity. Social knowledge, then, is best understood as a kind of self-awareness. Knowledge, for Marx, was internal in the same senses in which it was external for empiricist thinkers. First, persons are active and involved in forming or creating a conceptualized and meaningful world. Without involvement there can be no reality for us. Second, human beings are a part of the subject matter as knowing individuals—the subject of all specifically human knowledge. Moreover, through the appropriation, the incorporation, of experience, the appropriation of what empiricists have treated as external, we make both the natural and the social world a part of our humanness.

Praxis, appropriation, and knowledge, then, are three aspects of, or three ways of grasping, the processes that come to a focus in the contemporary social sciences as understood from a Marxian perspective. To recognize knowledge as the appropriation of internals is to comprehend objectivity, not as the verification of impressions of external objects, but as the reality and power of our thinking in practice.

It is to apply standards formulated not so much in terms of truth as in terms of "correct tendencies," "correct theses," conditional certitude, and so on—standards that incorporate (appropriate) both the observational and revolutionary aspects of Marx's science. These new terms move us beyond the earlier definition of knowledge and toward one that ultimately refuses to separate comprehension and thought from action. All this does not mean that the sole test for scientific analysis is its utility in changing the world. It does mean that only through conscious activity, activity changing both oneself and the world, can one learn to know *either* the social world or oneself.

If one recognizes the centrality of real, active human beings to the generation of knowledge (or the appropriation of experience), it is possible to understand objective science, both social and "natural," as an instrument for the systematic appropriation of experience. Because this experience has its own history and allows for the possibility of a full realization of human potential through the supersession of the social relations of people, science, understood in this sense, must be a force for change. As Marx put it, "where speculation ends—in real life—there real, positive science begins: the representation of the practical activity, of the practical process of development of men."[66]

Objectivity and Revolution

I have argued that objectivity and revolution, science and liberation, are integrally related in Marx's theory—in his vision of humanity and in his positing of human activity as an ontological as well as an epistemological category. Because self-realizing activity is fundamental to the definition of what it is to be human, the perversion of life activity in capitalism is the perversion of what women and men might become. To be objective in this situation, for Marx, means to expose the laws governing this perversion and theft, to grasp the possibility for the supersession of alienation, to appropriate this understanding, and to act on it.

The resolution of the problem of objectivity for Marx is only possible in a practical and political way. That is to say, the relation between objectivity and revolution is essentially a practical one. This does not mean that the authors of every successful revolution can necessarily claim to have completed an objective analysis of society. (Although they may have done so.) Rather, objectivity in Marxist theory must be understood as one way to express the significance of human activity as constitutive of social life. I have argued that the concept of objectivity performs this function along two general lines. Along the first, attention to objectivity illuminates our interaction with the material world on the basis of our needs and allows us to uncover the ways our relation to the material world can be perverted, the way it can be changed through our alienated activity into a relation to a world dominated by hostile and overpowering forces. Along the second line, attention to objectivity in Marxist theory points to the importance of concealed aspects of reality. It points to the mediated and therefore objective understanding made possible by adopting the standpoint of the working class. Along the second line as well, Marx's understanding of objectivity makes clear that the supersession of the social relations of capitalism in fact rather than simply in thought is required to fully appropriate this account of capitalism. Marx stated the case most clearly when he said:

> We have . . . shown that private property can be abolished only on condition of an all-round development of individuals, because the existing character of intercourse and productive forces is an all-round one, and only individuals that are developing in an all-round fashion can appropriate them, i.e. can turn them into free manifestations of their lives. We have shown that at the present time individuals *must* abolish private property, because the productive forces and forms of intercourse have developed so far that, under the domination of private property, they have become destructive forces, and because the contradiction between the classes has reached its extreme limit.[67]

Marx has made it clear that an objective account of capitalist society can lead only to the conclusion that this form of social interaction must be abolished. At the same time, it is only the possibility for the supersession of the social relations of capital embodied in the life experience of the working class that provides a position, a vantage point, from which to understand these relations in their real, if concealed, forms. Thus the struggle for objectivity is inseparable from the struggle for revolution. Each depends upon and presupposes the other. Indeed, the achievement of either requires the achievement of both.

NOTES

I would like to thank Zillah Eisenstein, Bertell Ollman, and Neil Smith for helpful comments on an earlier draft of this paper.

1. Lucio Colletti, *From Rousseau to Lenin* (New York: Monthly Review Press, 1972), p. 235. On this point, also see Georg Lukacs, *History and Class Consciousness* (Cambridge, Mass.: MIT Press, 1971), pp. 1–2.

2. See, for example, Ernest Nagel, *The Structure of Science* (New York: Harcourt, Brace, and World, 1961), pp. 485–490. The point of view he expressed is one I have referred to with the shorthand term "empiricism." Although it is obviously more accurate for some people than others, it seems a useful way to briefly characterize a point of view.

3. See David Hume, *A Treatise of Human Nature,* ed. L. S. Selby-Bigge (Oxford: Clarendon Press, 1888 ed.), pp. 69, 104.

4. Ibid., p. 458.

5. See, for example, Hume's discussion of human fallibility. Ibid., pp. 181ff.

6. Karl Marx, *Economic and Philosophic Manuscripts of 1844,* ed. Dirk Struik (New York: International Publishers, 1964), p. 165.

7. See Herbert Marcuse, *Studies in Critical Philosophy,* trans. Boris De Bres (Boston: Beacon Press, 1973), p. 14. Also see Marx, *Manuscripts of 1844,* pp. 113, 188.

8. Karl Marx, *Capital,* vol. 1 (New York: International Publishers, 1967), pp. 183–184.

9. Marx, *Manuscripts of 1844,* p. 111.

10. Here I will use praxis as the most general reference to human self-realizing activity. Marx often refers to this activity as "work" and sometimes even as "labor." There are, however, some distinctions that can be made among these concepts. See, for example, Bertell Ollman, *Alienation: Marx's Conception of Man in Capitalist Society* (New York: Cambridge University Press, 1971), pp. 99–105; and Karl Marx and Frederick Engels, *The German Ideology,* ed. C. J. Arthur (New York: International Publishers, 1970), p. 94.

11. Karl Marx, "Theses on Feuerbach," in Marx and Engels, *The German Ideology,* p. 121.

12. Marx, *Manuscripts of 1844,* p. 112.

13. Ibid., p. 114. See also p. 137, where Marx stated that the human essence of nature only exists for social man. On the issue of the relation of natural to human worlds, see the very interesting account by Alfred Schmidt, *The Concept of Nature in Marx,* trans. Ben Fowkes (London: New Left Books, 1971).

14. On this point see Marx's remark about educating the educator in the "Theses on Feuerbach," and Marx and Engels, *The German Ideology,* p. 51.

15. Marx, *Manuscripts of 1844,* p. 140.

16. Marx and Engels, *The German Ideology,* pp. 42, 59.

17. Marx, *Manuscripts of 1844,* p. 137. See also Lukacs, *History and Class Consciousness,* p. 19, where he argued that "only when the core of existence stands revealed as a social process can existence be seen as the product, albeit the hitherto unconscious product, of human activity. This activity will be seen in its turn as the element crucial for the transformation of existence."

18. Marx, *Manuscripts of 1844,* p. 177.

19. Karl Marx, *Grundrisse,* trans. Martin Nicolaus (Middlesex, England: Penguin Books, 1973), p. 162. See also Marx, *Manuscripts of 1844,* p. 141.

20. Marx, *Grundrisse,* p. 92.

21. Marx, *Manuscripts of 1844,* p. 137.

22. Ibid., p. 117.

23. Ibid., p. 110.

24. Ibid., p. 111.

25. Ibid., pp. 112–113.

26. Ibid., p. 114.

27. Ibid., p. 117.

28. Ibid.

29. Ibid., p. 136.

30. Ibid., p. 135. Marx's attention to practical activity is apparent in his vision of Communist society as the *"genuine* resolution of the conflict between man and nature and between man and man—the true resolution of the strife between existence and essence, . . . between the individual and the species. Communism is the riddle of history solved, and it knows itself to be this solution" (ibid.).

31. Ibid., p. 136.

32. I have not touched on one of the most important features of Marx's analysis of labor—the fact that labor power has both a use value and an exchange value. The use value of labor power could be the production of a truly human life, but the exchange value of labor has been used to subvert this life. The dual character of labor power is for Marx the source of surplus value—the source of the capitalist accumulation of wealth.

33. Although I am dividing them here for purposes of exposition, it should be clear that these aspects are not clearly or easily separable in Marx's thought. Indeed, one might treat each as a vantage point from which to understand different features of the totality of social relations. Even though they may be distinct, they should be recognized as parts of a unity. (See Marx, *Manuscripts of 1844*, p. 138.)

34. Lukacs, *History and Class Consciousness*, p. 27 (italics in the original).

35. Ibid., p. 13.

36. Ibid., p. 8.

37. Ibid., p. 13.

38. Ibid.

39. Ibid., Lukacs cited Marx's *Contribution to a Critique of Political Economy.* The same statement occurs in Marx, *Grundrisse*, p. 99.

40. See, for example, Lukacs, p. 154.

41. For an example that differs from Marx's account, see Alvin Gouldner's history of utilitarian culture in *The Coming Crisis of Western Sociology* (New York: Basic Books, 1970).

42. Marx and Engels, *The German Ideology*, p. 62.

43. Marx, *Grundrisse*, pp. 99, 93.

44. Marx, *Manuscripts of 1844*, p. 119. See also Ollman's discussion of relational concepts, in *Alienation*. See especially Marx's discussion of these relations in the Introduction to the *Grundrisse*, pp. 88–100.

45. Karl Marx, *Capital*, vol. 1 (Moscow: Foreign Language Publishing House, 1954), p. 20, quoted in Ollman, *Alienation*.

46. Marx and Engels, *The German Ideology*, p. 64. See also Marx, *Grundrisse*, p. 239. I believe it is important to note, once again, the shifts that take place in the last sentence of the extract. The simplistic first formulation is expanded, relocated, and changed.

47. Lukacs, *History and Class Consciousness*, pp. 12–13.

48. Marx, *Capital*, vol. I, p. 645 (italics mine). See also Marx, *Manuscripts of 1844*, for the same argument stated in other terms (pp. 148–49).

49. Marx, *Manuscripts of 1844*, p. 181.

50. Ibid., p. 140.

51. Ibid., pp. 180, 140.

52. See the quotation from Marx presented by David McClellan, *Karl Marx* (New York: Viking, 1976), pp. 31–32.

53. Marx, *Manuscripts of 1844*, p. 180. Lukacs, *History and Class Consciousness*, p. 100.

54. Lukacs, *History and Class Consciousness*, p. 5. This view is not unique to Marxism: See also Charles Taylor, "Neutrality in Political Science," in P. Laslett and W. G. Runciman, eds., *Philosophy, Politics, and Society* (Oxford: Blackwell, 1969). Marx remarked that it is a consequence of alienation that each sphere of life has its own and opposite yardstick (*Manuscripts of 1844*, p. 152).

55. Lukacs, *History and Class Consciousness*, p. 160.

56. Marx and Engels, *The German Ideology*, p. 102.

57. Lukacs, *History and Class Consciousness*, p. 149.

58. Marx, *Capital*, vol. 3, p. 209.

59. Lukacs, *History and Class Consciousness*, p. 150.

60. Ibid., p. 177.

61. Gouldner made a similar point in *The Coming Crisis of Western Sociology*, but although he argued for an awareness of internals, he meant something quite different.

62. Marx, *Manuscripts of 1844*, p. 139.

63. Ibid., p. 140. Marx and Engels went on to argue that "the appropriation of the productive forces is itself nothing more than the development of the individual capacities corresponding to the material instruments of production. The appropriation of a totality of instruments of production is, for this very reason, the development of a totality of capacities in the individuals themselves" (*The German Ideology*, pp. 92–93).

64. Lukacs, *History and Class Consciousness*, p. 159.

65. Ibid., p. 169.

66. Marx and Engels, *The German Ideology*, p. 48. Antonio Gramsci argued that "one can 'scientifically' foresee only the struggle, but not the concrete moments of the struggle, which cannot be the results of opposing forces in continuous movement, which are never reducible to fixed quantities since within them quantity is continually becoming quality. In reality, one can 'foresee' to the extent that one acts, to the extent that one applies a voluntary effort and therefore contributes concretely to creating the result 'foreseen.' Prediction reveals itself thus not as a scientific act of knowledge, but as the abstract expression of the effort made, the practical way of creating a collective will" (*Prison Notebooks*, ed. and trans. Quintin Hoare and Geoffrey Nowell Smith [New York: International Publishers, 1971], p. 438).

67. Marx and Engels, *The German Ideology*, p. 117.

six

The Feminist Standpoint: Developing the Ground for a Specifically Feminist Historical Materialism

The power of the Marxian critique of class domination stands as an implicit suggestion that feminists should consider the advantages of adopting a historical materialist approach to understanding phallocratic domination. A specifically feminist historical materialism might enable us to lay bare the laws of tendency which constitute the structure of patriarchy over time and to follow its development in and through the Western class societies on which Marx's interest centered. A feminist materialism might in addition enable us to expand the Marxian account to include all human activity rather than focusing on activity more characteristic of males in capitalism. The development of such a historical and materialist account is a very large task, one which requires the political and theoretical contributions of many feminists. Here I will address only the question of the

In Sandra Harding and Merrill B. Hintikka (eds.), *Discovering Reality*, 283–310. Copyright © 1983 by D. Reidel Publishing Company.

epistemological underpinnings such a materialism would require. Most specifically, I will attempt to develop, on the methodological base provided by Marxian theory, an important epistemological tool for understanding and opposing all forms of domination—a feminist standpoint.

Despite the difficulties feminists have correctly pointed to in Marxian theory, there are several reasons to take over much of Marx's approach. First, I have argued elsewhere that Marx's method and the method developed by the contemporary women's movement recapitulate each other in important ways.[1] This makes it possible for feminists to take over a number of aspects of Marx's method. Here, I will adopt his distinction between appearance and essence, circulation and production, abstract and concrete, and use these distinctions between dual levels of reality to work out the theoretical forms appropriate to each level when viewed not from the standpoint of the proletariat but from a specifically feminist standpoint. In this process I will explore and expand the Marxian argument that socially mediated interaction with nature in the process of production shapes both human beings and theories of knowledge. The Marxian category of labor, including as it does both interaction with other humans and with the natural world, can help to cut through the dichotomy of nature and culture, and, for feminists, can help to avoid the false choice of characterizing the situation of women as either "purely natural" or "purely social." As embodied humans we are of course inextricably both natural and social, though feminist theory to date has, for important strategic reasons, concentrated attention on the social aspect.

I set off from Marx's proposal that a correct vision of class society is available from only one of the two major class positions in capitalist society. On the basis of this meta-theoretical claim, he was able to develop a powerful critique of class domination. The power of Marx's critique depended on the epistemology and ontology supporting this meta-theoretical claim. Feminist Marxists and materialist feminists more generally have argued that the position of women is structurally different from that of men, and that the lived realities of women's lives are profoundly different from those of men.[2] They have not yet, however, given sustained attention to the epistemological consequences of such a claim. Faced with the depth of Marx's critique of capitalism, feminist analysis, as Iris Young has correctly pointed out, often

> accepts the traditional Marxian theory of production relations, historical change, and analysis of the structure of capitalism in basically unchanged form. It rightly criticizes that theory for being essentially gender-blind, and hence seeks to supplement Marxist theory of capitalism with feminist theory of a system of male domination. Taking this route, however, tacitly endorses the traditional Marxian position that 'the woman question' is auxiliary to the central questions of a Marxian theory of society.[3]

By setting off from the Marxian meta-theory I am implicitly suggesting that this, rather than his critique of capitalism, can be most helpful to feminists. I will explore some of the epistemological consequences of claiming that women's lives differ structurally from those of men. In particular, I will suggest that like the lives of proletarians according to Marxian theory, women's lives make available a particular and privileged vantage point on male supremacy, a vantage point which can ground a powerful critique of the phallocratic institutions and ideology which constitute the capitalist form of patriarchy. After a summary of the nature of a standpoint as an epistemological device, I will address the question of whether one can discover a feminist standpoint on which to ground a specifically feminist historical materialism. I will suggest that the sexual division of labor forms the basis for such a standpoint and will argue that on the basis of the structures which define women's activity as contributors to subsistence and as mothers one could begin, though not complete, the construction of such an epistemological tool. I hope to show how just as Marx's understanding of the world from the standpoint of the proletariat enabled him to go beneath bourgeois ideology, so a feminist standpoint can allow us to understand patriarchal institutions and ideologies as perverse inversions of more humane social relations.

The Nature of a Standpoint

A standpoint is not simply an interested position (interpreted as bias) but is interested in the sense of being engaged. It is true that a desire to conceal real social relations can contribute to an obscurantist account, and it is also true that the ruling gender and class have material interests in deception. A standpoint, however, carries with it the contention that there are some perspectives on society from which, however well-intentioned one may be, the real relations of humans with each other and with the natural world are not visible. This contention should be sorted into a number of distinct epistemological and political claims: (1) Material life (class position in Marxist theory) not only structures but sets limits on the understanding of social relations. (2) If material life is structured in fundamentally opposing ways for two different groups, one can expect that the vision of each will represent an inversion of the other, and in systems of domination the vision available to the rulers will be both partial and perverse. (3) The vision of the ruling class (or gender) structures the material relations in which all parties are forced to participate, and therefore cannot be dismissed as simply false. (4) In consequence, the vision available to the oppressed group must be struggled for and represents an achievement which requires both science to see beneath the surface of the social relations in which all are forced to participate, and the education which can only grow from struggle to change those relations. (5) As an engaged vision, the understanding of the oppressed, the adoption of a standpoint exposes the real relations among human beings as inhuman, points beyond the present, and carries a historically liberatory role.

The concept of a standpoint structures epistemology in a particular way. Rather than a simple dualism, it posits a duality of levels of reality, of which the deeper level or essence both includes and explains the "surface" or appearance, and indicates the logic by means of which the appearance inverts and distorts the deeper reality. In addition, the concept of a standpoint depends on the assumption that epistemology grows in a complex and contradictory way from material life. Any effort to develop a standpoint must take seriously Marx's injunction that "all mysteries which lead theory to mysticism find their rational solution in human practice and in the comprehension of this practice."[4] Marx held that the source both for the proletarian standpoint and the critique of capitalism it makes possible is to be found in practical activity itself. The epistemological (and even ontological) significance of human activity is made clear in Marx's argument not only that persons are active but that reality itself consists of "sensuous human activity, practice."[5] Thus, Marx can speak of products as crystallized or congealed human activity or work, of products as conscious human activity in another form. He can state that even plants, animals, light, etc. constitute theoretically a part of human consciousness, and a part of human life and activity.[6] As Marx and Engels summarize their position,

> As individuals express their life, so they are. What they are, therefore, coincides with their production, both with *what* they produce and with *how* they produce. The nature of individuals thus depends on the material conditions determining their production.[7]

This starting point has definite consequences for Marx's theory of knowledge. If humans are not what they eat but what they do, especially what they do in the course of production of subsistence, each means of producing subsistence should be expected to carry with it *both* social relations *and* relations to the world of nature, which express the social understanding contained in that mode of production. And in any society with systematically divergent practical activities, one should expect the growth of logically divergent world views. That is, each division of labor, whether by gender or class, can be expected to have consequences for knowledge. Class society, according to Marx, does produce this dual vision in the form of the ruling class vision and the understanding available to the ruled.

On the basis of Marx's description of the activity of commodity exchange in capitalism, the ways in which the dominant categories of thought simply express the mystery of the commodity form have been pointed out. These include a dependence on quantity, duality and opposition of nature to culture, a rigid separation of mind and body, intention and behavior.[8] From the perspective of exchange, where commodities differ from each other only quantitatively, it seems absurd to suggest that labor power differs from all other commodities. The sale and purchase of labor power from the perspective of capital is simply a contract between free agents, in which "the agreement [the parties] come to is but the form in which they give legal expression of their common will." It is a relation of equality,

> because each enters into relation with the other, as with a simple owner of commodities, and they exchange equivalent for equivalent. . . . The only force that brings them together and puts them in relation with each other, is the selfishness, the gain and the private interests of each. Each looks to himself only, and no one troubles himself about the rest, and just because they do so, do they all, in accordance with the pre-established harmony of things, or under the auspices of an all shrewd providence, work together to their mutual advantage, for the common weal and in the interest of all.

This is the only description available within the sphere of circulation or exchange of commodities, or as Marx might put it, at the level of appearance. But at the level of production, the world looks far different. As Marx puts it,

> On leaving this sphere of simple circulation or of exchange of commodities . . . we can perceive a change in the physiognomy of our *dramatis personae.* He who before was the money-owner, now strides in front as capitalist; the possessor of labor-power follows as his laborer. The one with an air of importance, smirking, intent on business; the other timid and holding back, like one who is bringing his own hide to market and has nothing to expect but— a hiding.

This is a vastly different account of the social relations of the buyer and seller of labor power.[9] Only by following the two into the realm of production and adopting the point of view available to the worker could Marx uncover what is really involved in the purchase and sale of labor power, that is, uncover the process by which surplus value is produced and appropriated by the capitalist, and the means by which the worker is systematically disadvantaged.[10]

If one examines Marx's account of the production and extraction of surplus value, one can see in it the elaboration of each of the claims contained in the concept of a standpoint. First, the contention that material life structures understanding points to the importance of the epistemological consequences of the opposed models of exchange and production.

labor & widgets appear equivalent, but differ at the level of appearance at the level of production

It is apparent that the former results in a dualism based on both the separation of exchange from use, and on the positing of exchange as the only important side of the dichotomy. The epistemological result if one follows through the implications of exchange is a series of opposed and hierarchical dualities—mind/body, ideal/material, social/natural, self/other—even a kind of solipsism—replicating the devaluation of use relative to exchange. The proletarian and Marxian valuation of use over exchange on the basis of involvement in production, in labor, results in a dialectical rather than dualist epistemology: the dialectical and interactive unity (distinction within a unity) of human and natural worlds, mind and body, ideal and material, and the cooperation of self and other (community).

As to the second claim of a standpoint, a Marxian account of exchange vs. production indicates that the epistemology growing from exchange not only inverts that present in the process of production but in addition is both partial and fundamentally perverse. The real point of the production of goods and services is, after all, the continuation of the species, a possibility dependent on their use. The epistemology embodied in exchange then, along with the social relations it expresses, not only occupies only one side of the dualities it constructs, but also reverses the proper ordering of any hierarchy in the dualisms: use is primary, not exchange.

The third claim for a standpoint indicates a recognition of the power realities operative in a community, and points to the ways the ruling group's vision may be *both* perverse *and* made real by means of that group's power to define the terms for the community as a whole. In the Marxian analysis, this power is exercised in both control of ideological production, and in the real participation of the worker in exchange. The dichotomous epistemology which grows from exchange cannot be dismissed either as simply false or as an epistemology relevant to only a few: the worker as well as the capitalist engages in the purchase and sale of commodities, and if material life structures consciousness, this cannot fail to have an effect. This leads into the fourth claim for a standpoint—that it is achieved rather than obvious, a mediated rather than immediate understanding. Because the ruling group controls the means of mental as well as physical production, the production of ideals as well as goods, the standpoint of the oppressed represents an achievement both of science (analysis) and of political struggle on the basis of which this analysis can be conducted.

Finally, because it provides the basis for revealing the perversion of both life and thought, the inhumanity of human relations, a standpoint can be the basis for moving beyond these relations. In the historical context of Marx's theory, the engaged vision available to the producers, by drawing out the potentiality available in the actuality, that is, by following up the possibility of abundance capitalism creates, leads toward transcendence. Thus, the proletariat is the only class which has the possibility of creating a classless society. It can do this simply (!) by generalizing its own condition, that is, by making society itself a propertyless producer.[11]

These are the general characteristics of the standpoint of the proletariat. What guidance can feminists take from this discussion? I hold that the powerful vision of both the perverseness and reality of class domination made possible by Marx's adoption of the standpoint of the proletariat suggests that a specifically feminist standpoint could allow for a much more profound critique of phallocratic ideologies and institutions than has yet been achieved. The effectiveness of Marx's critique grew from its uncompromising focus on material life activity, and I propose here to set out from the Marxian contention that not only are persons active, but that reality itself consists of "sensuous human activity, practice." But rather than beginning with men's labor, I will focus on women's life activity and on the institutions which structure that activity in order to raise the question of whether this activity can form the ground for a distinctive standpoint, that is, to determine whether it meets the requirements for a feminist standpoint. (I use the term, "feminist" rather than "female" here to indicate both the achieved character of a standpoint and that a standpoint by definition carries a liberatory potential.)

Women's work in every society differs systematically from men's. I intend to pursue the suggestion that this division of labor is the first and in some societies the only division of labor, and moreover, that it is central to the organization of social labor more generally. On the basis of an account of the sexual division of labor, one should be able to begin to explore the oppositions and differences between women's and men's activity and their consequences for epistemology. While I cannot attempt a complete account, I will put forward a schematic and simplified account of the sexual division of labor and its consequences for epistemology. I will sketch out a kind of ideal type of the social relations and world view characteristic of male and female activity in order to explore the epistemology contained in the institutionalized sexual division of labor. In so doing, I do not mean to attribute this vision to individual women or men any more than Marx (or Lukacs) meant their theory of class consciousness to apply to any particular worker or group of workers. My focus is instead on institutionalized social practices and on the specific epistemology and ontology manifested by the institutionalized sexual division of labor. Individuals, as individuals, may change their activity in ways which move them outside the outlook embodied in these institutions, but such a move can be significant only when it occurs at the level of society as a whole.

I will discuss the "sexual division of labor" rather than the "gender division of labor" to stress first my belief that the division of labor between women and men cannot be reduced to purely social dimensions. One must distinguish between what Sara Ruddick has termed "invariant and *nearly* unchangeable" features of human life, and those which despite being "*nearly* universal" are "certainly changeable."[12] Thus, the fact that women and not men *bear* children is not (yet) a social choice, but that women and not men rear children in a society structured by compulsory heterosexuality and male dominance is clearly a societal choice. A second reason to use the term "sexual division of labor" is to keep hold of the bodily aspect of existence—perhaps to grasp it over-firmly in an effort to keep it from evaporating altogether. There is some biological, bodily component to human existence. But its size and substantive content will remain unknown until at least the certainly changeable aspects of the sexual division of labor are altered.

On a strict reading of Marx, of course, my enterprise here is illegitimate. While on the one hand, Marx remarked that the very first division of labor occurred in sexual intercourse, he argues that the division of labor only becomes "truly such" when the division of mental and manual labor appears. Thus, he dismisses the sexual division of labor as of no analytic importance. At the same time, a reading of other remarks—such as his claim that the mental/manual division of labor is based on the "natural" division of labor in the family—would seem to support the legitimacy of my attention to the sexual division of labor and even add weight to the radical feminist argument that capitalism is an outgrowth of male dominance, rather than vice versa.

On the basis of a schematic account of the sexual division of labor, I will begin to fill in the specific content of the feminist standpoint and begin to specify how women's lives structure an understanding of social relations, that is, begin to follow out the epistemological consequences of the sexual division of labor. In addressing the institutionalized sexual division of labor, I propose to lay aside the important differences among women across race and class boundaries and instead search for central commonalities. I take some justification from the fruitfulness of Marx's similar strategy in constructing a simplified, two class, two man model in which everything was exchanged at its value. Marx's schematic accounting in Volume I of *Capital* left out of account such factors as imperialism, the differential wages, work, and working conditions of the Irish, the differences between women, men, and children, and so on. While all of these factors are important to the analysis of contemporary capitalism, none changes either Marx's theories of surplus value or alienation, two of the most fundamental features of the Marxian analysis of capitalism. My effort here takes a similar form in an attempt to move toward a theory of the extraction and appropriation of women's activity and women themselves. Still, I adopt this strategy with some reluctance, since it contains the danger of making invisible the experience of lesbians or women of color.[13] At the same time, I recognize that the effort to uncover a feminist standpoint assumes that there are some things common to all women's lives in Western class societies.

The feminist standpoint which emerges through an examination of women's activities is related to the proletarian standpoint, but deeper going. Women and workers inhabit a world in which the emphasis is on change rather than stasis, a world characterized by interaction with natural substances rather than separation from nature, a world in which quality is more important than quantity, a world in which the unification of mind and body is inherent in the activities performed. Yet, there are some important differences, differences marked by the fact that the proletarian (if male) is immersed in this world only during the time his labor power is being used by the capitalist. If, to paraphrase Marx, we follow the worker home from the factory, we can once again perceive a change in the *dramatis personae*. He who before followed behind as the worker, timid and holding back, with nothing to expect but a hiding, now strides in front while a third person, not specifically present in Marx's account of the transaction between capitalist and worker (both of whom are male) follows timidly behind, carrying groceries, baby and diapers.

The Sexual Division of Labor

Women's activity as institutionalized has a double aspect—their contribution to subsistence, and their contribution to childrearing. Whether or not all of us do both, women as a sex are institutionally responsible for producing both goods and human beings and all women are forced to become the kinds of people who can do both. Although the nature of women's contribution to subsistence varies immensely over time and space, my primary focus here is on capitalism, with a secondary focus on the Western class societies which preceded it.[14] In capitalism, women contribute both production for wages and production of goods in the home, that is, they, like men, sell their labor power and produce both commodities and surplus value, and produce use-values in the home. Unlike men, however, women's lives are institutionally defined by their production of use-values in the home.[15] And here we begin to encounter the narrowness of the Marxian concept of production. Women's production of use-values in the home has not been well understood by socialists. It is no surprise to feminists that Engels, for example, simply asks how women can continue to do the work in the home and also work in production outside the home. Marx too takes for granted women's responsibility for household labor. He repeats, as if it were his own, the question of a Belgian factory inspector: If a mother works for wages, "how will [the household's] internal economy be cared for; who will look after the young children; who will get ready the meals, do the washing and mending?"[16]

Let us trace both the outlines and the consequences of women's dual contribution to subsistence in capitalism. Women's labor, like that of the male worker, is contact with material necessity. Their contribution to subsistence, like that of the male worker, involves them in a world in which the relation to nature and to concrete human requirements is central, both in the form of interaction with natural substances whose quality, rather than quantity is important to the production of meals, clothing, etc., and in the form of close attention to the natural changes in these substances. Women's labor both for wages and even more in household production involves a unification of mind and body for the purpose of transforming natural substances into socially defined goods. This too is true of the labor of the male worker.

There are, however, important differences. First, women as a group work more than men. We are all familiar with the phenomenon of the "double day," and with indications that women work many more hours per week than men.[17] Second, a larger proportion of women's labor time is devoted to the production of use-values than men's. Only some of the goods women produce are commodities (however much they live in a society structured by commodity production and exchange). Third, women's production is structured by repetition in a different way than men's. While repetition for both the woman and the male worker may take the form of production of the same object, over and over—whether apple pies or brake linings—women's work in housekeeping involves a repetitious cleaning.[18]

Thus, the male worker in the process of production, is involved in contact with necessity, and interchange with nature as well as with other human beings but the process of production or work does not consume his whole life. The activity of a woman in the home as well as the work she does for wages keeps her continually in contact with a world of qualities and change. Her immersion in the world of use—in concrete, many-qualitied, changing material processes—is more complete than his. And if life itself consists of sensuous activity, the vantage point available to women on the basis of their contribution to subsistence represents an intensification and deepening of the materialist world view and consciousness available to the producers of commodities in capitalism, an intensification of class consciousness. The availability of this outlook to even non-working-class women has been strikingly formulated by Marilyn French in *The Women's Room*.

> Washing the toilet used by three males, and the floor and walls around it, is, Mira thought, coming face to face with necessity. And that is why women were saner than men, did not come up with the mad, absurd schemes men developed; they were in touch with necessity, they had to wash the toilet bowl and floor.[19]

The focus on women's subsistence activity rather than men's leads to a model in which the capitalist (male) lives a life structured completely by commodity exchange and not at all by production, and at the furthest distance from contact with concrete material life. The male worker marks a way station on the path to the other extreme of the constant contact with material necessity in women's contribution to subsistence. There are of course important differences along the lines of race and class. For example, working-class men seem to do more domestic labor than men higher up in the class structure—car repairs, carpentry, etc. And until very recently, the wage work done by most women of color replicated the housework required by their own households. Still, there are commonalities present in the institutionalized sexual division of labor which make women responsible for both housework and wage work.

The female contribution to subsistence, however, represents only a part of women's labor. Women also produce/reproduce men (and other women) on both a daily and a long-term basis. This aspect of women's "production" exposes the deep inadequacies of the concept of production as a description of women's activity. One does not (cannot) produce another human being in anything like the way one produces an object such as a chair. Much more is involved, activity which cannot easily be dichotomized into play or work. Helping another to develop, the gradual relinquishing of control, the experience of the human limits of one's action—all these are important features of women's activity as mothers. Women as mothers even more than as workers, are institutionally involved in processes of change and growth, and more than workers, must understand the importance of avoiding excessive control in order to help others grow.[20] The activity involved is far more complex than the instrumental working with others to transform objects. (Interestingly, much of women's wage work—nursing, social work, and some secretarial jobs in particular—requires and depends on the relational and interpersonal skills women learned by being mothered by someone of the same sex.)

This aspect of women's activity too is not without consequences. Indeed, it is in the production of men by women and the appropriation of this labor and women themselves by men that the opposition between feminist and masculinist experience and outlook is rooted, and it is here that features of the proletarian vision are enhanced and modified for the woman and diluted for the man. The female experience in reproduction represents a unity with nature which goes beyond the proletarian experience of interchange with nature. As another theorist has put it, "reproductive labor might be said to combine the functions of the architect and the bee: like the architect, parturitive woman knows what she is doing; like the bee, she cannot help what she is doing." And just as the worker's acting on the external world changes both the world and the worker's nature, so too "a new life changes the world and the consciousness of the woman."[21] In addition, in the process of producing human beings, relations with others may take a variety of forms with deeper significance than simple cooperation with others for common goals—forms which range from a deep unity with another through the many-leveled and changing connections mothers experience with growing children. Finally, the female experience in bearing and rearing children involves a unity of mind and body more profound than is possible in the worker's instrumental activity.

Motherhood in the large sense, that is, motherhood as an institution rather than experience, including pregnancy and the preparation for motherhood almost all female children receive as socialization, results in the construction of female existence as centered with a complex relational nexus.[22] One aspect of this relational existence is centered on the experience of living in a female rather than male body. There are a series of boundary challenges inherent in the female physiology—challenges which make it impossible to maintain rigid separation from the object world. Menstruation, coitus, pregnancy, childbirth, lactation—all represent challenges to bodily boundaries.[23] Adrienne Rich has described the experience of pregnancy as one in which the embryo was both inside and

> daily more separate, on its way to becoming separate from me and of itself.
> In early pregnancy the stirring of the fetus felt like ghostly tremors of my
> own body, later like the movements of a being imprisoned in me; but both
> sensations were *my* sensations, contributing to my own sense of physical and
> psychic space.[24]

In turn, the fact that women but not men are primarily responsible for young children means that the infant first experiences itself as not fully differentiated from the mother, and then as an I in relation to an It that it later comes to know as female.[25]

Jane Flax and Nancy Chodorow have argued that the object relations school of psychoanalytic theory puts forward a materialist psychology, one which I propose to treat as a kind of empirical hypothesis. If the account of human development provided by object relations is correct, one ought to expect to find consequences—both psychic, and social. According to object relations theory, the process of differentiation from a woman by both male and female children reinforces boundary confusion in female egos and boundary strengthening in males. Individuation is far more conflictual for male than for female children, in part because both mother and son experience the other as a definite "other." The experience of oneness on the part of both mother and infant seems to last longer with girls.[26]

The complex relational world inhabited by women has its start in the experience and resolution of the oedipal crisis, cleanly resolved for the boy, whereas the girl is much more likely to retain both parents as love objects. The nature of the crisis itself differs by sex: the boy's love for the mother is an extension of mother-infant unity and thus essentially threatening to his ego and independence. Male ego-formation necessarily requires repressing this first relation and negating the mother.[27] In contrast, the girl's love for the father is less threatening both because it occurs outside this unity and because it occurs at a later stage of development. For boys, the central issue to be resolved concerns gender identification; for girls the issue is psychosexual development.[28] Chodorow concludes that girls' gradual emergence from the oedipal period takes place in such a way that empathy is built into their primary definition of self, and they have a variety of capacities for experiencing another's needs or feelings as their own. Put another way, girls, because of female parenting, are less differentiated from others than boys, more continuous with and related to the external object world. They are differently oriented to their inner object world as well.[29]

The more complex female relational world is reinforced by the process of socialization. Girls learn roles from watching their mothers; boys must learn roles from rules which structure the life of an absent male figure. Girls can identify with a concrete example present in daily life; boys must identify with an abstract set of maxims only occasionally concretely present in the form of the father. Thus, not only do girls learn roles with more interpersonal and relational skills, but the process of role learning itself is embodied in the concrete relation with the mother. The male, in contrast, must identify with an abstract, cultural stereotype and learn abstract behaviors not attached to a well-known person. Masculinity is idealized by boys whereas femininity is concrete for girls.[30]

Women and men, then, grow up with personalities affected by different boundary experiences, differently constructed and experienced inner and outer worlds, and preoccupations with different relational issues. This early experience forms an important ground for the female sense of self as connected to the world and the male sense of self as separate, distinct, and even disconnected. By retaining the preoedipal attachment to the mother, girls come to define and experience themselves as continuous with others. In sum, girls enter adulthood with a more complex layering of affective ties and a rich, ongoing inner set of object relations. Boys, with a simpler oedipal situation and a clear and early resolution, have repressed ties to another. As a result, women define and experience themselves and men do not.[31]

Abstract Masculinity and the Feminist Standpoint

This excursion into psychoanalytic theory has served to point to the differences in the male and female experience of self due to the sexual division of labor in childrearing. These different (psychic) experiences both structure and are reinforced by the differing patterns of male and female activity required by the sexual division of labor, and are thereby replicated as epistemology and ontology. The differential male and female life activity in class society leads on the one hand toward a feminist standpoint and on the other toward an abstract masculinity.

Because the problem for the boy is to distinguish himself from the mother and to protect himself against the real threat she poses for his identity, his conflictual and oppositional efforts lead to the formation of rigid ego boundaries. The way Freud takes for granted the rigid distinction between the "me and not-me" makes the point well: "Normally, there is nothing of which we are more certain than the feeling of ourself, of our own ego. This ego appears to us as something autonomous and unitary, marked off distinctly from everything else." At least toward the outside, "the ego seems to maintain clear and sharp lines of demarcation."[32] Thus, the boy's construction of self in opposition to unity with the mother, his construction of identity as differentiation from the other, sets a hostile and combative dualism at the heart of both the community men construct and the masculinist world view by means of which they understand their lives.

I do not mean to suggest that the totality of human relations can be explained by psychoanalysis. Rather I want to point to the ways male rather than female experience and activity replicates itself in both the hierarchical and dualist institutions of class society and in the frameworks of thought generated by this experience. It is interesting to read Hegel's account of the relation of self and other as a statement of male experience: the relation of the two consciousnesses takes the form of a trial by death. As Hegel describes it, "each seeks the death of the other."

> Thus, the relation of the two self-conscious individuals is such that they provide themselves and each other through a life-and-death struggle. They must engage in this struggle, for they must raise their certainty *for themselves* to truth, both in the case of the other and in their own case.[33]

The construction of the self in opposition to another who threatens one's very being reverberates throughout the construction of both class society and the masculinist world view and results in a deep-going and hierarchical dualism. First, the male experience is characterized by the duality of concrete versus abstract. Material reality as experienced by the boy in the family provides no model, and is unimportant in the attainment of masculinity. Nothing of value to the boy occurs with the family, and masculinity becomes an abstract ideal to be achieved over the opposition of daily life.[34] Masculinity must be attained by means of opposition to the concrete world of daily life, by escaping from contact with the female world of the household into the masculine world of public life. This experience of two worlds, one valuable, if abstract and deeply unattainable, the other useless and demeaning, if concrete and necessary, lies at the heart of a series of dualisms—abstract/concrete, mind/body, culture/nature, ideal/real, stasis/change. And these dualisms are overlaid by gender: only the first of each pair is associated with the male.

Dualism, along with the dominance of one side of the dichotomy over the other, marks phallocentric society and social theory. These dualisms appear in a variety of forms—in philosophy, technology, political theory, and the organization of class society itself. One can, for example, see them very clearly worked out in Plato, although they appear in many other forms.[35] There, the concrete/abstract duality takes the form of an opposition of material to ideal, and a denial of the relevance of the material world to the attainment of what is of fundamental importance: love of knowledge, or philosophy (masculinity). The duality between nature and culture takes the form of a devaluation of work or necessity, and the primacy instead of purely social interaction for the attainment of undying fame. Philosophy itself is separate from nature, and indeed, exists only on the basis of the domination of (at least some) of the philosopher's own nature.[36] Abstract masculinity, then, can be seen to have structured Western social relations and the modes of thought to which these relations give rise at least since the founding of the *polis*.

The oedipal roots of these hierarchical dualisms are memorialized in the overlay of female and male connotations: it is not accidental that women are associated with quasi-human and non-human nature, that the female is associated with the body and material life, that the lives of women are systematically used as examples to characterize the lives of those ruled by their bodies rather than their minds.[37]

Both the fragility and fundamental falseness of the masculinist ideology and the deeply problematic nature of the social relations from which it grows are apparent in its reliance on a series of counterfactual assumptions and contentions. Consider how the following contentions are contrary to lived experience: the body is both irrelevant and in opposition to the (real) self, an impediment to be overcome by the mind; the female mind either does not exist (Do women have souls?) or works in such incomprehensible ways as to be unintelligible (the "enigma of woman"); what is real and primary is imperceptible to the senses and impervious to nature and natural change. What is remarkable is not only that these contentions have absorbed a great deal of philosophical energy, but, along with a series of other counterfactuals, have structured social relations for centuries.

Interestingly enough the epistemology and society constructed by men suffering from the effects of abstract masculinity have a great deal in common with that imposed by commodity exchange. The separation and opposition of social and natural worlds, of abstract and concrete, of permanence and change, the effort to define only the former of each pair as important, the reliance on a series of counter factual assumptions—all this is shared with the exchange abstraction. Abstract masculinity shares still another of its aspects with the exchange abstraction: it forms the basis for an even more problematic social synthesis. Hegel's analysis makes clear the problematic social relations available to the self which maintains itself by opposition: each of the two subjects struggling for recognition risks its own death in the struggle to kill the other, but if the other is killed the subject is once again alone.[38] In sum, then, the male experience when replicated as epistemology leads to a world conceived as, and (in fact) inhabited by, a number of fundamentally hostile others whom one comes to know by means of opposition (even death struggle) and yet with whom one must construct a social relation in order to survive.

The female construction of self in relation to others leads in an opposite direction—toward opposition to dualisms of any sort, valuation of concrete, everyday life, sense of a variety of connectednesses and continuities both with other persons and with the natural world. If material life structures consciousness, women's relationally defined existence, bodily experience of boundary challenges, and activity of transforming both physical objects and human beings must be expected to result in a world view to which dichotomies are foreign. Women experience others and themselves along a continuum whose dimensions are evidenced in Adrienne Rich's argument that the child carried for nine months can be defined "*neither* as me or as not-me," and she argues that inner and outer are not polar opposites but a continuum.[39] What the sexual division of labor defines as women's work turns on issues of change rather than stasis, the changes involved in producing both use-values and commodities, but more profoundly in the activity of rearing human beings who change in both more subtle and more autonomous ways than any inanimate object. Not only the qualities of things but also the qualities of people are important in women's work: quantity becomes peripheral. In addition, far more than the instrumental cooperation of the workplace is required; the mother-child relation and the maintenance of the family, while it has instrumental aspects, is not defined by them. Finally, the unity of mental and manual labor, and the directly sensuous nature of much of women's work leads to a more profound unity of mental and manual labor, social and natural worlds, than is experienced by the male worker in capitalism. The unity grows from the fact that women's bodies, unlike men's, can be themselves instruments of production: in pregnancy, giving birth or lactation, arguments about a division of mental from manual labor are fundamentally foreign.

That this is indeed women's experience is documented in both the theory and practice of the contemporary women's movement and needs no further development here.[40] The more important question here is whether female experience and the world view constructed by female activity can meet the criteria for a standpoint. If we return to the five claims carried by the concept of a standpoint, it seems clear that women's material life activity has important epistemological and ontological consequences for both the understanding and construction of social relations. Women's activity, then, does satisfy the first requirement of a standpoint.

I can now take up the second claim made by a standpoint: that the female experience not only inverts that of the male, but forms a basis on which to expose abstract masculinity as both partial and fundamentally perverse, as not only occupying only one side of the dualities it has constructed, but reversing the proper valuation of human activity. The partiality of the masculinist vision and of the societies which support this understanding is evidenced by its confinement of activity proper to the male to only one side of the dualisms. Its perverseness, however, lies elsewhere. Perhaps the most dramatic (though not the only) reversal of the proper order of things characteristic of the male experience is the substitution of death for life.

The substitution of death for life results at least in part from the sexual division of labor in childrearing. The self surrounded by rigid ego-boundaries, certain of what is inner and what is outer, the self experienced as walled city, is discontinuous with others. Georges Bataille has made brilliantly clear the ways in which death emerges as the only possible solution to this discontinuity and has followed the logic through to argue that reproduction itself must be understood not as the creation of life, but as death. The core experience to be understood is that of discontinuity and its consequences. As a consequence of this experience of discontinuity and aloneness, penetration of ego-boundaries, or fusion with another is experienced as violent. Thus, the desire for fusion with another can take the form of domination of the other. In this form, it leads to the only possible fusion with a threatening other: when the other ceases to exist as a separate, and for that reason threatening, being. Insisting that another submit to one's will is simply a milder form of the destruction of discontinuity in the death of the other since in this case one is no longer confronting a discontinuous and opposed will, despite its discontinuous embodiment. This is perhaps one source of the links between sexual activity, domination, and death.

Bataille suggests that killing and sexual activity share both prohibitions and religious significance. Their unity is demonstrated by religious sacrifice since the latter:

> is intentional like the act of the man who lays bare, desires and wants to penetrate his victim. The lover strips the beloved of her identity no less than the bloodstained priest his human or animal victim. The woman in the hands of her assailant is despoiled of her being . . . loses the firm barrier that once sep-

arated her from others . . . is brusquely laid open to the violence of the sexual urges set loose in the organs of reproduction; she is laid open to the impersonal violence that overwhelms her from without.[41]

Note the use of the term "lover" and "assailant" as synonyms and the presence of the female as victim.

The importance of Bataille's analysis lies in the fact that it can help to make clear the links between violence, death, and sexual fusion with another, links which are not simply theoretical but actualized in rape and pornography. Images of women in chains, being beaten, or threatened with attack carry clear social messages, among them that "the normal male is sexually aggressive in a brutal and demeaning way."[42] Bataille's analysis can help to understand why "men advertise, even brag, that their movie is the 'bloodiest thing that ever happened in front of a camera.'"[43] The analysis is supported by the psychoanalyst who suggested that although one of the important dynamics of pornography is hostility, "one can raise the possibly controversial question whether in humans (especially males) powerful sexual excitement can ever exist without brutality also being present."[44]

Bataille's analysis can help to explain what is erotic about "snuff" films, which not only depict the torture and dismemberment of a woman, but claim that the actress is *in fact* killed. His analysis suggests that perhaps she is a sacrificial victim whose discontinuous existence has been succeeded in her death by "the organic continuity of life drawn into the common life of the beholders."[45] Thus, the pair "love-assailant" is not accidental. Nor is the connection of reproduction and death.

"Reproduction," Bataille argues, "implies the existence of *discontinuous* beings." This is so because, "Beings which reproduce themselves are distinct from one another, and those reproduced are likewise distinct from each other, just as they are distinct from their parents. Each being is distinct from all others. His birth, his death, the events of his life may have an interest for others, but he alone is directly concerned in them. He is born alone. He dies alone. Between one being and another, there is a *gulf*, a discontinuity."[46] (Clearly it is not just a gulf, but is better understood as a chasm.) In reproduction sperm and ovum unite to form a new entity, but they do so from the death and disappearance of two separate beings. Thus, the new entity bears within itself "the transition to continuity, the fusion, fatal to both, of two separate beings."[47] Thus, death and reproduction are intimately linked, yet Bataille stresses that "it is only death which is to be identified with continuity." Thus, despite the unity of birth and death in this analysis, Bataille gives greater weight to a "tormenting fact: the urge towards love, pushed to its limit, is an urge toward death."[48] Bataille holds to this position despite his recognition that reproduction is a form of growth. The growth, however, he dismisses as not being "ours," as being only "impersonal."[49] This is not the female experience, in which reproduction is hardly impersonal, nor experienced as death. It is, of course, in a literal sense, the sperm which is cut off from its source, and lost. No wonder, then, at the masculinist occupation with death, and the feeling that growth is "impersonal," not of fundamental concern to oneself. But this complete dismissal of the experience of another bespeaks a profound lack of empathy and refusal to recognize the very being of another. It is a manifestation of the chasm which separates each man from every other being and from the natural world, the chasm which both marks and defines the problem of community.

The preoccupation with death instead of life appears as well in the argument that it is the ability to kill (and for centuries, the practice) which sets humans above animals. Even Simone de Beauvoir has accepted that "it is not in giving life but in risking life that man is raised above the animal: that is why superiority has been accorded in humanity not to the sex that brings forth but to that which kills."[50] That superiority has been accorded to the sex which kills is beyond doubt. But what kind of experience and vision can take reproduction, the creation of new life, and the force of life in sexuality, and turn it into death—not just in theory but in the practice of rape, pornography, and sexual murder? And why give pride of place to killing? This is not only an inversion of the proper order of things, but also a refusal to recognize the real activities in which men as well as women are engaged. The producing of goods and the reproducing of human beings are certainly life-sustaining activities. And even the deaths of the ancient heroes in search of undying fame were pursuits of life, and represented the attempt to avoid death by attaining immortality. The search for life, then, represents the deeper reality which lies beneath the glorification of death and destruction.

Yet one cannot dismiss the substitution of death for life as simply false. Men's power to structure social relations in their own image means that women too must participate in social relations which manifest and express abstract masculinity. The most important life activities have consistently been held by the powers that be to be unworthy of those who are fully human most centrally because of their close connections with necessity and life: motherwork (the rearing of children), housework, and until the rise of capitalism in the West, any work necessary to subsistence. In addition, these activities in contemporary capitalism are all constructed in ways which systematically degrade and destroy the minds and bodies of those who perform them.[51] The organization of motherhood as an institution in which a woman is alone with her children, the isolation of women from each other in domestic labor, the female pathology of loss of self in service to others—all mark the transformation of life into death, the distortion of what could have been creative and communal activity into oppressive toil, and the destruction of the possibility of community present in women's relational self-definition. The ruling gender's and class's interest in maintaining social relations such as these is evidenced by the fact that when women set up other structures in which the mother is not alone with her children, isolated from others—as is frequently the case in working-class communities or communities of people of color—these arrangements are categorized as pathological deviations.

The real destructiveness of the social relations characteristic of abstract masculinity, however, is now concealed beneath layers of ideology. Marxian theory needed to go beneath the surface to discover the different levels of determination which defined the relation of capitalist and (male) worker. These levels of determination and laws of motion or tendency of phallocratic society must be worked out on the basis of female experience. This brings me to the fourth claim for a standpoint—its character as an achievement of both analysis and political struggle occurring in a particular historical space. The fact that class divisions should have proven so resistant to analysis and required such a prolonged political struggle before Marx was able to formulate the theory of surplus value indicates the difficulty of this accomplishment. And the rational control of production has certainly not been achieved.

Feminists have only begun the process of revaluing female experience, searching for common threads which connect the diverse experiences of women, and searching for the structural determinants of the experiences. The difficulty of the problem faced by feminist theory can be illustrated by the fact that it required a struggle even to define household labor, if not done for wages, as work, to argue that what are held to be acts of love instead must be recognized as work whether or not wages are paid.[52] Both the valuation of women's experience, and the use of this experience as a ground for critique are required. A feminist standpoint may be present on the basis of the common threads of female experience, but it is neither self-evident nor obvious.

Finally, because it provides a way to reveal the perverseness and inhumanity of human relations, a standpoint forms the basis for moving beyond these relations. Just as the proletarian standpoint emerges out of the contradiction between appearance and essence in capitalism, understood as essentially historical and constituted by the relation of capitalist and worker, the feminist standpoint emerges both out of the contradiction between the systematically differing structure of male and female life activity in Western cultures. It expresses female experience at a particular time and place, located within a particular set of social relations. Capitalism, Marx noted, could not develop fully until the notion of human equality achieved the status of universal truth.[53] Despite women's exploitation both as unpaid reproducers of the labor force and as a sex-segregated labor force available for low wages, then, capitalism poses problems for the continued oppression of women. Just as capitalism enables the proletariat to raise the possibility of a society free from class domination, so too, it provides space to raise the possibility of a society free from all forms of domination. The articulation of a feminist standpoint based on women's relational self-definition and activity exposes the world men have constructed and the self-understanding which manifests these relations as partial and perverse. More important, by drawing out the potentiality available in the actuality and thereby exposing the inhumanity of human relations, it embodies a distress which requires a solution. The experience of continuity and relation—with others, with the natural world, of mind with body—provides an ontological base for developing a non-problematic social synthesis, a social synthesis which need not operate through the denial of the body, the attack on nature, or the death struggle between the self and other, a social synthesis which does not depend on any of the forms taken by abstract masculinity.

What is necessary is the generalization of the potentiality made available by the activity of women—the defining of society as a whole as propertyless producer both of use-values and of human beings. To understand what such a transformation would require we should consider what is involved in the partial transformation represented by making the whole of society into propertyless producers of use-values, that is, socialist revolution. The abolition of the division between mental and manual labor cannot take place simply by means of adopting worker-self-management techniques, but instead requires the abolition of private property, the seizure of state power, and lengthy post-revolutionary class struggle. Thus, I am not suggesting that shared parenting arrangements can abolish the sexual division of labor. Doing away with this division of labor would of course require institutionalizing the participation of both women and men in childrearing; but just as the rational and conscious control of the production of goods and services requires a vast and far-reaching social transformation, so the rational and conscious organization of reproduction would entail the transformation both of *every* human relation, and of human relations to the natural world. The magnitude of the task is apparent if one asks what a society without institutionalized gender differences might look like.

Conclusion

An analysis which begins from the sexual division of labor—understood not as taboo, but as the real, material activity of concrete human beings—could form the basis for an analysis of the real structures of women's oppression, an analysis which would not require that one sever biology from society, nature from culture, an analysis which would expose the ways women both participate in and oppose their own subordination. The elaboration of such an analysis cannot but be difficult. Women's lives, like men's, are structured by social relations which manifest the experience of the dominant gender and class. The ability to go beneath the surface of appearances to reveal the real but concealed social relations requires both theoretical and political activity. Feminist theorists must demand that feminist theorizing be grounded in women's material activity and must as well be a part of the political struggle necessary to develop areas of social life modeled on this activity. The outcome could be the development of a political economy which included women's activity as well as men's, and could as well be a step toward the redefining and restructuring of society as a whole on the basis of women's activity.

Generalizing the activity of women to the social system as a whole would raise, for the first time in human history, the possibility of a fully human community, a community structured by connection rather than separation and opposition. One can conclude then that women's life activity does form the basis of a specifically feminist materialism, a materialism which can provide a point from which both to critique and to work against phallocratic ideology and institutions.

My argument here opens a number of avenues for future work. Clearly, a systematic critique of Marx on the basis of a more fully developed understanding of the sexual division of labor is in order. And this is indeed being undertaken by a number of feminists. A second avenue for further investigation is the relation between exchange and abstract masculinity. An exploration of Mauss's *The Gift* would play an important part in this project, since he presents the solipsism of exchange as an overlay on and substitution for a deeper-going hostility, the exchange of gifts as an alternative to war. We have seen that the necessity for recognizing and receiving recognition from another to take the form of a death struggle memorializes the male rather than female experience of emerging as a person in opposition to a woman in the context of a deeply phallocratic world. If the community of exchangers (capitalists) rests on the more overtly and directly hostile death struggle of self and other, one might be able to argue that what underlies the exchange abstraction is abstract masculinity. One might then turn to the question of whether capitalism rests on and is a consequence of patriarchy. Perhaps then feminists can produce the analysis which could amend Marx to read: "Though class society appears to be the source, the cause of the oppression of women, it is rather its consequence." Thus, it is "only at the last culmination of the development of class society [that] this, its secret, appear[s] again, namely, that on the one hand it is the *product* of the oppression of women, and that on the other it is the *means* by which women participate in and create their own oppression."[54, 55]

NOTES

I take my title from Iris Young's call for the development of a specifically feminist historical materialism. See 'Socialist Feminism and the Limits of Dual Systems Theory,' in *Socialist Review* 10, 2/3 (March-June, 1980). My work on this paper is deeply indebted to a number of women whose ideas are incorporated here, although not always used in the ways they might wish. My discussions with Donna Haraway and Sandra Harding have been intense and ongoing over a period of years. I have also had a number of important and useful conversations with Jane Flax, and my project here has benefitted both from these contacts, and from the opportunity to read her paper, 'Political Philosophy and the Patriarchal Unconscious: A Psychoanalytic Perspective on Epistemology and Metaphysics.' In addition I have been helped immensely by collective discussions with Annette Bickel, Sarah Begus, and Alexa Freeman. All of these people (along with Iris Young and Irene Diamond) have read and commented on drafts of this paper. I would also like to thank Alison Jaggar for continuing to question me about the basis on which one could claim the superiority of a feminist standpoint and for giving me the opportunity to deliver the paper at the University of Cincinnati Philosophy Department Colloquium; and Stephen Rose for taking the time to read and comment on a rough draft of the paper at a critical point in its development.

1. See my 'Feminist Theory and the Development of Revolutionary Strategy,' in Zillah Eisenstein, ed., *Capitalist Patriarchy and the Case for Socialist Feminism* (New York: Monthly Review, 1978).

2. The recent literature on mothering is perhaps the most detailed on this point. See Dorothy Dinnerstein, *The Mermaid and the Minotaur* (New York: Harper and Row, 1976); Nancy Chodorow, *The Reproduction of Mothering* (Berkeley: University of California Press, 1978).

3. Iris Young, 'Socialist Feminism and the Limits of Dual Systems Theory,' in *Socialist Review* 10, 2/3 (March-June, 1980), p. 180.

4. Eighth Thesis on Feuerbach, in Karl Marx, 'Theses on Feuerbach,' in *The German Ideology*, C. J. Arthur, ed. (New York: International Publishers, 1970), p. 121.

5. *Ibid.* Conscious human practice, then, is at once both an epistemological category and the basis for Marx's conception of the nature of humanity itself. To put the case even more strongly, Marx argues that human activity has both an ontological and epistemological status, that human feelings are not "merely anthropological phenomena," but are "truly ontological affirmations of being." See Karl Marx, *Economic and Philosophic Manuscripts of 1844*, Dirk Struik, ed. (New York: International Publishers, 1964), pp. 113, 165, 188.

6. Marx, *1844*, p. 112. Nature itself, for Marx, appears as a form of human work, since he argues that humans duplicate themselves actively and come to contemplate themselves in a world of their own making. (*Ibid.*, p. 114.) On the more general issue of the relation of natural to human worlds, see the very interesting account by Alfred Schmidt, *The Concept of Nature in Marx*, tr. Ben Foukes (London: New Left Books, 1971).

7. Marx and Engels, *The German Ideology*, p. 42.

8. See Alfred Sohn Rethel, *Intellectual and Manual Labor: A Critique of Epistemology* (London: Macmillan, 1978). I should note that my analysis both depends on

...hn-Rethel's. Sohn-Rethel argues that commodity ex-
...f all class societies—one which comes to a head in capi-
...dvanced form in capitalism. His project, which is not
...commodity exchange, a characteristic of all class soci-
...of abstraction, (b) that this abstraction contains the for-
...he cognitive faculty of conceptual thinking, and (c) that
...n exchange, an abstraction in practice, is the source of
the ideal abstraction basic to Greek philosophy and to modern science. (See *Ibid.*, p. 28.) In addition to a different purpose, I should indicate several major differences with Sohn-Rethel. First, he treats the productive forces as separate from the productive relations of society and ascribes far too much autonomy to them. (See, for example, his discussions on pp. 84–86, 95.) I take the position that the distinction between the two is simply a device used for purposes of analysis rather than a feature of the real world. Second, Sohn-Rethel characterizes the period preceding generalized commodity production as primitive communism. (See p. 98.) This is however an inadequate characterization of tribal societies.

9. Karl Marx, *Capital,* vol. I (New York: International Publishers, 1967), p. 176.

10. I have done this elsewhere in a systematic way. For the analysis, see my discussion of the exchange abstraction in *Money, Sex, and Power: An Essay on Domination and Community* (New York: Longman, Inc., 1983).

11. This is Iris Young's point. I am indebted to her persuasive arguments for taking what she terms the "gender differentiation of labor" as a central category of analysis (Young, 'Dual Systems Theory,' p. 185). My use of this category, however, differs to some extent from hers. Young's analysis of women in capitalism does not seem to include marriage as a part of the division of labor. She is more concerned with the division of labor in the productive sector.

12. See Sara Ruddick, 'Maternal Thinking,' *Feminist Studies* 6, 2 (Summer, 1980), p. 364.

13. See, for discussions of this danger, Adrienne Rich, 'Disloyal to Civilization: Feminism, Racism, Gynephobia,' in *On Lies, Secrets, and Silence* (New York: W. W. Norton & Co., 1979), pp. 275–310; Elly Bulkin 'Racism and Writing: Some Implications for White Lesbian Critics,' in *Sinister Wisdom*, No. 6 (Spring, 1980).

14. Some cross-cultural evidence indicates that the status of women varies with the work they do. To the extent that women and men contribute equally to subsistence, women's status is higher than it would be if their subsistence-work differed profoundly from that of men; that is, if they do none or almost all of the work of subsistence, their status remains low. See Peggy Sanday, 'Female Status in the Public Domain,' in Michelle Rosaldo and Louise Lamphere, eds., *Women, Culture, and Society* (Stanford: Stanford University Press, 1974), p. 199. See also Iris Young's account of the sexual division of labor in capitalism, mentioned above.

15. It is irrelevant to my argument here that women's wage labor takes place under different circumstances than men's, that is, their lower wages, their confinement to only a few occupational categories, etc. I am concentrating instead on the formal, structural features of women's work. There has been much effort to argue that women's domestic labor is a source of surplus value, that is, to include it within the scope of Marx's value theory as productive labor, or to argue that since it does not produce surplus value it belongs to an entirely different mode of pro-

duction, variously characterized as domestic or patriarchal. My strategy here is quite different from this. See, for the British debate, Mariarosa Dalla Costa and Selma James, *The Power of Women and the Subversion of the Community* (Falling Wall Press, Bristol, 1975); Wally Secombe, 'The Housewife and Her Labor Under Capitalism,' *New Left Review* 83 (January-February, 1974); Jean Gardiner, 'Women's Domestic Labour,' *New Left Review* 89 (March, 1975); and Paul Smith, 'Domestic Labour and Marx's Theory of Value,' in Annette Kuhn and Ann Marie Wolpe, eds., *Feminism and Materialism* (Boston: Routledge and Kegan Paul, 1978). A portion of the American debate can be found in Ira Gerstein, 'Domestic Work and Capitalism,' and Lisa Vogel, 'The Earthly Family,' *Radical America* 7, 4/5 (July-October, 1973); Ann Ferguson, 'Women as a New Revolutionary Class,' in Pat Walker, ed., *Between Labor and Capital* (Boston: South End Press, 1979).

16. Frederick Engels, *Origins of the Family, Private Property and the State* (New York: International Publishers, 1942); Karl Marx, *Capital,* vol. I, p. 671. Marx and Engels have also described the sexual division of labor as natural or spontaneous. See Mary O'Brien, 'Reproducing Marxist Man,' in Lorenne Clark and Lynda Lange, eds., *The Sexism of Social and Political Theory: Women and Reproduction from Plato to Nietzsche* (Toronto: University of Toronto Press, 1979).

17. For a discussion of women's work, see Elise Boulding, 'Familial Constraints on Women's Work Roles,' in Martha Blaxall and B. Reagan, eds., *Women and the Workplace* (Chicago: University of Chicago Press, 1976), esp. the charts on pp. 111, 113.

An interesting historical note is provided by the fact that even Nausicaa, the daughter of a Homeric king, did the household laundry. (See M. I. Finley, *The World of Odysseus* [Middlesex, England: Penguin, 1979], p. 73.) While aristocratic women were less involved in actual labor, the difference was one of degree. And as Aristotle remarked in *The Politics,* supervising slaves is not a particularly uplifting activity. The life of leisure and philosophy, so much the goal for aristocratic Athenian men, then, was almost unthinkable for any woman.

18. Simone de Beauvoir holds that repetition has a deeper significance and that women's biological destiny itself is repetition. (See *The Second Sex,* tr. H. M. Parshley [New York: Knopf, 1953], p. 59). But see also her discussion of housework in *Ibid.,* pp. 434ff. There her treatment of housework is strikingly negative. For de Beauvoir, transcendence is provided in the historical struggle of self with other and with the natural world. The oppositions she sees are not really stasis vs. change, but rather transcendence, escape from the muddy concreteness of daily life, from the static, biological, concrete repetition of "placid femininity."

19. Marilyn French, *The Women's Room* (New York: Jove, 1978), p. 214.

20. Sara Ruddick, 'Maternal Thinking,' presents an interesting discussion of these and other aspects of the thought which emerges from the activity of mothering. Although I find it difficult to speak the language of interests and demands she uses, she brings out several valuable points. Her distinction between maternal and scientific thought is very intriguing and potentially useful (see esp. pp. 350–353).

21. O'Brien, 'Reproducing Marxist Man,' p. 115, n. 11.

22. It should be understood that I am concentrating here on the experience of women in Western culture. There are a number of cross-cultural differences which can be expected to have some effect. See, for example, the differences which

emerge from a comparison of childrearing in ancient Greek society with that of the contemporary Mbuti in central Africa. See Phillip Slater, *The Glory of Hera* (Boston: Beacon, 1968) and Colin Turnbull, 'The Politics of Non-Aggression,' in Ashley Montagu, ed., *Learning Non-Aggression* (New York: Oxford University Press, 1978).

23. See Nancy Chodorow, 'Family Structure and Feminine Personality,' in Michelle Rosaldo and Louise Lamphere, *Woman, Culture, and Society* (Stanford: Stanford University Press, 1974), p. 59.

24. *Of Woman Born* (New York: Norton, 1976), p. 63.

25. See Chodorow, *The Reproduction of Mothering*, and Flax, 'The Conflict Between Nurturance and Autonomy in Mother-Daughter Relations and in Feminism,' *Feminist Studies* 4, 2 (June, 1978). I rely on the analyses of Dinnerstein and Chodorow but there are difficulties in that they are attempting to explain why humans, both male and female, fear and hate the female. My purpose here is to invert their arguments and to attempt to put forward a positive account of the epistemological consequences of this situation. What follows is a summary of Chodorow, *The Reproduction of Mothering*.

26. Chodorow, *Reproduction*, pp. 105–109.

27. This is Jane Flax's point.

28. Chodorow, *Reproduction*, pp. 127–131, 163.

29. *Ibid.*, p. 166.

30. *Ibid.*, pp. 174–178. Chodorow suggests a correlation between father absence and fear of women (p. 213), and one should, treating this as an empirical hypothesis, expect a series of cultural differences based on the degree of father absence. Here the ancient Greeks and the Mbuti provide a fascinating contrast. (See above, note 22.)

31. *Ibid.*, p. 198. The flexible and diffuse female ego boundaries can of course result in the pathology of loss of self in responsibility for and dependence on others. (The obverse of the male pathology of experiencing the self as walled city.)

32. Sigmund Freud, *Civilization and Its Discontents* (New York: Norton, 1961), pp. 12–13.

33. Hegel, *Phenomenology of Spirit* (New York: Oxford University Press, 1979), trans. A. V. Miller, p. 114. See also Jessica Benjamin's very interesting use of this discussion in 'The Bonds of Love: Rational Violence and Erotic Domination,' *Feminist Studies* 6, 1 (June, 1980).

34. Alvin Gouldner has made a similar argument in his contention that the Platonic stress on hierarchy and order resulted from a similarly learned opposition to daily life which was rooted in the young aristocrat's experience of being taught proper behavior by slaves who could not themselves engage in this behavior. See *Enter Plato* (New York: Basic Books, 1965), pp. 351–355.

35. One can argue, as Chodorow's analysis suggests, that their extreme form in his philosophy represents an extreme father-absent (father-deprived?) situation. A more general critique of phallocentric dualism occurs in Susan Griffin, *Woman and Nature* (New York: Harper & Row, 1978).

36. More recently, of course, the opposition to the natural world has taken the form of destructive technology. See Evelyn Fox Keller, 'Gender and Science,' *Psychoanalysis and Contemporary Thought* 1, 3 (1978), reprinted in this volume.

37. See Elizabeth Spelman, 'Metaphysics and Misogyny: The Soul and Body in Plato's Dialogues,' mimeo. One analyst has argued that its basis lies in the fact that "the early mother, monolithic representative of nature, is a source, like nature, of ultimate distress as well as ultimate joy. Like nature, she is both nourishing and disappointing, both alluring and threatening . . . The infant loves her . . . and it hates her because, like nature, she does not perfectly protect and provide for it . . . The mother, then—like nature, which sends blizzards and locusts as well as sunshine and strawberries—is perceived as capricious, sometimes actively malevolent." Dinnerstein, p. 95.

38. See Benjamin, p. 152. The rest of her analysis goes in a different direction than mine, though her account of *The Story of O* can be read as making clear the problems for any social synthesis based on the Hegelian model.

39. *Of Woman Born,* pp. 64, 167. For a similar descriptive account, but a dissimilar analysis, see David Bakan, *The Duality of Human Existence* (Boston: Beacon, 1966).

40. My arguments are supported with remarkable force by both the theory and practice of the contemporary women's movement. In theory, this appears in different forms in the work of Dorothy Riddle, 'New Visions of Spiritual Power,' *Quest: a Feminist Quarterly* 1, 3 (Spring, 1975); Susan Griffin, *Woman and Nature,* esp. Book IV: 'The Separate Rejoined'; Adrienne Rich, *Of Woman Born,* esp. pp. 62–68; Linda Thurston, 'On Male and Female Principle,' *The Second Wave* 1, 2 (Summer, 1971). In feminist political organizing, this vision has been expressed as an opposition of leadership and hierarchy, as an effort to prevent the development of organizations divided into leaders and followers. It has also taken the form of an insistence on the unity of the personal and the political, a stress on the concrete rather than on abstract principles (an opposition to theory), and a stress on the politics of everyday life. For a fascinating and early example, see Pat Mainardi, 'The Politics of Housework,' in Leslie Tanner, ed., *Voices of Women's Liberation* (New York: New American Library, 1970).

41. George Bataille, *Death and Sensuality* (New York: Arno Press, 1977), p. 90.

42. Women Against Violence Against Women Newsletter, June, 1976, p. 1.

43. *Aegis: A Magazine on Ending Violence Against Women,* November/December 1978, p. 3.

44. Robert Stoller, *Perversion: The Erotic Form of Hatred* (New York: Pantheon, 1975), p. 88.

45. Bataille, p. 91. See pp. 91ff for a more complete account of the commonalities of sexual activity and ritual sacrifice.

46. *Death and Sensuality,* p. 12 (italics mine). See also de Beauvoir's discussion in *The Second Sex,* pp. 135, 151.

47. Bataille, p. 14.

48. *Ibid.,* p. 42. While Adrienne Rich acknowledges the violent feelings between mothers and children, she quite clearly does not put these at the heart of the relation (*Of Women Born*).

49. Bataille, pp. 95–96.

50. *The Second Sex,* p. 58. It should be noted that killing and risking life are ways of indicating one's contempt for one's body, and as such are of a piece with the Platonic search for disembodiment.

51. Consider, for example, Rich's discussion of pregnancy and childbirth, Ch. VI and VII, *Of Woman Born*. And see also Charlotte Perkins Gilman's discussion of domestic labor in *The Home* (Urbana, Ill.: The University of Illinois Press, 1972).

52. The Marxist-feminist efforts to determine whether housework produces surplus value and the feminist political strategy of demanding wages for housework represent two (mistaken) efforts to recognize women's non-wage activity as work. Perhaps domestic labor's non-status as work is one of the reasons why its wages—disproportionately paid to women of color—are so low, and working conditions so poor.

53. *Capital*, vol. I, p. 60.

54. The phrase is O'Brien's, p. 113.

55. See Marx, *1844*, p. 117.

seven

Louis Althusser's Structuralist Marxism: Political Clarity and Theoretical Distortions

The petty bourgeois is composed of On The One Hand and On The Other Hand. This is so in his economic interests and therefore in his politics, in his scientific, religious and artistic views. It is so in his morals, in everything. He is a living contradiction. If, like Proudhon, he is in addition a gifted man, he will soon learn to play with his own contradictions and develop them according to circumstances into striking, ostentatious, now scandalous or now brilliant paradoxes. Charlatanism in science and accommodation in politics are inseparable from such a point of view.
—Karl Marx, *The Poverty of Philosophy* (202)

Signification as play, the irreducibility of difference, the subversion of the subject, the deconstruction of truth—these themes came to dominate French thought in the 1960's and early seventies . . . [and] even Marxism . . . was not immune to their attractions.
—Alex Callinicos, *Is There a Future for Marxism?* (81)

In *Rethinking Marxism* 4, no. 4 (Winter 1991).

In his book *In the Tracks of Historical Materialism*, Perry Anderson notes that Western Marxism is the product of "repeated defeats of the labour movement in the strongholds of advanced capitalism in continental Europe" (1984, 15). He cites the defeat of proletarian insurgencies from 1918 to 1922, the collapse of the Popular Fronts of the late thirties, and the failure of the Resistance movements to attain political power immediately following World War II. The situation for Marxism has not improved in recent years, with the demise of strong Communist parties in Western Europe, the failure of Eurocommunism, and most recently the Eastern European revolutions and the collapse of the Soviet Union.

One response has been to declare Marxism dead and, in many cases, to adopt some variant of poststructuralism. However, as Cornel West has stated, "despite its blindness and inadequacies—especially in regard to racism, patriarchy, homophobia, and ecological abuse—Marxist thought is an indispensable tradition for freedom fighters who focus on the fundamental issues of jobs, food, shelter, literacy, health and child care for all" (1991, xiv). I believe it is important to enter into a dialogue with the tradition, to (as West does) treat Marxism as an intellectual weapon, to analyze how the defeats of Marxism in the West have come to be inscribed in its theories, and to expose the ways in which some theoretical moves foreclose new possibilities both intellectually and politically.

In such a dialogue, the figure of Louis Althusser is particularly important as an instance of the problems Marxists have encountered in retaining both Marx's politics and the science of history that emerged from his work. Althusser has been very influential in English- as well as French-speaking contexts as even a very brief survey of the literature of Marxism will demonstrate.[1] He has been credited with setting the theoretical agenda for a time in Europe and to some degree in North America (Freedman 1990, 309). His work has been the subject of a number of important debates and at least one writer has credited him with attempting to "constitute Marxist philosophy" (Therborn 1976, 55). And in recent years, his work on ideological state apparatuses has been widely influential across disciplines. Thus, one finds feminist authors such as Teresa de Lauretis arguing that Althusser's work on ideology can potentially illuminate how concrete individuals are constituted as gendered subjects (1987, 6).

Althusser's structural Marxism is also interesting in light of the emergence of poststructuralism and its current attractiveness to many radical critics. A number of writers have recognized the "anemic" politics of postmodernist and poststructuralist approaches (Anderson 1984; Callinicos 1982; Elliott 1987; Hartsock 1990), but some believe these approaches can be grafted onto intellectual work with a more explicitly political goal (e.g., Fraser and Nicholson 1989). While many postmodernist theorists do not claim to have radical political commitments, Althusser obviously did.

Moreover, his structuralism represents only the first steps along the road later taken by poststructural thinkers in which the subject is subverted and truth deconstructed. Thus, an analysis of the political difficulties generated by his theoretical positions can highlight some of the central problems in attempting a liberatory politics based on the theoretical moves of both structuralism and poststructuralism. That is, if Althusser, given his political commitments, forecloses important political and intellectual directions, can we really expect political guidance from his intellectual successors?

Althusser represents a particularly interesting figure since he insisted that theory itself is an important aspect of class struggle, or more precisely, that philosophy is, in the last instance, class struggle in theory; that his own work must be understood as an intervention in a particular political conjuncture. In addition, Althusser insisted that Marxism is a science, and was himself concerned with the harmful political results of collapsing the scientific and political aspects of Marxist theory into each other. He argued against those who have reduced Marxist theory to economic determinism on the one hand or to an ethico-religious humanism on the other.

Yet in spite of his important contributions in each of these areas, and the basic correctness of the political (if not theoretical) directions he took, Althusser's formulations distort Marx's theory. In an effort to defend Marx against those who reduced Marxism to only one of the two aspects, or those who ignored one of these two aspects of Marx's work, Althusser split them apart. In stressing the double nature of Marx's work, Althusser, especially in his early writing (*For Marx, Reading Capital*), lost sight of the connection between Marx's theory and his politics. In his later works (*Lenin and Philosophy, Essays in Self-Criticism*), Althusser attempted to reintroduce class struggle in the form of a self-criticism for his "theoreticist deviation," but failed to reestablish the dialectical unity of science and politics. Thus, in his insistence that Marxism cannot be reduced to either one, he took the position that the terms themselves are irreducible and ended up reproducing dualisms fundamental to liberal theory—the opposition of subject to object, and the observer to the external world. The impact of his argument is to separate science from politics and thereby to undermine the liberatory significance of Marxism.

Althusser's incorrect understandings, however, are instructive. They demonstrate the extent to which our lives and thought are dominated by the dualisms of liberal theory, and make clear the difficulty of maintaining the dialectical tension between Marxism as a theory of liberation and Marxism as a systematic analysis of capitalism. But because Marxism is indeed a political science, theoretical errors "inevitably" involve political mistakes. Therefore, Althusser's work, as a contribution to Marxist theory, must be evaluated not only on the basis of its theoretical fidelity to

Marx's "problematic" and the possible advances it offers Marxist theory, but also in terms of its consequences for politics.

Althusser's Marxism

For Marx, to describe the social relations of capitalism is at one and the same time to justify revolution. But as should be clear, the unity of theory and practice is not an identity but a set of distinctions within a unity. Its different moments and aspects are structured and complex, and cannot be reduced to a simple statement. I will examine Althusser's understanding of the fundamental features of Marxism and look as well at the kinds of political consequences that the adoption of his views would encourage in the contemporary world. Althusser himself argued that "public positions must always be judged against the system of positions actually held and against the effects they produce. For example, to look at only one side of the question, you may declare yourself for Marxist theory and yet defend this theory on the basis of positivist, therefore non-Marxist positions— with all the consequences. Because you cannot really defend Marxist theory and science except on the basis of dialectical materialist (therefore non-speculative and non-positivist) positions, trying to appreciate that quite *extraordinary*, because unprecedented, reality: Marxist theory as a *revolutionary* theory, Marxist science as a *revolutionary* science" (1976, 115). Althusser argued as well that "The class struggle has not only an economic form and a political form but also a theoretical form" (1976, 38). Thus,

> every interpretation of Marxist theory involves not only theoretical stakes but also political and historical. Theoretical positions in philosophy have led to real defeats and victories in politics" (1976, 186).[2]

Althusser is correct that the nature of Marxism is such that if we fail to understand theory as an aspect of class struggle we will fail to understand the logic of arguments such as those Althusser puts forward. He described his own work as an effort to advance and "defend the simple idea that a Marxist cannot fight, in what he writes or in what he does, without thinking out the struggle; without thinking out the conditions, the mechanism, and the stakes of the battle in which he is engaged and which engages him" (1976, 168).[3] He insisted that his texts, then, must be understood as political interventions, as efforts to defend Marxism against the dangers of bourgeois ideology.

The reader who is already familiar with the debates about Althusser will find that I share a number of the specific criticisms made by others. For example, like several others, I take a critical view of Althusser's use of the production process as the model for theoretical practice.[4] My argument against the adoption of Althusser's views, however, is based on my criticism of his destruction of the dialectical unity of theory and practice or, in his terms, science and revolution. In that context, Althusser's use of the production process as a model becomes simply another instance of a more general pattern.

In addition, I have ignored a number of important debates because they do not bear directly on the issue of the relations between theory and social change. I have left aside questions of Althusser's Stalinism, and though I discuss his claim that there was an epistemological break in Marx's thought, I do not address the question of whether or not he was correct. My purpose here is to stress the importance of maintaining the links between intellectual work and political practice in Marxism, to indicate some of the ways one can lose sight of this unity, and to point to the unfortunate philosophical and political consequences of this loss.[5] Finally, by pointing to some of the difficulties that flow from Althusser's structuralism, I intend to raise questions about poststructuralism.

My account here is focused largely on the positions taken in Althusser's early works. While some have suggested that there may be an epistemological break or fundamental change in his thought between his early and later work, I see little evidence of such a change.[6] Where relevant, I have noted his later formulation. In general, however, even his own admissions of error did not lead him to make fundamental changes in his ideas. Thus, for example, despite his admission of a "theoreticist deviation," the basic features of his position changed very little even though, in some cases, major changes would seem to have been required by Althusser's own admissions of error. The *Essays in Self-Criticism* should be understood, then, to be clarifications of his earlier positions rather than a formulation of alternative views.

Althusser suggested three themes that tie his essays together and that can help us understand the general structure of his thought (1976, 175ff.). Each of them should be viewed as aspects of his arguments against reductionism; each path represents his attempt to insist on *both* the scientific and revolutionary character of Marxism. Yet along each path we can see the fundamental separation of science from social change in Althusser's work. Althusser suggested the concept of "the last instance," "theoretical anti-humanism," and "the process of production of knowledge" as three paths across his essays. Let us examine each in turn.

The Last Instance

Althusser argued that each social formation is complex—an overdetermined, structured whole. The exact structures of the whole in any particular instance cannot be determined in advance: the role of primary and secondary contradictions may change; and the whole itself can be said to be determined by the economic mode of production only in the last instance (an instance, Althusser argued, that never occurs in pure form). Along this path, to support his argument, Althusser introduced the concept of overdetermination. In addition, he argued for the differentiation of Marx's dialectic from Hegel's by means of the epistemological break between the simple dialectic of Hegel and the complex one of Marx. This "path" must be understood as an attempt to combat economism—a position that collapses Marx's political side into an account of the development of the productive forces. At the same time, along this path Althusser developed several theses that are also important in his opposition to humanism.

Contradiction and Overdetermination

Althusser used Lenin's accounts of the situation in Russia on the eve of the revolution to argue that the central contradiction between the forces and relations of production cannot in and of itself induce a revolutionary situation. If this contradiction is to become a "ruptural principle," there must be an "accumulation of circumstances" into a single national crisis. "If as in this situation, a vast accumulation of 'contradictions' comes into play *in the same court,* some of which are radically heterogeneous—of different origins, different sense, different *levels* and *points* of application—but which nevertheless 'merge' into a ruptural unity, we can no longer talk of the sole, unique power of the general 'contradiction.' Of course, the basic contradiction dominating the period . . . is active in all these 'contradictions' and even in their 'fusion.' But strictly speaking it cannot be claimed that these contradictions and their fusion are merely the *pure phenomena* of the general contradiction . . . the 'contradiction' is inseparable from the total structure of the social body in which it is found, inseparable from its formal *conditions* of existence, and even from the *instances* it governs; it is radically *affected by them,* determining, but also determined in one and the same movement, and determined by the various *levels* and *instances* of the social formation it animates; it might be called *overdetermined in its principle*" (Althusser 1970, 100–101).

Althusser is arguing here against those who would reduce Marxism to the simple contradiction between capital and labor, those who make Marxism into economic determinism by stressing only the development of the productive forces. He is correct that contradictions other than the general antithesis of capital and labor not only exist but are not totally dependent on the capital-labor relation. They have a certain autonomy. Moreover, the social totality within which the different contradictions are active is both determined by the general contradiction and determinant of it. The totality is cause, effect, and context, all at once.

Because of the complexity of real social situations, the "lonely hour of the 'last instance' never comes" (Althusser 1970, 113). That is, we never confront economic factors in isolation from other social relations. Thus, Althusser suggested that after a revolution, one is not simply dealing with survivals from the old system, anomalies with no relation to a new mode of production. (Here Althusser is arguing against Stalin.) Rather, Althusser argued, we must recognize that a revolution in the mode of production does not necessarily and automatically modify all the social relations of a society. Often ideologies and other aspects of society remain unchanged. In addition, the revolutionary society itself may reactivate older structures (Althusser 1970, 115–16): The continuation of patriarchal family structures in the Soviet Union is only one example of these processes.

Thus, for Althusser, the social whole is complex. Kolakowski charges that Althusser was simply restating the commonsense argument that there are always many factors at work. But Althusser did more than this. He argued that the complex whole is structured in dominance (Althusser 1970, 202).[7] There are two aspects of this structure. First, the concept of overdetermination designates "the reflection in contradiction itself of its conditions of existence, that is, of its situation in the structure in dominance of the complex whole" (Althusser 1970, 209). An important feature of the position of any contradiction is what Althusser called the unevenness in the determination of the contradiction itself. To put it more simply, Althusser was arguing that any situation contains both primary and secondary contradictions. Moreover, each contradiction has both primary and secondary aspects. He did not, however, mean to say that the relations among primary and secondary contradictions or primary and secondary aspects of a contradiction are simple or mechanical. Althusser insisted that the secondary contradictions are essential even to the existence of the principal contradiction, that they constitute its conditions of existence just as the principal contradiction constitutes the condition of existence of the secondary ones.

A second aspect of the structure of the whole is that for Althusser, in a real historical situation, two processes occur: one opposite may pass into the position of another (something Althusser called "displacement"), or opposites may form an identity (a process he called "condensation"). In both cases, however, the structure itself remains constant (Althusser 1970, 211).

In the essay on contradiction and overdetermination, Althusser's categories begin to move and flow in a way readers of Marx will find familiar. However, his formulations present several problems. First, they are marred by his insistence on the certainty of finding a single primary and several secondary contradictions in any and every situation. At least in principle, one cannot expect that a single contradiction will *always* be dominant. One cannot predict in advance a single structure for every social relation. Althusser allowed himself to fall into the same mechanical reasoning he attempted to combat. He argued for a close analysis of the real social situation, by insisting that one cannot name *in advance* the determining factors one will find, and indeed, suggested that one can never find the *single* factor that represents the determination of a crisis by the economy. His argument is supported by his contention that any situation contains both primary and secondary contradictions and that the relations between them are not simple and mechanical but complex and changing. However, when Althusser asserted that in any situation one can find only *one* principle and several contradictions, he stepped back from the conclusion toward which he himself had pointed. Althusser laid out the answers in advance of real analysis, on the basis of an *a priori* principle.[8] This mechanical insistence on the necessity of finding one primary and several secondary contradictions is certainly foreign to Marx's own practice of using a single social relation as a starting point for unravelling the totality.

Second, Althusser's understanding of the relation of opposites is devoid of a sense of dialectical (inner) unity. He focused on processes that he treated as distinct entities and that have essentially *external* relations to each other. Althusser's contradictions, unlike the relations Marx brings to view, do not contain their opposites *within* themselves, but must "change places" with their opposites. Oppositions may also, according to Althusser, "condense" to form a (simple) identity. Here too, Marx's understanding that social relations contain their opposites within themselves is abandoned. Thus, Althusser could not see, as Marx did, the accumulation of misery, toil, ignorance, brutality, and mental degradation contained within the process of accumulation of wealth. His understanding of contradictions cannot support such a close, indeed internal, relation of opposites.

In spite of the ways Althusser's formulations undermine his own argument, we should recognize the correctness of his basic direction, if not of his conclusions. By calling attention to the structured complexity of situations and by emphasizing that one cannot see the configuration of a situation in advance, Althusser attempted to make an important and useful point against economic determinism in Marxist theory.

Althusser went on to argue that it is precisely the structured complexity of primary and secondary contradictions that differentiates Marx's dialectic from that of Hegel (Althusser 1970, 107, 209). His differentiation of Marx from Hegel brings us to our next topic, the epistemological break. Althusser used the concept of the epistemological break in Marx's work in two arguments: against economic determinism, on one hand, and against humanism, on the other.

The Epistemological Break

Althusser argued that Marxism is only scientific because of the epistemological break between the idealist, Hegelian, Feuerbachian, "pre-Marxist" notions of Marx prior to 1845 and the period of scientific Marxism or the science of historical materialism after that time. Through his argument for the epistemological break, Althusser joined the debate over the early versus the late Marx which had raged for decades. Many people have been involved in this argument—Leszek Kolakowski, Ernest Mandel, Istvan Meszaros, Galvano Della Volpe, Lucio Colletti, to name only a few. Although I take the position that there are important developments in the thought of Marx, but no fundamental break between the young Marx and Marx proper, I do not intend to enter the debate here. My criticism of Althusser's use of the "epistemological break" does not turn on my disagreement with him about the relation of the young Marx to the old.

Althusser used the term "epistemological break" to call attention to a "mutation in the theoretical problematic contemporary with the foundation of a scientific discipline" (Althusser 1970, 32). The epistemological break, as he quite correctly made clear, is not a question of simply finding Marxist and pre-Marxist elements in Marx's thought, but rather refers to a change in the basic problematic that structures the work as a whole (Althusser 1970, 68). On the basis of the changed problematic, Althusser argued that one can differentiate the "enslaved thought" of the young Marx from the "free thought" of Marx (Althusser 1970, 83). Thus, while the *1844 Manuscripts* rest on the concepts of "human essence," "alienated labor," and "alienation," the *German Ideology* makes use of other concepts such as "mode of production" and "division of labor." These changes in basic concepts represented for Althusser a shift to a terrain "on which the new concepts, after much elaboration, can lay down the foundations of *a scientific* theory, or (another metaphor) 'open the road' to the development of what will, irresistibly, become a science, an unusual science, a *revolutionary science,* but a theory which contains what we recognize in the sciences, because it provides *objective knowledge (connaissances objectives)*" (Althusser 1970, 85).

Althusser stressed the differences between Marx's early work, which he saw as based on concepts such as "human essence" and "alienated labor," and Marx's later works in which, although alienation is present as a category, it is not a major concern. In this way, Althusser laid the groundwork for an argument against a Marxist humanism based on Marx's early works, a humanism that he believed downgrades the importance of class struggle by stressing the importance of the links among all human beings and by failing to give enough attention to the divisions and dehumanization that result from class society. At the same time, his insistence that Marx's dialectic opened a new continent to science, and that it allowed for the posing of the real problems of history, allowed Althusser to argue that Marx's dialectic differs from that of Hegel. It also links the thesis of the epistemological break to his argument about complexity and overdetermination. In this latter context, the thesis of the epistemological break served Althusser in his struggle against economism.

Althusser argued that Marx's dialectic did not simply take the form "the-sis/antithesis/synthesis" and did not represent the development of a sin-gle essence through history, thus marking his critique of essentialism. Hu-manists, Althusser implied, have substituted the development of the human essence for the Hegelian development of the world spirit; economic determinists have substituted the development of the productive forces. Both groups, then, have failed to recognize the fundamental differences be-tween Marx's dialectic and that of Hegel. Althusser argued that the episte-mological break contained three "elements." First, it contained the element provided by the development of a theory based on "radically new con-cepts: the concepts of social formation, productive forces, relations of pro-duction, superstructure, ideologies, determination in the last instance by the economy, specific determination of the other levels, etc." rather than a theory based on human nature or alienation. Second, it contained a radical critique of the "*theoretical* pretensions of every philosophical humanism." Third, it contained the "definition of humanism as an *ideology*."[9]

Althusser argued that the epistemological break occurs in the *German Ideology*. The "Theses on Feuerbach" mark its earlier limit. The break con-cerns what Althusser described as "two distinct theoretical disciplines": the theory of history (historical materialism) and a new philosophy (di-alectical materialism) (Althusser 1970, 33). This division between philoso-phy and the science of history, seemingly an innocuous academic exercise, proves to be the source of some of Althusser's most radical divergences from Marx's theory. Perhaps as a consequence of these divergences, it proves to be a division Althusser was constantly forced to rework. A set of contradictory positions grows from Althusser's insistence on the concep-tual distinction between philosophy (dialectical materialism) and science (historical materialism), and his attempt to constitute each as a distinct theoretical practice. The difficulties are exacerbated by Althusser's self-confessed theoreticism and by his later efforts to reintroduce class struggle into his work and to link philosophy and science with it.

In his later work, Althusser recognized that for Marx, philosophy, sci-ence, and revolution were closely linked. He also correctly saw the sup-pression of distinctions among these domains as indicative of "rightist" or "leftist deviations." The first reduces philosophy to science; the second reduces science to philosophy (Althusser 1971, 14). But Althusser's argu-ment for the *distinctness* and autonomy of each practice is one that isolates each practice from the others, and treats each as an entity in itself. Thus, for example, Althusser at first cautioned us that the new philosophy was only implicit in the new science and might even "confuse itself with it" (Althusser 1970, 33; italicized in original). Later, however, he maintained that philosophy lags behind science, and is, in effect, *produced* in the theo-retical domain by the conjuncture of the effects of the class struggle and the effects of scientific practice (Althusser 1971, 15, 107). Although Althusser was attempting to argue in this way for the separation of philosophy from science, and for its constitution as a separate and autonomous discipline, he made philosophy into a phenomenon that simply results from a conjuncture of processes outside it, and therefore lacks autonomy.

He created still more difficulties with his suggestion that philosophy is distinguished from science by the fact that it has no history and therefore, strictly speaking, no object. Althusser then differentiated science, which has an object, from politics, which has a stake and an aim. But then he suggested that philosophy is like politics in that it too has a stake—"scientific practice" (Althusser 1971, 55–57, 61). To make his confusion even more apparent, Althusser then argued that there are two decisive nodal points: (1) the relation between philosophy and science, and (2) the relation between philosophy and politics. As he put it, "everything revolves around this double relation" (Althusser 1971, 65). Here he has lost track of the relation he posited previously, in which philosophy is an effect produced by science and politics. Perhaps in recognition of these difficulties, Althusser took yet another position with regard to philosophy in his *Essays in Self-Criticism*. While he admitted that there are arguments for the idea that philosophy lags behind science, he indicated that one can also argue that Marx's scientific breakthrough was based on and presupposed a philosophical revolution. Moreover, he indicated that what lay beneath the philosophical change was Marx's political development. Here, then, Althusser has argued that philosophy is not (at least in this situation) an *effect* of scientific practice and class struggle, but that both philosophy *and* scientific practice depend on class struggle.

Althusser preserved the separation he made among philosophy, politics, and science at some cost. The accounts he gave are not only contradictory, but also run counter to his own contention that the science of historical materialism is an autonomous realm which defines its own standards. Althusser obviously fell into a morass in attempting to specify the manifold (and as he saw them, external) relations of dialectical materialism (philosophy), historical materialism (science), and politics. The cases against humanism and economic determinism not only do not require such extreme and rigid oppositions among different spheres of activity but, indeed, cannot be made on this basis.

The distinction between dialectical and historical materialism is foreign to Marx's own ideas and, significantly, never appears in his work. The term "historical materialism" comes from Engels, and "dialectical materialism" from Plekanov (Bottomore 1956, 20). The distinction was then taken up by Lenin, in *Materialism and Empirio-Criticism*, and codified by Stalin, in *Historical and Dialectical Materialism*. Marx, himself, refused such rigid distinctions. At the same time, however, he did not argue for the simple *identity* of philosophy and science (or of science and politics). Marx spoke of "'distinctions within a unity,' 'members of a totality,' 'identities' which were not simple but 'mediated.'"[10] Marx does not provide a set of consistent, mutually exclusive categories into which one can "sort" action and experience. For Marx, the boundaries among science, philosophy, and politics are elastic and permeable. The three are not, as they are for Althusser, separate, though related activities, each of which can be clearly distinguished from the others.[11] Rather, they are aspects of a dialectical unity in which science, philosophy, and revolution are internally related. For example, in Marx's Introduction to the *Grundrisse*, ironically cited so frequently by Althusser, one finds an intermingling of philosophy, science, and even politics. There Marx is concerned not to specify relations among (fixed and unchanging) spheres but rather to explore the inner relations of a unified, though not necessarily uniform, whole.

Marx's own theory indicated, on one hand, that from the vantage point of human activity as ontology, to possess a scientifically correct account of reality was at the same time to be a revolutionary. On the other hand, by taking up the vantage point of the working class, a revolutionary class position, Marx demonstrated that revolutionary activity both required and helped to generate such an account. That is, the two vantage points allow for different views of the same terrain. Althusser, in contrast, gave a far more instrumental and one-sided account of these relations: the working class needs objective and scientific knowledge in order to win.[12] Marx's work in *Capital* has become a tool to be selected or rejected. It is no longer analysis and critique of capitalist production and justification for social change all at the same time.

Although he recognized the problems created by his formulation of the epistemological break as a "simple theoretical fact," and later argued that class struggle must be brought back into his work, Althusser left the links among the separate spheres of science, philosophy, and politics unspecified. One might almost say he treated them as nonexistent. The commonality among the separate spheres consists simply in the fact that each sphere has a common structure—that of production. Although Althusser appears to endorse the idea that Marxism is a revolutionary science, his insistence on the separate activities of philosophy, politics, and science depart from Marx's own account. Althusser's continual attempts to restate the proper relation among what he understood to be three (distinct) activities, and his contradictory accounts of the roles of each sphere in relation to the others suggests that he recognized the difficulties.

Science and Ideology

We cannot conclude this discussion of Althusser's understanding of the epistemological break without touching on the question of the relation between science and ideology—since the break between the thought of the Marx who was not Marx (pre-Marx) and Marx consists in the passage from ideology into science.[13]

In *For Marx*, Althusser argued that he was about to set out on a reading of Marx that would allow him to distinguish science from ideology in Marx's own work (Althusser 1970, 39). Because every ideology is false, Althusser argued, one must not examine it in terms of its relation to a truth other than itself but must instead look at its relation to the ideological field and to the social structures that sustain it and are reflected in it. Here too one can see the kind of statement that poststructuralists make. An ideology must be recognized to be a result of forces other than itself. It is not autonomous; its "motor principle" is outside it (Althusser 1970, 63). To make clear the status of a body of thought, to expose the basic problematic that lies beneath the ideology, Althusser proposed that we compare the problems posed by the ideologue with the real problems posed for her/him by her/his time (Althusser 1970, 67–68). By this means, Althusser pointed to one of the important and defining features of ideology—its unconsciousness of itself.

Althusser then put forward a second formulation: the unconsciousness of ideology does not indicate that it is simply false. Ideology is an expression of the way people live their relation to their world, the expression of the not-necessarily-conscious structures that define the lives of all human beings. It is, Althusser argued, both a real relation and an imaginary one. More precisely, it is the "(overdetermined) unity of the real relation and the imaginary relation" (Althusser 1970, 234). The bourgeoisie, for example, "*lives* in the ideology of *freedom*, the relation between it and its conditions of existence: that is *its* real relation (the law of a liberal capitalist economy) *but invested in an imaginary relation* (all men are free including free laborers)" (Althusser 1970, 234). But ideology for Althusser is not simply a feature of capitalist society: it is a "system of mass representations." Ideology presents the forms in which people *always* live their lives. Since it represents a real, lived relation to the world, Althusser argues it will be essential even in communist society (Althusser 1970, 235, 252).

Because it was based on the unscientific concepts of "human essence" and "alienation," Marx's work prior to 1845 must be analyzed as ideology. Althusser argued that although Marx's work was ideology, Marx was involved in a "retreat" from the massive ideology of German philosophy. This retreat from ideology coincided with Marx's discovery of the organized working class and of a class struggle "obeying its own laws and ignoring philosophy and philosophers." Marx then had to "think" what Althusser refers to as a "double reality" (Althusser 1970, 81; italics in original). Moreover, Marx had to think this double reality in concepts left over from his own past as an ideologue, concepts that were not adequate to the task Marx set for them. Only by moving to adopt the standpoint of the proletariat as represented in the political action of the organized working class was Marx able to move from ideology to science. The analysis of the social world from a proletarian class position was essential to the foundation of a science of history, "that is, to an analysis of the mechanisms of class exploitation and domination" (Althusser 1976, 160).[14]

Ideology differs from science in its practico-social function (function as knowledge). Ideology refers to the *lived* relation to the world, whereas science, because it refers to the production of knowledge, has, by implication, a much more distant relation to life. Ideology and science are thus fundamentally separated in Althusser's thought.[15] Each is given its own sphere of activity, or practice. Althusser's understanding of ideology led to two errors in his treatment of Marx's own evolution. First, Althusser treated the epistemological break as the mark of Marx's passage from error to truth, his passage from ideology to science. As he later admitted, he reduced the break between bourgeois ideology and Marxism to the opposition of truth and error, and thereby made the opposition into a theoretical rather than practical and political one. Science for Althusser is, in this context, the discovery (production) of truth. But Althusser's categories cannot allow for the appropriation of Marx's science in a practical way. To the extent that appropriating Marx's science in a practical way affects real life, it takes, for Althusser, the form of ideological practice and can no longer be scientific. This seems the only possible conclusion to be drawn from his insistence that even inhabitants of a communist society will live their relation to the world through ideology.

Second, in what was perhaps an attempt to reintroduce class struggle into his work, Althusser suggested that since ideology is a feature of all social relations, Marx's break with bourgeois ideology consisted simply in taking up "proletarian ideology" (Althusser 1976, 120–24). Althusser wished to reject what he called the theoreticist deviation embodied in his contrast of truth (in the form of science) with error (in the form of ideology). Yet by opposing bourgeois to proletarian ideologies, he ends up in relativism (Benton 1984, 179). The importance of totality, of the mediate and therefore objectively correct understanding of reality available from the perspective of the proletariat, has disappeared. The practical, political struggle has been transformed into the opposition of two (presumably) equally valid ideologies, two lived relations to the world.

Along the first path across Althusser's essays, the path of the last instance, we have encountered a number of irreducible dualisms: the static and rationalist opposition of truth (science) to error (ideology), the insistence on the "double reality" Marx has to theorize (the capitalist *and* the proletarian realities), the tangled separation of philosophy both from science and from class struggle, and the delineation of a realm of science as opposed to a realm of ideology. Although Althusser later modified his positions on some of these questions, the fundamentally dualistic character of his views remained unchanged. In *Lenin and Philosophy* he said he was too abrupt in stating that the epistemological break occurred in 1845. Rather, he argued, it began in 1845 and Marx's whole intellectual history can be seen as the continuing and difficult rupture with his past (Althusser 1971, 93–101). Second, in his *Essays in Self-Criticism*, he argued that he formulated the concept of the epistemological break in a "theoreticist" way. That is, he reduced the antagonism "between Marxism and bourgeois ideology to the antagonism between science and ideology" (Althusser 1976, 123). Moreover, Althusser noted that he formulated the distinction between science in general and ideology in general as the distinction between truth and error. Thus, Althusser admitted, he ended up in a "rationalist-speculative" formulation which left class struggle out of account (Althusser 1976, 106).

Althusser argued that all the effects of this theoreticism derive from his rationalist-speculative interpretation. All this is a useful corrective to the views he set out in *For Marx* and *Reading Capital*, but none of his corrections overcome the irreducible dualisms of this thought. Nor do they reestablish the ruptured connection between systematic analysis and political struggle. That is to say, he is still involved in the search for mutually exclusive categories and the use of the principle of analysis—the belief that wholes are made up of fundamentally simple parts which can be separated from each other and examined, the belief that elements may be broken out of the whole without fundamentally altering them. This view differs profoundly from Marx's understanding of the dialectical unity of opposites, and of the essentially inner relations of capitalist society. It represents, rather, several common features of the bourgeois ideology Althusser was attempting to combat.[16]

In his own defense, Althusser explained his purposes along the first path across his essays:

> I wanted to defend Marxism against the real dangers of *bourgeois* ideology: it was necessary to stress its revolutionary new character; it was therefore necessary to "prove" that there is an antagonism between Marxism and bourgeois ideology, that Marxism could not have developed in Marx or in the labour movement except given a radical and unremitting *break* with bourgeois ideology, an unceasing struggle against the assaults of this ideology. This theses was correct. It still is correct (1976, 105).

At the same time, Althusser indicated that he did not see clearly in 1965 what made Marxist science different from other sciences—that it was "a *revolutionary* science. Not simply a science which revolutionaries can use in order to make revolution, but a science which they can use because it rests on *revolutionary class theoretical positions*" (Althusser 1976, 130).

I have argued that along the path of the last instance, Althusser is indeed involved in a "theoreticist deviation." The importation of class struggle as an afterthought does not lead to the reconstitution of Marxism as a practical political science.

Theoretical Antihumanism

Althusser pointed out a second path across his essays, one that is also a part of his fight against reductionism—the path of what he termed Marx's theoretical antihumanism. And as Althusser remarks in the *Essays on Self-Criticism*, "just for the pleasure of watching the ideological fireworks with which it was met, I would have had to invent this thesis if I had not already put it forward" (Althusser 1976, 195). He argued that liberation from Stalinism gave rise to a liberal and ethical reaction in Marxist circles in which Marx's early works were used as support for the reduction of Marxism to a moral theory with a human subject at its heart.[17] In opposition to this kind of humanism, Althusser argued that the idea that human beings are at the center of the world is linked to the rise of the bourgeoisie. It expresses their aspirations by basing all social understanding on the view that to be a person is to be a free subject—an individual free to possess, to sell, and to buy (Althusser 1976, 201). Marx, Althusser stressed, began his analysis of capital from the perspective of the real dehumanization and lack of humanity of workers, not "from man but from the economically given period of society" (Althusser 1976, 201). In *Capital*, where he focused on the production relations that structure the social formation as a whole, Marx dealt with individuals as "personifications of economic categories, embodiments of particular class relations and class interests."[18] Thus, Althusser argued, Marx's science is fundamentally opposed to theoretical humanism.

Although this brief statement gives the general tenor of the argument, and provides a sense of its base in Marx's own writing, Althusser's argument against theoretical humanism in fact has several elements. First, Althusser argued that to ground explanation in the concept of a human being as "originating subject," as the source of her/his own needs, thoughts, and acts, tempts one to believe in the "omnipotence of liberty or of creative labor" (Althusser 1976, 205). It leads one to ignore the class basis of the development and practice of humanism in the West. In a second and related argument, Althusser argued that by ignoring the importance of class relations, humanists commit the same error as the classical bourgeois economists Marx criticized for beginning their analyses with population. They fail to recognize that the concrete (in this case, the concrete human individual) is the result rather than the starting point of analysis (Althusser 1976, 205). Thus, Althusser suggested that humanism fails as an account of the real social relations of bourgeois society. This is one reason why Althusser argued that Marx's break with humanism was one of the elements of Marx's epistemological break with bourgeois ideology in general.

This leads Althusser to a third, though closely related criticism. Humanism represents a concept developed by the ruling class as a description of their social reality. Theorists such as Hobbes and Locke began from the free and separate individual who was the embodiment of human nature, the possessor of his/her own needs, desires, and capabilities. The stress on the free subject and on the human essence expressed an aspiration of the bourgeoisie, but also expressed what was both an imaginary and a lived relation to the world (Althusser 1976, 198).[19] Because humanism takes up these fundamentally capitalist ideas, Althusser was correct to criticize humanism for falling into a fundamental antinomy of liberal thought. He argues that humanism is an empiricist/idealist outlook because "if the essence of man is to be a universal attribute, it is essential that *concrete subjects* exist as absolute givens; this implies an *empiricism of the subject*." Yet to argue that each individual must carry within him/herself the "whole human essence," even if only in principle, implies "an idealism of the essence" (Althusser 1970, 228). Althusser's critique of humanism here comes close to restating Marx's point in the "Theses on Feuerbach" that the human essence must not be understood as an abstraction inherent in each single individual.

These several critiques of humanism are part of Althusser's correct argument, first, that humanism downgrades the importance of classes in any systematic analysis; and second, that to begin at this point is to mistake the proper method of political economy and to fall into inconsistency. One cannot begin from the essence of humanity, but can only arrive at concrete humanity as an end point. The proper starting point for analysis is quite different: it is the social relations of production.

A second critique of humanism emerges in the essays in *Reading Capital*, where humanism is criticized under the heading of historicism. In this context, too, Althusser is involved in an argument against reductionism— here, an argument against the reduction of historical materialism to dialectical materialism (or what he termed in other contexts the reduction of science to philosophy) and the "flattening" of scientific knowledge down to "politico-economic practice" (Althusser and Balibar 1970, 136, 133). Humanism and historicism indicate that the actors of history are also its subjects, that is, they are "actors of roles of which they are the authors, too" (Althusser and Balibar 1970, 139). Althusser argued that both humanism and historicism assume that most people have far more power than they do in reality. At worst, then, humanism can become a Marxist variant of blaming the victim for her/his own plight. Althusser is attempting to call attention to the situation of an individual confronted with and indeed constructed by inexorable and impersonal social forces.

As in the case of the "epistemological break," Althusser chose provocative terms which indicate a more extreme opposition than he was in fact suggesting. Stress should be put on the term "theoretical." Althusser's Marx is working against the *theoretical* "pretensions of the humanist conception to explain society and history, starting out from the human essence, from the free human subject, the subject of needs, of labour, of desire, the subject of moral and political action" (Althusser 1976, 201). He was arguing against humanism as a basis for scientific knowledge. As Althusser explained, theoretical antihumanism does not indicate a contempt for human beings. *Capital* must be understood as a work that was written in order to end the suffering of an exploited class. Althusser was also careful to explain that he recognizes that humanist ideologies, even if they support the ideological hegemony of the capitalist class, may also express a revolt against that class (Althusser 1976, 200). His purpose was simply to point to the scientific achievements of Marxism, and to argue that Marx arrived at a scientific analysis of the social relations of capitalism through a critique of the philosophy of the human essence (Althusser 1970, 223).

The theses of the epistemological break and the distinction between science and ideology clearly have important roles to play in Althusser's account of Marx's theoretical antihumanism. Both serve to emphasize his argument for the fundamental disjunction between Marxism and the bourgeois science that preceded it. The epistemological break for Althusser established a complex, rather than a simple dialectic, and together with Althusser's distinction between science and ideology, allowed him to define Marx's earlier work as ideology. Althusser's work on contradiction and overdetermination becomes relevant as well, in the form of his argument that only by "displacing" the concept of humanity and having its place taken by the analysis of social relations can one arrive at the knowledge of the concrete (Althusser 1970, 243).

Althusser's account of Marx's theoretical antihumanism represents an important and fundamentally correct direction. It could serve as an entry point for a discussion of the importance of mediation in constructing an objective account of the social world by calling attention to Marx's insistence on the necessity for beginning an analysis with social relations and arriving at a reproduction of concrete reality only as a terminal point. Althusser was correct as well to argue against those who downgrade the importance of class divisions or who overemphasize the power individuals have over their own circumstances. The problems in Althusser's formulation of Marx's theoretical antihumanism lie in other directions.

The single most important difficulty grows out of Althusser's argument that social relations include not only the social relations among groups of people but also include relations between human beings and things. Althusser included within the latter the relation to the means of production, and thus divided social relations into two distinct categories. This represents an important departure from Marx's own views. Marx argued that human labor occurs as an interaction with (nonhuman) nature but transforms nature in such a way that it comes to be the embodiment of human activity in other forms. Nature itself comes to appear as a form of human work, and human beings must, conversely, be recognized as natural beings as well as social animals.[20]

Neither humankind nor the natural world can be understood without the other; each has become what it is, been shaped and even created by the other. While both humankind and the natural, material world are indissolubly interdependent, neither can successfully be reduced to the other.[21] The process of human creative activity, or work, involves both the incorporation of human powers into natural objects and their reconstitution as social use-values. At the same time, the process of realizing human powers changes humankind itself.[22] The commonplace opposition of the social and natural worlds, and the sense that natural forces must be brought under human control, was an important feature of the ideology developed by the emerging bourgeoisie as they worked to develop technological control of nature. In separating relations to human beings from relations with (natural) objects, Althusser, however, did more than simply take over one element of this world view. By splitting the social from the "natural" world, Althusser failed to recognize the ontological importance of human activity, and thus, its character as constitutive of the human world in *both* its social and natural aspects. The result is that in breaking the dialectical unity of humankind with nature, Althusser also severed the links between Marx's science of history and political struggle. *Capital* is a justification for revolution only if Marx's analysis of the laws governing capitalist production is at the same time an analysis of the laws governing the theft and destruction of the worker's humanity. *Capital* can provide this double analysis only if one accepts the world-constitutive (ontological) character of human activity. Althusser failed to grasp the fact that the ontological character of human activity, as developed in Marx's account of alienation, is fundamental to Marx's project.

Althusser's argument for Marx's theoretical antihumanism, insofar as it depends on his thesis of the disjunction between science and ideology, suffers as well from the effects of his self-confessed theoreticist deviation. Here, these effects consist in his stress on the scientific character of Marxism to the exclusion of its political aspect. This one-sided view takes the form of an emphasis on the importance of classes but not of class struggle. In addition I have argued that Althusser's insistence on the epistemological break and on the lack of theoretical importance of the concept of alienation in Marx's later work is the basis for a disjunction between science and revolution. By refusing alienation an important *theoretical* role in *Capital,* Althusser once again separates Marxism as a science from Marxism as a theory of revolution. Finally, Althusser's failure to grasp the meaning of dialectical unity appears once again in his use of the concept "displacement" to refer to Marx's substitution of social relations for the concept of human essence as a starting point for his analysis (Althusser 1970, 167). Althusser used the concept of displacement to refer to the shift of one opposite into the place of the other, but dialectical unity does not refer to objects that can shift positions but rather refers to relations that include within themselves both aspects of a polarity.

Thus, Marx described his own move in the *German Ideology* not as a result of shifting two (by implication separate) parts of an opposition, but rather, as a move based on the recognition of the real relations behind (and contained within) the apparent ones. This is why Marx could state that "This sum of productive forces, capital funds, and social forms of intercourse . . . is the real basis of what the philosophers have conceived as the 'substance' and 'essence of man'" (Marx and Engels 1970, 59).

The Production of Knowledge: Theoretical Practice and Political Practice

The third path Althusser suggested, that of the process of production of knowledge, is the locus of the most pernicious effects of his one-sided stress on Marxism as a scientific account of capitalist production. Along this path, he extended his thesis of the epistemological break in Marx's work, along with his distinction between ideology and science, to develop the concept of theoretical practice. He argued that knowledge is the result of a process of production in the realm of thought, and undertook a literal transposition of Marx's account of the process of material production into what Althusser saw as the separate and distinct world of thought and knowledge. The raw materials of knowledge are transformed into knowledge(s), the product, through a process of theoretical labor or theoretical practice. Knowledge, then, is the product of a theoretical labor, and since this labor takes place entirely in thought, the product as well can exist only in thought.

There are several aspects of Althusser's argument which must be taken up in turn. First, there is his argument that the practice of the production of knowledge is distinct from other social practices and is linked with them by the fact that every social practice takes the common form of production. This represents Althusser's interpretation and distortion of Marx's argument that production is the single most important and determinant practice among the social practices in any society (Althusser 1970,

167). Second, we should look more closely at Althusser's distinction between the real object and the object of knowledge produced by theoretical practice, and his idea that theoretical practice generates its own standards. Finally, we can link the theses of the epistemological break and Althusser's distinction between science and ideology with his efforts to develop the concept of theoretical practice.

Althusser began to present the concept of theoretical practice in the context of setting out Marx's differences from Hegel. He argued that the solutions to theoretical problems already exist in Marxist practice. In every case, however, they must be posed and resolved in *theoretical* form. This "ultimately means to express theoretically the 'solution' existing in the practical state, that Marxist practice had found for a real difficulty it has encountered in its development" (Althusser 1970, 165).

Theoretical practice for Althusser is one of a number of distinct social practices—that is, it is a "process of *transformation* of a determinate given raw material into a determinate *product*, a transformation effected by a determinate human labour, using determinate means (of 'production')" (Althusser 1970, 166). Political practice represents another practice that proceeds on the same model and produces not knowledge but revolutions. Althusser suggests here a division of labor among Marxists between "a man of science who applies himself to the constitution and development of a science, or a political man who applies himself to the development of the class struggle."[23] Clearly, Althusser understood the social world to be made up of a variety of autonomous spheres, each of which takes its form from the process of material, economic (in the narrow sense) production. Indeed, he indicated four major autonomous spheres of practice, each of which is fundamentally constituted by a separate process of production—economic, political, ideological, and theoretical.[24]

Althusser used the concept of theoretical practice to argue that the production of knowledge involves a transformation, and to indicate that theorizing is a legitimate activity (or work). Although Althusser argued that Marxist theorists are merely expressing something in theory that has already been worked out in practice, this theoretical expression requires real theoretical labor—theoretical practice. It takes the dual form of the production of a knowledge and the critique of illusion (Althusser 1970, 166, 189).

Althusser described the process of theoretical practice or production as one that includes three "generalities." Generality I is the precondition for scientific labor, the raw material to be transformed into knowledge. Generality II refers to the work done—although Althusser was unclear about whether this is simply the means of production or the labor process itself. Generality III is the knowledge produced through this process of transformation. Althusser insists on two main propositions: (1) that there is "never an identity of essence between Generality I and Generality III, but always a real transformation"; and (2) "the work whereby Generality I becomes Generality III . . . whereby the 'abstract' becomes the 'concrete' only involves the process of theoretical practice, that is, it takes place 'within knowledge'" (Althusser 1970, 185).

Although this form of argument may strike the reader as unnecessarily complex, Althusser indicated that he presented the argument in this form for two purposes: (1) to support his argument that theoretical practice involves real labor, evidenced by the transformation of the materials worked on in a process of production; and (2) to emphasize that Marxism is a science rather than a technique, that scientific Marxism is not simply the application of formulae to situations but involves a real analysis of the complexities of those situations (Althusser 1970, 170).

The work takes place entirely in thought, and the objects produced exist only in thought. Thus, Althusser argues that one must not confuse *"two different concretes:* the *concrete-in-thought* which is a knowledge, and the concrete-reality which is its object. The process that produces the concrete-knowledge takes place wholly in the theoretical practice" (Althusser 1970, 186). This mode of appropriating the concrete-in-thought, then, differs from the mode of appropriating real objects: thought objects can only be appropriated in thought. Althusser is supporting a division of the world into two opposing realms: a world of thought on the one hand—with its own objects, practices, mode of appropriation, and so on, and a world of real objects (by implication physical ones), attached to their own practices. The opposition of these two worlds represents an important distortion of Marx's own views—one we can perhaps clarify by looking at the sources in Marx's work from which Althusser seems to have drawn support.

In constructing his model of theoretical practice, Althusser took his inspiration not only from Marx's argument that production is the determinant moment of social relations but also from Marx's statement that the proper scientific method consists not of the evaporation of the concrete to produce abstractions (such as the "division of labor" or "money") but rather requires one to begin from these abstractions to arrive at the "reproduction of the concrete by way of thought" (Marx 1973, 100–101).[25] One arrives at the concrete through a process of (re)constructing and concentrating the many determinations at work. It is a result rather than a beginning. Marx goes on to argue against those to whom the "movement of the categories appears as the real act of production." Althusser's distinction between the concrete-in-thought and the concrete-reality is an effort to restate Marx's argument that "the totality as it appears in the head, as a totality of thoughts, is a product of a thinking head, which appropriates the world in the only way it can, a way different from the artistic, religious, practical, and mental appropriation of this world. The real subject retains its autonomous existence outside the head just as before; namely, as long as the head's conduct is merely speculative, merely theoretical" (Marx 1973, 101–2). The distortion represented by Althusser's account stems from the fact that he seems to have missed Marx's last phrases. Science for Marx is not speculative but must be practical as well. Indeed, Marx argued that science only begins where speculation ends and argued as well that one can only appropriate the world by changing it in reality, not simply by interpreting it differently, or changing it in thought.[26]

Whereas for liberal theory the objects of which we have knowledge are simply external to us, Marx recognized a more complex relationship. We must appropriate objects of knowledge in a practical as well as speculative way; we must in addition recognize both the social and natural worlds as aspects of ourselves, as our own creations, and even as extensions of ourselves. While Althusser was correct to stress the production of knowledge as real activity, as production in thought, he failed to grasp the fact that we come to know the world as whole human beings with all our senses. Indeed, we come to know the world by appropriating it and in that *appropriation* we cannot help but recognize our involvement and participation.

Althusser's separation of the concrete-in-thought from concrete reality and his argument for theoretical practice as a process analogous to the process of production form a part of his argument for the autonomy of different spheres of social life. The argument for autonomy, in turn, must be seen at least in part as an effort to support his argument against the simplistic analyses of economic determinism. In terms of theoretical practice, Althusser argued that "demonstration and proof are the product of definite and specific material and theoretical apparatuses and procedures, internal to each science" (Althusser 1976, 170).

As in the case of the distinction between the object of knowledge and the real object, Althusser based his argument for the autonomy of theoretical practice, or of science, on one of Marx's arguments. Althusser took off from Marx's statement that the "order of succession" of economic categories, "is determined ... by their relation to one another in modern bourgeois society, which is precisely the opposite of that which seems to be their natural order or which corresponds to historical development" (Marx 1973, 107).[27] This statement is one of the bases for Althusser's emphasis on the autonomy of science. It forms the basis of his argument that the order of categories in a science differs from their order of historical genesis, and by implication, that activity in any sphere other than science cannot provide a guide to the practice of science (Althusser and Balibar 1970, 46).

Thus, theoretical practice must be understood to contain within itself the criteria with which to "validate the quality of its product, that is, the criteria of the scientificity of the products of scientific practice." Once a science is truly constituted it has no need for verification from what Althusser terms "external practices."[28] The theoretical practice, for example, of the experimental sciences is formed by experiments that are both the forms of the theoretical practice and the criteria of its validity. The same is true of historical materialism: Althusser paraphrases Lenin's famous statement when he says, "It has been possible to apply Marx's theory with success because it is 'true'; it is not true because it has been applied with success" (Althusser and Balibar 1970, 59).[29]

Althusser's argument for understanding the creation of knowledge as a process of production both forms a part of his general argument against reductionism and also depends on his other theses. In his *Essays in Self-Criticism*, he stated that along the path of the process of production of knowledge he wished to make several arguments. First, he wanted to argue against empiricism—against the notion that the path to knowledge is the path of rising from the simple to the combined. Second, he wanted to argue against those who felt that Marxist science was complete and needed simply to be applied. Third, Althusser attempted to take up the double opposition to empiricism and to Hegel contained in Marx's argument that the progression from the abstract to the concrete took place in thought, and that this movement did not produce the material world but was a process of coming to know it (Althusser 1976, 189ff.). Thus Althusser saw his distinction between the object of knowledge and the real object as an attempt to stress Marx's break with bourgeois ideology, and thus to support his own argument of the epistemological break (Althusser 1976, 194).

In every case, along this path, Althusser's purposes support the main lines of Marxist theory. Many of his concerns are similar to the questions I have raised. His formulations, however, cannot serve these ends, and indeed, because they represent distortions of Marx's theory, have very different theoretical consequences from those Althusser might wish.

The concept of creating knowledge through a transposition of the process of production lies at the heart of Althusser's understanding of theoretical practice. His error is located in his efforts to simply take over the *form* of production and argue that this form is replicated in every social practice. Marx made clear that the process of production structures all aspects of social life. This does not mean, however, that all areas of social practice simply mirror the production process. The problems inherent in Althusser's argument for autonomous but identically constructed spheres of production can be clarified by examining Marx's own argument that production was the determinant moment in social relations.

Marx argued that production and consumption are related to each other through three identities which form a totality. First, there is an immediate identity in which production is consumption and consumption is production. Second, each mediates the other—production creates the material of consumption. It "not only supplies a material for the need but supplies a need for the material." Consumption mediates production in that "it creates for the products a subject for whom they are products." Third, each "creates the other in completing itself, and creates itself as the other." "Consumption accomplishes the act of production only in completing the product as product by dissolving it, by consuming its independently material form, by raising the inclination developed in the first act of production, through the need for repetition, to its finished form; it is thus not only the concluding act in which the product becomes product, but also that in which the producer becomes producer. On the other side, production produces consumption by creating the specific manner of consumption; and, further, by creating the stimulus of consumption, the ability to consume, as a need" (Marx 1973, 91–93). "The conclusion we reach is not that production, distribution, exchange and consumption are identical, but that they all form the members of a totality, distinctions within a unity. Production predominates not only over itself, in the antithetical definition of production, but over the other moments as well" (Marx 1973, 99).

The relations of different realms, even within what Althusser would no doubt term the economic sphere, are thus not simple replications of the form of the production process. The different moments form a complex whole; relations among the parts include immediate identity, the creation by each process of its opposite, and the mediation of each process by the others. We should search for this complex interrelation rather than for Althusser's simple replication of the process of production (Generalities I to III) in all our social relations. Althusser's formulation of theoretical practice as an act of production does not include the other moments described by Marx and ignores the complex and mediated relations of processes. Moreover, it once again breaks the links between theory and practice in Marx's work. Theoretical practice, according to Althusser, contains its own theory and its own practice, along with its own criteria for validation. As Althusser describes it, the sphere of theoretical practice is in effect not simply autonomous but independent of other spheres of activity. Althusser has subdivided the social world and built identical houses on undifferentiated plots of land.

Althusser later admits he used the analogy to the process of production "mechanically" (Althusser 1976, 189). And perhaps, he says, even "forced" Marx's texts. In justification he suggested that it was a way of pointing out that knowledge does not transform the real object and that knowledge is the outcome of a process that takes place only in thought. Althusser recognized that this argument might lead to nominalism and even to idealism, but felt it to be an important aspect of his struggle against humanism (Althusser 1976, 189–92, 195).

Althusser, however, has done far more than simply "force a little" Marx's texts. His mechanical transposition of the process of production into other (separate) spheres of social life, along with his lack of attention to the interrelations among these spheres, reproduces two important features of liberal capitalist ideology. First, he reproduces an understanding of social life as a series of (disconnected) arenas. While Althusser does not reproduce the division between public and private, subjective and objective, he does stress both the separation and the autonomy (almost independence) of different social spheres.[30] Their only link, as he sees it, is the fact that they share a common structure—the structure of production. Second, in using the labour process in production as the fundamental form of all human activity, Althusser has made the same move as liberal theorists who argue that the market is the fundamental basis for human interaction, and that all forms of social relations can be understood on this model; that the market is the prototypical pattern of interaction.[31]

The fundamental separation of theory and practice is made even more apparent in Althusser's distinction between the real object and the object of knowledge. Here, understanding of the world is once again fundamentally separated from participation in it.[32] Human relations to the social world become fundamentally external. By implication, the only practice that can have an effect on knowledge is the practice of theoretical production—production in thought. Once again, what was for Marx a dialectical unity, a set of distinctions within a totality, has been split apart into separate spheres. Althusser's argument indicates, contrary to his own statement, that practice does not contain answers to questions, answers that must be appropriated by theory; the answers to our questions can be "produced," manufactured through a process that takes place in thought alone. The role of practice has been reduced to that of raw material which must be transformed before it can teach us anything. This is hardly what Marx had in mind when he stated that all the "mysteries which lead theory to mysticism find their rational solution in human practice and in the comprehension of this practice" (Marx 1970, 122).

To the extent that Althusser's understanding of theoretical practice depends on some of his other theses, it suffers from the defects of those theses as well. Althusser's understanding of theoretical practice was both supported by and depended on the thesis of the epistemological break, and also functioned as a support for his attempt to differentiate Marx's science of history from ideology. The argument for theoretical practice was also an argument against reductionism (against those who considered Marxism to be a science which had only to be applied), and an attempt to stress the importance of continuing to develop theory. Thus the argument cannot be isolated from other features of Althusser's Marxism.

Overall, Althusser's formulations express a dualistic vision of the world—a kind of division of labor within Marxism, a specialization in either science or politics. As such, they support a distinction between science and politics alien to Marx's work and profoundly hostile to Marx's project.

In later formulations, Althusser attempted to give more weight to political practice, and argued that one must directly experience two realities: "the reality of theoretical practice (science, philosophy) in its concrete life; the reality of the *practice of revolutionary class struggle* in its concrete life, in close contact with the masses" (Althusser 1970, 20; italics in original). He also attempted once again to work out the links between philosophy and politics, and to argue in more specific terms that philosophy represents politics in the domain of theory. "Philosophy represents politics in the domain of theory, or to be more precise: *with the sciences* and, *vice versa*, philosophy represents scientificity in politics, with the classes engaged in the class struggle" (Althusser 1971, 65).

By the time Althusser came to write the *Essays in Self-Criticism* he had moved to the point where he argued that the category of theoretical practice was a poor one, and represented his theoreticist tendency (Althusser 1976, 123). The reason he gave for rejecting the category, however, is that he confused scientific and philosophic practice. It is important, he argued, to avoid making philosophy into science or politics. Philosophy, however, he now says, is not simply an outcome of other forces but is itself, in the last instance, a self-contained class struggle in theory (Althusser 1976, 150).

Althusserian Politics

I have been concerned to show how Althusser distorted Marxist theory. Others have been more explicit about the specifically structuralist directions he took and have pointed to the political trajectory of Althusser and some of his post-Althusserian followers. I have argued that Althusser's formulations lead in the direction of cutting off theory from politics. There are three sorts of evidence that support this analysis: Althusser's own political history; others' views of the political consequences of his thought; and the ideas of some of his followers—most importantly, Barry Hindess and Paul Hirst.

Althusser's political activity has been described as "naive and sporadic" (Benton 1984, 15) and his politics as "oddly apolitical" (Callinicos 1982, 59). While he worked for theoretical autonomy from the French Communist Party (PCF) he was unwilling to challenge its political authority. In addition, Althusser was notably absent during the events of May '68. Although he was ill at the time, even the next spring he did not seem to have understood the extent to which students and part of the working class had moved far past the PCF (Elliott 1987, 241). There seems to be agreement that when the "ruptural unity" Althusser had theorized occurred in May '68, its theorist ignored it. "The 'most important event in Western history' since 1945 found Althusser politically wanting" (Elliott 1987, 243).

But this may have been an individual failure to understand political events. What is more important is the direction in which his theoretical works point. A number of commentators have argued that Althusser's arguments preclude real analysis, and tend toward both idealist and relativist conclusions. There is, first, his argument for the irreducible heterogeneity of the social world, for different spheres with different standards, but with the same identical structure—that of production. Althusser knows in advance of analysis the form any practice will take. What is pregiven is the process of transforming a raw material into a product, effected by human labor (Callinicos 1982, 63).

Althusser's development of the concept of theoretical practice as distinct from political practice, even in the context of Althusser's own struggle against reductionism leads to a new kind of reductionism—a reduction of the dialectical unity of science/philosophy and politics to two realities, each of which has lost connection with the other. Because Althusser does not make the dialectical unity of theory and practice central to his account of science, he allows historical materialism to become simply a science (almost) like any other. It becomes a self-contained arena of production that differs from other self-contained arenas only because knowledges rather than chairs are produced. This stress on science as its own self-contained reality can only support academic Marxism. It suggests that the only appropriate standards are those internal to the practice of producing scientific knowledge and thereby supports the production of knowledge in isolation from organizational ties to struggles for liberation.

Third, there is Althusser's formulation of history as a process without a subject, that is, his reduction of agency to structure. Perry Anderson states that Althusser abolished subjects except as an illusory effect of ideology and notes that a short time later his former student, Foucault, proclaimed the end of man (1984, 38; Elliott 1987, 325). This reduction had several consequences: Althusser was unable to conceptualize struggle and change (Callinicos 1987, 3). In addition, Althusser's argument that subjects are constituted by means of ideological state apparatuses indicates that subjects acquire subjectivity simultaneously with their subjection to authority. The structure is primary and it is difficult to see how any oppositional subjects could be formed (Benton 1984, 139; Callinicos 1987, 155, 236).

Fourth, Althusser's formulations lead him into both relativism and idealism. Relativism emerges first in his argument that each practice has standards interior to it, and cannot be judged by standards appropriate to other practices, that is, that each practice has its own time and history. Ted Benton has argued that structuralism itself generates pressures toward relativism. He notes the impact of decentering the subject as a bestower of meaning and excluding the idea of reference from the theory of meaning. The result is that all that is left is an understanding of language as a system of mutually defining differences (Benton 1984, 180). The idealist strains emerge in Althusser's tendency to collapse the base into the superstructure. In his emphasis on the ideological state apparatuses, the economy is occluded, and even the state comes to take a minor role (Callinicos 1982, 76; Elliott 1987, 233).

But it is with the work of Hindess and Hirst in their trajectory from "hyper-" to "post-Althusserianism" (Elliott 1987, 5) that one can see even more clearly the effects of Althusser's ideas as they extend his work in more poststructuralist directions. Hindess and Hirst have come to see Marxist theory as an obstacle to socialist politics (Benton 1984, 182). In their work, language has become both "absolutized" and "unhinged from reality" (Anderson 1984, 45; Callinicos 1982, 169). Hindess and Hirst argue that there is no access to reality independent of discourse. The entities discourse refers to are constituted in and by it (an echo of Althusser's view of the constitution of subjects and a theme familiar in poststructuralism). Thus, they end up committed to a dualist ontology with, on one side, discourse and, on the other, an external reality to which discourse has no access. The result is the abandonment of the view that theoretical work can provide knowledge of a realty beyond itself. They have been charged with attacking all conceptual thought (Callinicos 1982, 189). And at least one commentator has wondered why such a position is any less dogmatic than claims that reality is knowable (Benton 1984, 182, 195).

The relativism of their position is much more apparent than Althusser's: once discourse is set free from any anchorage in the real, criteria that enable us to choose among discourses vanish (Callinicos 1982, 173). And the tendencies toward idealism in Althusser become more evident. Hindess and Hirst have argued that the "forms of thought must determine the order of connections in the real: the logical relations of inclusion and exclusion between concepts determine what is and is not possible in reality." The result is a collapse of the real into theoretical discourse (Benton 1984, 184).

Althusser argued in his own defense that the principle tendency of his work was to defend Marxism against the most threatening forms of bourgeois ideology—humanism, historicism, pragmatism, evolutionism, philosophical idealism, and so on. But he admitted that the secondary, theoreticist tendency of his work was harmful (Althusser 1976, 149). Although I cannot share this evaluation of his work, Althusser's statements of intent can be important guides for political thinking. Thus, for example, Althusser argued that along the path of the process of knowledge he tried to show that theory was itself a practice in opposition to pragmatism, that he tried to argue that Marxist theory should not be a slave to pragmatic tactical political decisions (Althusser 1976, 169). Along this path, Althusser argued that his motive was to develop what he called a "radical double opposition to empiricism, and to Hegel" (Althusser 1976, 190).[33]

What was at stake was the relative autonomy of theory. Althusser made similar arguments for the positions he took along the other paths. His theoretical antihumanism was, he said, an attempt to combat dogmatism not from the Right but from the Left (Althusser 1976, 170). His thesis of "determination in the last instance by the economy" was intended to oppose both economism and idealism. The argument for determination by the economy was an argument against idealism, an attempt to put himself on the side of materialism. The argument for the last instance was an effort to call attention to the complexity of the process and thereby to argue against economism (Althusser 1976, 177). He made much the same arguments for his other theses.

These statements along with Althusser's argument for the importance of thinking in extremes, are perhaps the most important contribution Althusser made. The enemies Althusser was attempting to combat are real enemies, and we should take his political thought, but not his theoretical advice.

NOTES

I would like to thank Jack Amariglio for encouraging me to revise this paper, and David Ruccio for his comments and suggestions. Karen Stuhldreher made very important contributions as my research assistant and Ann Buscherfeld typed the text and gave computer advice.

1. His influence is very strong in the work of such figures as Nicos Poulantzas (1975a, 1975b, 1974) and Etienne Balibar (1977). In addition, the bibliography at the end of Althusser's *Essays in Self-Criticism* lists 58 works *on* Althusser.

2. See also the introduction to the same essays by Grahame Lock on the question of what is termed the "Stalinian deviation," and Althusser's own statement on the relation of philosophy and politics in *Lenin and Philosophy* (1971, 42–45). On this point Althusser finds much support in Marxist theory. The polemics against Eduard Bernstein and other reformists rested on theoretical (rather than simply tactical) differences.

3. On Althusser's attempts to defend Marxism against bourgeois ideology, see Althusser (1976, 105, 115–17, 143, 186).

4. See Callinicos (1976, 75), Benton and Therborn (1977, 184), and Glucksmann (1972, 69–71).

5. On Althusser's relation to Stalinism, see Gerratana (1977, 101–2) and the "Introduction" by Grahame Lock (Althusser 1976, 1–32); Callinicos (1976, chap. 4) also addresses this question. On the question of Althusser's structuralism, see Glucksmann (1972). For humanist responses, see Kolakowski (1971) and Korac

(1969). For an argument against Althusser's thesis of the epistemological break, see for example Meszaros (1970).

6. Geras (1972, 86) made this suggestion. See also McLennan (1978, 135–43).

7. See also Kolakowski (1971, 120).

8. Benton (1984) makes a similar point.

9. I am uncertain of Althusser's definition of the concept of "elements" in Marxist theory, but my own reading of Marx is much more sympathetic to the concept of aspects and elements. The remarks about the three "elements" of the epistemological break come from Althusser (1970, 227).

10. For illustrations of these terms, see Marx's Introduction to the *Grundrisse* (1973, 81–115).

11. Althusser's account of the relations among these activities is especially important in *Lenin and Philosophy* (1971, 11–22); see also Althusser (1971, 107–26).

12. On this point, see for example the entry for "theory" in the glossary at the end of *For Marx* (1970, 256); see also Althusser (1976, 116).

13. See the very interesting discussions of this question by Benton and Therborn (1972, 186ff.) and Callinicos (1976, 60–66).

14. See also Althusser (1970, 157 and 1971, 100).

15. See also Althusser (1970, 243, 231).

16. See Unger (1975) on this point for a far more comprehensive discussion.

17. In this argument Althusser took the position, no doubt related to the 1936 Congress of the CPSU and perhaps later repudiated, that the dictatorship of the proletariat is superseded by a kind of humanism in the USSR (but not China). On this point, see the essay "Marxism and Humanism" (Althusser 1970).

18. See, for example, Marx (1967a, 10).

19. See also MacPherson (1962).

20. See Schmidt (1971) and Marx (1964, 112, 114, 13).

21. The attempt to reduce the social to the natural world or, more precisely, to study it in the same categories as the natural world is, of course, one of the major efforts of Western social science. Behaviorists and other positivist social scientists are still continuing their efforts to reduce the social world to the kinds of terms found in the natural sciences.

22. See, for example, Marx (1967a, 177).

23. See Althusser (1970, 174, 199, 210 and 1971, 75).

24. See Althusser and Balibar (1970, 58) and "Glossary" in Althusser (1970).

25. This passage is cited in Althusser (1970, notes to 185).

26. See, for example, Marx and Engels (1970, 41, 18).

27. See also Marx (1967b, 209).

28. See also Althusser (1970, 253) and Althusser and Balibar (1970, 59).

29. See also Althusser (1976, 170) where he remarks that Marx's theory does not depend for its truth on verification.

30. On this point see Unger (1975, 29–62, 104–44).

31. See, for example, Parsons (1969), Boulding (1969), Mayhew (1974), and Buchanon and Tullock (1965).

32. See, for an extreme extension of this position, Hindess (1977).

33. In opposition to empiricism, Althusser is arguing that seeing the importance of the production of knowledge is a "way of recalling Lenin's astonishing

remark, that Marx *only laid the foundation stones* of a theory which we must at all costs develop in every direction. It is a way of saying: Marxist theory can fall behind history and even behind itself, if ever it believes that it has arrived" (Althusser 1976, 195). The opposition to Hegel contained in Althusser's understanding of the process of production of knowledge was the stress on the dual nature of the process—the continued existence of the concrete objects and the creation of an object of knowledge.

REFERENCES

Althusser, L. 1970. *For Marx.* Trans. B. Brewster. New York: Vintage Books.

_____. 1971. *Lenin and Philosophy.* Trans. B. Brewster. New York: Monthly Review Press.

_____. 1976. *Essays in Self-Criticism.* Trans. G. Lock. London: New Left Books.

_____. 1977. "On the Twenty-Second Congress of the French Communist Party." Trans. B. Brewster. *New Left Review,* no. 104 (July–August): 2–25.

Althusser, L. and Balibar, E. 1970. *Reading Capital.* Trans. B. Brewster. London: New Left Books.

Amariglio, J. 1987. "Marxism Against Economic Science, Althusser's Legacy." *Research in Political Economy* 10: 159–94.

Anderson, P. 1976. *Considerations on Western Marxism.* London: New Left Books.

_____. 1980. *Arguments Within English Marxism.* London: Verso.

_____. 1984. *In the Tracks of Historical Materialism.* Chicago: University of Chicago Press.

Balibar, E. 1977. *Dictatorship of the Proletariat.* Trans. G. Lock. London: New Left Books.

Benton, T. 1984. *The Rise and Fall of Structural Marxism.* London: Macmillan.

Benton, T. and Therborn, G. 1977. *Philosophical Foundations of the Three Sociologies.* London: Routledge and Kegan Paul.

Borger, R. and Cioffi, F. 1970. *Explanation in the Behavioral Sciences.* Cambridge: Cambridge University Press.

Bottomore, T. B. 1956. *Karl Marx: Selected Writings in Sociology and Social Philosophy.* New York: McGraw-Hill.

_____. 1968. *Critics of Society: Radical Thought in North America.* New York: Pantheon Books.

Boulding, K. 1969. "Toward a Pure Theory of Threat Systems." In *Political Power,* ed. R. Bell, D. V. Edwards, and R. Harrison, 285–92. New York: Free Press.

Buchanon, J. and Tullock, G. 1965. *The Calculus of Consent.* Ann Arbor: University of Michigan Press.

Callinicos, A. 1976. *Althusser's Marxism.* London: Pluto Press.

_____. 1978. "Althusser's Marxism and British Social Science." *Radical Sciences Journal* 6–7.

_____. 1982. *Is There A Future for Marxism?* Atlantic Highlands, N.J.: Humanities Press.

_____. 1987. *Making History.* London: Polity Press.

Clecak, P. 1974. *Radical Paradoxes: Dilemmas of the American Left, 1945–1970.* New York: Harper and Row.

Colletti, L. 1972. *From Rousseau to Lenin.* New York: Monthly Review Press.

de Lauretis, T. 1987. *Technologies of Gender.* Bloomington: Indiana University Press.

Elliot, G. 1987. *Althusser: The Detour of Theory.* New York: Verso.

Engels, F. 1972a. "Socialism: Utopian and Scientific." In *The Marx-Engels Reader,* ed. R. Tucker. New York: W. W. Norton.

_____. 1972b. "Social Relations in Russia." In *The Marx-Engels Reader,* ed. R. Tucker. New York: W. W. Norton.

Fraser, N. and Nicholson, L. 1989. "Social Criticism Without Philosophy." In *Feminism/Postmodernism,* ed. L. Nicholson, 19–38. New York: Routledge.

Freedman, C. 1990. "The International Marxism of Louis Althusser." *Rethinking Marxism* (Fall–Winter): 309–28.

Geras, N. 1972. "Althusserian Marxism." *New Left Review,* no. 71 (January–February).

Gerratana, V. 1977. "Althusser and Stalinism." *New Left Review,* no. 72 (March–April).

Glucksmann, A. 1972. "A Ventriloquist Structuralism." *New Left Review,* no. 72 (March–April).

Goldmann, L. 1969. *The Human Sciences and Philosophy.* Trans. H. White and R. Anchor. London: Jonathan Cape.

Gouldner, A. 1971. *The Coming Crisis in Western Sociology.* New York: Basic Books.

Gramsci, A. 1971. *Selections From the Prison Notebooks.* Trans. Q. Hoare and G. N. Smith. New York: International Publishers.

Hartsock, N. 1990. "Postmodernism and Political Change." *Cultural Critique* 14 (Fall–Winter): 15–33.

Hindess, B. 1977. *Philosophy and Methodology in the Social Sciences.* Atlantic Highlands, N.J.: Humanities Press.

Kavanagh, J. H. 1982. "Marxism's Althusser: Towards A Politics of Literary Theory." *Diacritics* 12: 25–45.

Kolakowski, L. 1971. "Althusser's Marx." In *The Socialist Register,* ed. R. Miliband and J. Saville, 111–28. London: Merlin Press.

Korac, V. 1969. "The Phenomenon of 'Theoretical Anti-Humanism'." *Praxis* 5 (3–4).

Kovesi, J. 1968. *Moral Notions.* New York: Humanities Press.

Lasch, C. 1969. *The Agony of the American Left.* New York: Vintage Books.

Lenin, V. I. 1929. *What Is To Be Done?* New York: International Publishers.

_____. 1962. *Left-Wing Communism.* Moscow: Progress Publishers.

_____. 1970. *The Proletarian Revolution and the Renegade Kautsky.* Moscow: Progress Publishers.

Lukacs, G. 1971. *History and Class Consciousness.* Cambridge, Mass.: MIT Press.

Luxemburg, R. 1971. "Social Reform or Revolution." In *Selected Writings of Rosa Luxemburg,* ed. D. Howard, 52–134. New York: Monthly Review Press.

MacPherson, C. B. 1962. *The Political Theory of Possessive Individualism.* London: Oxford University Press.

Marcuse, H. 1973. *Studies in Critical Philosophy.* Trans. J. de Bres. Boston: Beacon Press.

Marx, K. 1964. *Economic and Philosophic Manuscripts of 1844*. Ed. D. Struik. New York: International Publishers.

_____. 1967a. *Capital*. Vol. 1. New York: International Publishers.

_____. 1967b. *Capital*. Vol. 3. New York: International Publishers.

_____. 1970. "Theses on Feuerbach." In *The German Ideology*, ed. C. J. Arthur, 121–24. New York: W. W. Norton.

_____. 1972a. "Introduction." In *The Marx-Engels Reader*, ed. R. Tucker. New York: W. W. Norton.

_____. 1972b. "Introduction to a Critique of Hegel's Philosophy of Right." In *The Marx-Engels Reader*, ed. R. Tucker. New York: W. W. Norton.

_____. 1973. *Grundrisse*. Trans. M. Nicolaus. Middlesex: Penguin Books.

Marx, K. and Engels, F. 1970. *The German Ideology*. Ed. C. J. Arthur. New York: International Publishers.

Mayhew, D. 1974. *Congress: The Electoral Connection*. New Haven: Yale University Press.

McLennan, G. 1978. "Will the Real Louis Althusser Please Stand Up?" *Radical Science Journal* 6–7: 135–43.

Meszaros, I. 1970. *Alienation: Marx's Theory of Alienation*. New York: Harper and Row.

Ollman, B. 1971. *Alienation: Marx's Conception of Man in Capitalist Society*. New York: Cambridge University Press.

Parsons, T. 1969. "On the Concept of Political Power." In *Political Power*, ed. R. Bell, D. V. Edwards, and R. Harrison. New York: Free Press.

Poulantzas, N. 1974. *Fascism and Dictatorship*. Trans. J. White. London: New Left Books.

_____. 1975a. *Political Power and Social Change*. Trans. T. O'Hagan. London: New Left Books.

_____. 1975b. *Classes in Contemporary Capitalism*. Trans. D. Fernbach. London: New Left Books.

Resnick, R. and Wolff, R. 1991. "Althusser's Contribution." In *Rethinking Marxism* 4 (Spring): 13–16.

Schmidt, A. 1971. *The Concept of Nature in Marx*. Trans. B. Fowkes. London: New Left Books.

Therborn, G. 1976. *Science, Class, and Society*. London: New Left Books.

Unger, R. 1975. *Knowledge and Politics*. Glencoe: Free Press.

West, C. 1991. *The Ethical Dimensions of Marxist Thought*. New York: Monthly Review Press.

Part Three

Structuralism, Poststructuralism, and Politics

As women's studies became both more entrenched and more legitimate in colleges and universities, and as I became, finally, a women's studies faculty member in 1984, feminist scholarship came to be more engaged with the concerns of the university. As someone who had been involved with feminist organizations outside the university until that time (for me a matter of intellectual and political survival at a school where women's studies did not yet exist), I was concerned about the increasing separation of feminist theory from the political practices that had been its roots. Theory can contribute in an important way to politics by helping people see the logic of what they are doing. Somebody needs to step back and ask what it means, for example, that we decided to organize things in one way rather than another. What vision of the world led to this type of action? But it is all too rare for activists to have this kind of time.

The division between academic theorists and activists was brought home to me in several ways, but two examples seem most relevant here. In the mid-eighties I cotaught a course on feminist theory in the social sciences. My colleague and I planned to work through the literature in political science, sociology, economics, anthropology, and psychology, and we organized the course by disciplines. When we had put together our first effort at a syllabus, we realized that the then-burning questions in feminist theory—issues of race and sexuality—were absent. Feminist work oriented toward academic social sciences, although critical and important, turned out to be structured more by the concerns of the disciplines than by the concerns of feminist theory based on political practices and struggles that were both internal and external to the academy. This of course should not be surprising. A part of becoming more legitimate in

167

academia required that feminist theorists be able to be credible within existing disciplines. And it is important to remember that most women's studies positions in most universities are in fact controlled by existing departments. To staff their interdisciplinary courses, women's studies programs usually depend on faculty whose formal appointments are in various departments.

A second experience was coteaching a graduate course in which humanities students outnumbered social scientists three to one. It was a very useful and for me disturbing set of insights into the state of feminist theory in some fields. The humanities students insisted that one should not name anything because things are constantly shifting: "You can't talk about 'we' because who are 'we'?" Even if "we "referred to twenty graduate students at the University of Washington, everyone was too multidimensional to be pushed into any common identity/subjectivity.

Theories of difference have important contributions to make, but they have too often become immobilizing. The immobilization seems to come from at least two different perspectives. First, there is the issue of how anyone can speak for someone else. This is one way in which the difference dialogue gets translated in the U.S. context, in which individualism is all but sacrosanct. Second, these theories are also immobilizing because women's studies students learn about difference in a very academic setting. This is not their fault, but what they are learning are theories detached from activism. They learn the difference discourse in theory courses , but not in terms of differences within coalitions where daily activities must take account of differences. As Charlotte Bunch has put it, we need to ask how we can come together. This need not require a single voice. But it does require "knowing the difference between solidarity speaking, coalition speaking, and claiming or co-opting other's lives."[1]

In addition, we face the question of audience. As feminist theory has come to be more legitimately academic, its audience has also changed. The audience for many feminist theorists, myself included, is now mostly other academics. Some of us have been saying that feminist theory is valuable to the extent that it speaks to the practitioners and activists. But the academy is definitely not oriented in that way. My own work too has shifted, and thus the essays in this section are very much addressed to an academic audience. At the same time, it is unrealistic for each of us to go out and organize and then write theory in our spare time, as many of us did earlier.

Chapter 7, on Althusser, which concludes Part 2, should stand in many ways as a good introduction to Part 3. The problems I found with his interpretation of Marxism (the problem is not interpretation per se, since I have arguably done the same) are some of the same problems I found with both structuralism and poststructuralism. My purpose in analyzing

Althusser is the same as my purpose in all of these essays: to understand how some theories can support, empower, and guide activism and how other theories can work against effective action. Althusser tore apart the intricate weave of practices and theories in Marx's work. He wanted to respond to the popularity of structuralist theory and to insist on both the scientific and the revolutionary character of Marxism, but he ended up with separate and divergent categories: science and ideology, politics and theory, philosophy and history, production and consumption. These for Marx were dialectical categories in which each not only appeared as its opposite but contained the opposite within it. Thus, to give just one example, in a dialectical understanding of Marxist theory, it is evident that the means by which capitalism creates wealth are at the same time the means for the creation of poverty.

The fundamental difficulty, as I see it, was well stated by the editors of *Rethinking Marxism:* "To call into question Althusser's theoreticist and anti-dialectical errors is to call into question any political theory or activity founded upon it." Thus, this applies not only to Althusser, but also to non-Marxist structuralists such as Lévi-Strauss and to poststructuralist theorists, as structuralism represents only the first steps on the road taken by poststructuralist theorists, a road in which the subject is subverted and truth deconstructed rather than redefined. An analysis of the political problems generated by these theoretical positions can highlight some of the central problems one confronts in attempting a liberatory politics based on the theoretical moves of both structuralism and poststructuralism. "That is, if Althusser, given his political commitments, forecloses important political and intellectual directions, can we really expect political guidance from his intellectual successors?"[2]

Lévi-Strauss is not so much a successor to Althusser as an illustration of some of the problems of a non-Marxist structuralism. Several aspects of his account are very problematic, although they are also important in shaping both Gayle Rubin's classic argument and the arguments of poststructuralist thinkers. In particular, I find much congruence between Lévi-Strauss's contentions that superstructures are faulty acts that have somehow "made it" socially and Foucault's similar claims. In his attention to symbol systems, the symbols become more real than what they symbolize; "reality" becomes problematic, and history disappears into myth. Indeed, people disappear and become instead symbols spoken by myths. And here we have a form of the death of the subject, which is later elaborated in the work of theorists such as Foucault. I include a critique of Rubin's essay (Chapter 9) because I think it is very important to look at the baggage that comes with adopting a particular mode of thought. Any mode of thought, or approach to theory, carries some baggage with it— and that baggage is always both good and bad. One needs to look carefully at the assumptions and perspectives to determine how integral they are to an account of the world. In the case of her use of Lévi-Strauss, I believe Rubin imported some unwanted (and to some degree unnecessary) assumptions and conclusions.

Chapter 10, "Postmodernism and Political Change," makes a case that the adoption of the postmodern perspectives of theorists like Richard Rorty, or the poststructuralist perspectives of Foucault, will not provide helpful resources for feminist theory. I believe that the impulse for U.S. feminist theorists to look for work that stressed heterogeneity, incommensurability, and the lack of definitive answers arose from a recognition of the validity of critiques of white feminist theorists by theorists of color. But postmodernist theories stress resistance and subversion, not transformation. They also emphasize local and even individual knowledge. For those of us who want to change the world, however, more-systematic understandings are important. And these understandings are more available from the perspectives of those who have been marginalized and excluded.

The third essay in Part 3, "The Feminist Standpoint Revisited" (Chapter 11), represents my effort to rewrite and to correct, from the vantage point of the nineties, the argument I made in "The Feminist Standpoint" (reprinted herein as Chapter 6). As I have reflected on discussions of standpoint theories over the years, I have come to believe that it is the intertwining of issues of politics with the more traditional philosophical questions concerning "truth" and knowledge, along with their conflicting criteria for claims of epistemological validity, that have been responsible for much of the controversy and confusion. That is, standpoint theories must be recognized as essentially contested in much the same way that the concept of power is essentially contested. Chapter 11 also represents a continuation of my interest in epistemology and ontology, which marks the other essays included here.

NOTES

1. Charlotte Bunch, "Bringing Together Feminist Theory and Practice: A Collective Interview," *Signs: Journal of Women in Culture and Society* 21 (Summer 1996), 936.

2. Nancy Hartsock, "Louis Althusser's Structural Marxism: Political Clarity and Theoretical Distortions," *Rethinking Marxism* 4, no. 4 (Winter 1991), 11–12. See Chapter 7 herein.

eight

↴

The Kinship Abstraction in Feminist Theory

Like the lives of proletarians as described by Marx, women's lives make available a particular and privileged vantage point on phallocratic social relations and ideology. I propose to use the accounts I have developed of the world views of both the exchange abstraction and abstract masculinity to examine a category central to masculinist ideologies, that of kinship and the family. Claude Lévi-Strauss's work has frequently been used as a starting point for a feminist theory of the patriarchy. This theory, however, emerges from a phallocratic perspective that ignores women's lives and instead treats women as unreal beings who are at bottom simply symbols created by the male mind. Just as Marx's understanding of the world from the standpoint of the proletariat enabled him to get beneath bourgeois ideology, so a feminist standpoint can allow us to see patriarchal ideologies as inversions of real social relations.

A number of feminist theorists have been impressed with Claude Lévi-Strauss's theory that the exchange of women marks the human transition from nature to culture and have credited him with laying the basis for developing a political economy of sex.[1] They are not alone in admiring his work. Lévi-Strauss has been credited with so much by so many that it appears as if his outlook is so amorphous that one sees only one's own views reflected back from a reading of his work. His elusiveness (and seductiveness) is demonstrated by the fact that a single author can variously characterize him as a return to Rousseau by way of Plato; as having

---

In Nancy C. M. Hartsock, *Money, Sex, and Power: Toward a Feminist Historical Materialism* (New York: Longman, 1983).

been influenced by geology, Marx, and Freud; and as attempting to synthesize the responsibilities of the anthropologist with both Marxist thought and the Buddhist tradition.[2] Others have suggested that Lévi-Strauss has affinities with Kant; has been influenced by Rousseau; has formulated a Hobbesian social contract; and/or has synthesized Freud, Rousseau, and Marx. He has even been explored as a sociobiologist.[3] Given the diversity—and even oppositions of these commentators to each other—one wonders what to make of this.

On the basis of my own reading of Lévi-Strauss (I begin to think most readings of his work are idiosyncratic), I argue that his theorization of the exchange of women must be set within the context of his more general theory and that far from being an adequate starting point for feminist theory, it leads toward a phallocratic mystification of women's material lives and a location of women's oppression in the sphere of ideology rather than material social relations. If one addresses Lévi-Strauss's work from the insistently materialist vantage point provided by a feminist standpoint, if one reads him with feet firmly planted in the coarsely sensuous ground of female existence, his work can be shown to articulate a series of artificial and ahistorical dualisms: culture/nature, mind/body, abstract/concrete, science/savage thought, stasis/change, saying/doing, quantity/quality, exchange/use, strangers/kin. An understanding of social life based on these dualisms can posit only a fragile and problematic social synthesis, one that sees contracts and the exchanges constructed by them not as "secondary creations" but as the "basic material of social lie."[4] Some of these dualisms have their source in the exchange abstraction. Others are more easily located in abstract masculinity. The various faults to which I point are prominent in different areas of his theory—some emerge most explicitly in his discussion of language and symbol systems, others in his discussion of kinship, and still others in his description of the scientific enterprise in which he sees himself engaged. Because feminists have been most influenced by Lévi-Strauss's kinship theory, my attention focuses there, and my attention to other aspects of his thought serves to situate the kinship theory on more general terrain in order to demonstrate the full extent of its perniciousness. I argue, then, that despite his own protestations of being more faithful to Marx than his critics, Lévi-Strauss, because of his search for an eternal and natural human nature, and because of his stress on what he takes to be the creations of the human mind, cannot be considered a Marxist. And despite his sadness at what he sees as the loss of the West's "opportunity of remaining female," and despite his lauding of Buddhism as the hope for the world because it integrates excess by means of "the unifying reassurance implicit in the promise of a return to the maternal breast," his work must be understood as an expression of abstract masculinity.[5]

If this reading of Lévi-Strauss can be supported, it would not only cast doubt on his claims to be carrying on Marxist theory by contributing to the development of a theory of superstructure or by carrying on the work of Lewis Henry Morgan, but also would lay the basis for an overdue rejection of his work as a basis for developing a political economy of sex.[6]

Language, Symbols, and Values

Let us begin with Lévi-Strauss's work on symbol systems, since he sets out from language and linguistics. It is on the basis of his work in linguistics that Lévi-Strauss is able to argue that language, cooking, and the incest taboo represent a series of isomorphisms. All are created by the human mind, and each is what one commentator described as a screen to filter "the anonymous natural world and turn it into names, signs, and qualities. They change the shapeless torrent of life into a discrete quantity and into families of symbols."[7]

As Lévi-Strauss moves through what he sees as three sets of symbol systems sharing a single structure, one can perhaps best describe his trajectory in the terms a feminist poet used to describe the male mind. It is decided, she intones, that "there are three degrees of abstraction, each leading to higher truths. The scientist peels away uniqueness, revealing category; the mathematician peels away sensual fact, revealing number; the metaphysician peels away even number and reveals the fruit of pure being."[8] This is indeed what Lévi-Strauss believes his work does—revealing the underlying categories that structure human thought, developing what one commentator has termed "the rudiments of a semantic algebra,"[9] and finally, by means of an encounter with Buddhism, reaching true being and recognizing that the creations of the human mind are simply "the transient efflorescence of a creation in relation to which they have no meaning, except perhaps that of allowing to play its [destructive] part in creation."[10]

The voyage begins by way of an analogy between anthropology and linguistics. Lévi-Strauss points out that anthropology and linguistics share something fundamental: "*Both* language and culture are the products of activities which are basically similar. I am now referring to this uninvited guest which has been seated during this Conference beside us and which is *the human mind.*"[11] The human mind demands order, and this demand for order forms the basis for both primitive and scientific thought. Thus, life is ruled by a universal and unconscious reason, identical for both the savage and the civilized.[12] Both forms of thought center on an insistence on differentiation, on a "logical subordination of resemblance to contrast." In both systems, in cooking rules and in kinship systems built on the model of the incest taboo, one finds, he argues, the dichotomizing activity to be fundamental.[13] All classification proceeds by pairs of contrasts, and the progressive purification of reality by means of abstraction ends in a "final term," which takes the form of a simple binary opposition.[14] Thus, dualism is not only intentionally present in his work but also structures it fundamentally. Dualism forms the basis for a grid that produces meaning itself.[15]

Despite their similar structure, however, the scientific and savage mind proceed along different paths: The one is timeless, the other located in history; the one supremely concrete, the other supremely abstract; the one proceeding from sensible qualities, the other from formal properties; the one producing the neolithic arts, the other, contemporary science.[16] While the savage *'bricoleur'* speaks only through the medium of things, as opposed to the scientist who abstracts, both science and mythic thought are held to operate by reducing multiplicity to a few basic principles.

In both cases, the mind's demand for order follows universal and natural paths dependent on the construction of the human brain, a physico-chemical object. The structure then is not historical but natural, and in it resides the real human nature.[17] One critic has pointed out some of the inconsistencies that result from reliance on the assumptions (1) that "what is universally true must be natural," and (2) that "what distinguishes the human being from the man-animal is the distinction between culture and nature, that is, that the humanity of man is that which is non-natural."[18] Lévi-Strauss's preoccupation with the latter assumption emerges in his claim that language represents the shift from animality and nature to culture, the relation to the natural world is without the symbolization present in every social act.[19] The problem is compounded by the artificiality with which Lévi-Strauss holds that the human mind creates culture by intentional act. Culture, according to Lévi-Strauss, is an artificial creation of the human mind, an activity of creating aloneness out of social being by dichotomizing the world into my tribe and yours, thereby creating strangers who must be made if not kin, relatives by marriage.

This creation of strangers who are made affines on the basis of the universal dichotomizing needs of the human brain is of particular interest here. Lévi-Strauss contends that the study of kinship presents the anthropologist with a situation that formally resembles that of the structural linguist. "Like phonemes, kinship terms are elements of meaning; like phonemes, they acquire meaning only if they are integrated into systems. 'Kinship systems,' like 'phonemic systems,' are built by the mind on the level of unconscious thought."[20] The transformation of raw sound into phoneme is reproduced in the transformation of animal sexuality into a matrimonial system, an operation that selects and combines either verbal signs or signs in the form of women.[21]

Thus he proposes to treat the kinship system as a kind of language, a "set of processes, permitting the establishment, between individuals and groups, of a certain type of communication. That the mediating factor, in this case, should be the *women of the group*, who are circulated between clans, lineages, or families, in place of the *words of the group*, which are *circulated* between individuals, does not at all change the fact that the essential aspect of the phenomenon is identical in both cases."[22] Not only can kinship be treated as a language, but the study of women in the communication system between men may afford an image of the relationship that might have existed at an early period in the development of language between human actors and their words.[23] Lévi-Strauss's interest in kinship, then, can be seen to flow logically (if not historically or biographically) from this interest in the nature of symbol systems. Most particularly, he sees a study of kinship as a means for moving outside history, a means for understanding better the timelessness of the savage mind. The equation is thus posited:

$$\frac{\text{women}}{\text{men}} \quad = \quad \frac{\text{words}}{\text{savage.}}$$

Kinship and language, then, both mediate between nature and culture and divide the human from the natural or animal world. Lévi-Strauss holds that matrimonial exchange of women falls midway between nature and culture. Women are "natural products naturally procreated by other biological individuals," as opposed to the goods and services which are "social products culturally manufactured by technical agents."[24] The *system* of women functions, then, as a "middle term between the system of (natural) living creatures and the system of (manufactured) objects."[25]

Let us look a bit more closely at the ways this discussion of symbol systems expresses the perspective of abstract masculinity and the exchange abstraction by exploring the dualisms that emerge from this account. We can then see how these are both replicated and expanded in Lévi-Strauss's account of the exchange of women. The most prominent aspects of the two abstractions appear in his stress on the need to translate concrete, sensual qualities into abstract quantity and symbols, his separation of mind from body, his contradictory separation of natural and social, his opposition of doing to saying, and change to stasis (history vs. myth). These dualisms lead him, like the adherents of the exchange abstraction or the abstract masculinity discussed above, into idealism and into a series of contradictions and counterfactual statements.

Lévi-Strauss's first move toward abstraction is his reduction of the immense variety of societies and histories to a dichotomy—primitive thought vs. civilized or scientific thought. He then, however, discovers that this dichotomy is part of a second opposition, that of nature to culture. He contends that the products of culture—myths, language, kinship, cooking—obey natural laws.[26] Thus, despite the status of language and kinship as intentional human inventions for the purpose of taking control of nature, Lévi-Strauss can also hold that they are themselves "natural," since they result from "objective structure of the psyche and of the brain."[27] Thus, what one commentator referred to as Lévi-Strauss's "formalistic search for binary oppositions and their multiple permutations and combinations" must instead be understood as an effort to uncover natural and universal features of the human mind.[28]

Lévi-Strauss's resolution of the opposition, nature/culture, by means of positing a formal structural commonality, and his location of this commonality in physico-biochemical structure of the brain, forms the base for several further, and ironically idealist, dualisms and counterfactuals. Lévi-Strauss's working out of what one commentator was tempted to call a "transcendent object," as opposed to the Kantian transcendent subject, leads him into a mind/body dualism in which the mind almost disappears and then reemerges as all of reality becomes a metaphor. The mind, which Lévi-Strauss has referred to as an external presence, as the creator of culture, symbol systems, and kinship, is contradictorily defined as a "function of inert matter."[29] Perhaps the most telling statement of the opposition and separation of mind and body, and the subordination of the former to the latter, appears in Lévi-Strauss's description of his own existence as merely a "stake" in "the struggle between another society, made up of several thousand million nerve cells lodged in the ant-hill of my skull, and my body, which serves as its robot."[30] The human subject, in a world of other subjects, has been supplanted by an anthill and a robot! The rigid masculine ego boundaries, the opposition of self and other, here take the form of a rigid separation of and struggle between the mind and body. Further, the activities of the feeling and thinking mind are reduced to the actions of several thousand million uncomprehending and scurrying ants in combat with a robot. And this is so despite Lévi-Strauss's contention that the mind is logically prior to social relations.[31]

The primacy of the physico-chemical object leads Lévi-Strauss away from history. If inert matter is the source of being, then one can recover it only by moving outside of history. This is so because, Lévi-Strauss claims, the meaning given by history is never "*the right one:* superstructures are *faulty acts* which have 'made it' socially. Hence it is vain to go to historical consciousness for the truest meaning."[32] Thus, despite the fact that the scientist is condemned to live in history, he must see it as myth. Episodes in history can be expected to "resolve themselves into cerebral, hormonal, or nervous phenomena, which themselves have reference to the physical or chemical order."[33]

It is mythic thought that can provide a lever to extract oneself from history, mythic thought that provides a "machine for the suppression of time." The machine, however, as Lévi-Strauss describes it, operates without human knowledge or interference. If the human creations of myth, symbols, and kinship merely replicate and work out the inbuilt dichotomous passages of the human brain, he can conclude that nature speaks with itself through man without his being aware, that man is a "moment" in a message that nature sends and receives.[34] Perhaps one can now better understand Lévi-Strauss's contention that the creations of the human mind are simply "the transient efflorescence of a creation in relation to which they have no meaning."

Myths, then, must be understood as a kind of paralanguage; the words of the myth do not express its meaning. The true meaning is unconscious, and not accessible to the group that invented the myth. This group, the originators of the myth, does not know its meaning. The conclusion to be drawn is shocking: "Myths communicate with each other by means of men and without men knowing it."[35] The fetishism of such a position is astounding. Not only have relations between persons vanished as accessible objects of knowledge, but persons themselves have become, directly, the instruments of that which they themselves produced as passive instruments of nature. Man himself now becomes, like goods, words, and women, a sign of exchange.[36]

This is a critical step in the eventual evaporation of matter itself into metaphor in Lévi-Strauss's system. The logic moves from inert chemical reactions toward the use of real human beings by the symbols they themselves originally produced. Nature no longer consists of real trees, animals, and insects; these have been transformed into "equations" and "metaphors." Culture becomes a metaphor of the human mind, which is a metaphor of cellular chemical reactions, which in turn are simply to be understood as another metaphor.[37] As one commentator put is succinctly, for Lévi-Strauss, "the symbols are more real than what they symbolize."[38] Metaphors build on each other and come to relate only to each other. Thus, *Tristes Tropiques* concludes, in the excellent paraphrase of an enthusiastic commentator, with these claims:

> Time is also a metaphor and its passage is as illusory as our efforts to halt it: it neither flows nor stops. Our very mortality is illusory: every man who dies assures the survival of the species, each species which becomes extinct confirms the persistence of a movement which rushes timelessly toward an ever-imminent and always unreachable immobility."[39]

(At this point the ghost of Karl Marx can be heard to exclaim, "What horseshit!")

Lévi-Strauss can now be seen to reproduce a variant of the world view of abstract masculinity: He values the abstract and unattainable over the concrete; devalues material life activity in favor of the production of symbols; holds that the body is irrelevant to the real self, an impediment to be overcome by the mind; and contends that what is real is imperceptible to the senses, is unconscious, and accessible only to a mind detached from participation. The human mind's demand for order leads to a one-sided stress on abstraction, formal properties, and self-moving symbol systems at the expense of concrete, many-qualitied, material life.

The fundamental perverseness of such a vision is apparent in several formulations. For example, the relation of mind to body does not even take the form of the struggle of reason to master the appetites, but is instead a struggle between an anthill and a robot; the relation of humans to their own symbolic activity is one in which the signs themselves use human beings, instead of vice versa; material life is evaporated into a series of metaphors; history is abandoned in favor of myth. The masculinist inversion of life into death takes the form in Lévi-Strauss's work of the death of subjectivity both in his contention that myths speak to each other through the medium of men, and without men knowing it, and in his argument that life can in the end be understood as the operation of inert matter.

As I have noted, abstract masculinity has a great deal in common with the perspective imposed by commodity exchange. The separation and opposition of social and natural worlds, of abstract and concrete, of permanence and change, the effort to define only the former of each pair as important, the reliance on a series of counterfactual assumptions characteristic of both structure Lévi-Strauss's work. His work represents still another shared aspect. Both abstract masculinity and the exchange abstraction form the basis for a problematic, fragile, and conflictual social synthesis. The problematic nature of this synthesis, along with the dualism of exchange vs. use and strangers vs. kin, emerges most clearly in the context of Lévi-Strauss's argument that kinship is constituted by the exchange of women.[40]

The Exchange of Women as Social Contract

In *The Elementary Structures of Kinship*, Lévi-Strauss stated that his task was to demonstrate that all kinship systems and types of marriage hitherto excluded from the category of marriage were part of the general classification "methods of exchange."[41] There is, however, a deeper purpose of his work, one to which he frequently alludes: He is concerned with the creation and maintenance of the human group. The exchange of women (and, he notes, "the rule of exogamy which expresses it"), "provides the means of binding men together, and superimposing upon the natural links of kinship the henceforth artificial links—artificial in the sense that they are removed from chance encounters or the promiscuity of family life—of alliance governed by rule."[42] Human society, then, is an artificial creation, separated from the natural world by the intervention of purposeful human will, which replaces chance by organization. The incest taboo, then, can be described as man's "first 'no' against nature," an expression of "the transition from the natural fact of consanguinity to the cultural fact of alliance."[43]

Exchange for Lévi-Strauss is fundamental to purposeful human activity, since it forces natural sentiments and biological relationships into artificial social structures. And purposeful human activity, in turn, is essential, since, as Lévi-Strauss notes, without purposeful intervention, human society might not exist.[44] (One must remind oneself that human society both is and is not artificial for Lévi-Strauss. On the one hand, it requires purposeful intervention; on the other, this intervention can only take the form of imposing a dichotomy, which can then be resolved. The need to impose such a dichotomy is located in the physico-chemical structure of the brain itself.)

Regularized exchange of women results from the scarcity of women, which in turn results from a "natural and universal" feature of human existence—the "deep polygamous tendency, which exists among all men, always makes the number of available women seem insufficient. Let us add that even if there were as many women as men, those women would not all be equally desirable. . . . Hence, the demand for women is in actual fact, or to all intents and purposes, always in a state of disequilibrium and tension." Thus, Lévi-Strauss claims, monogamy is not itself an institution "but merely incorporates the limit of polygamy in societies where, for highly varied reasons, economic and sexual competition reaches an acute form."[45] In addition, the social division of labor in primitive societies makes women highly valued members of the family. The human group, then, controls women as a scarce and essential valuable and "institutes freedom of access for every individual [male] to the women of the group." In so doing, the groups create a system in which "all men are in equal competition for all women."[46] In the light of these contentions, it is curious that women but not children are circulating commodities. Indeed, Lévi-Strauss himself notes that pygmy societies, because of their division of labor, consider women *and children* to be the most valuable of the family group.[47] One can only conclude that this is a result of Lévi-Strauss's unwillingness to see any males as commodities.

Lévi-Strauss characterizes the situation as an equal competition, even though few men are allowed to practice polygamy. He argues that the chief's privilege of polygamy is part of a collective bargain, or primitive social contract. "By recognizing the privilege, the group has exchanged the *elements of individual security*" which accompany the rule of monogamy for a "*collective security* arising out of political organization." In return for his services, the chief receives several women from the group, which has suspended the "common law" for him. "Polygamy, therefore, does not run counter to the demand for an equitable distribution of women. It merely superimposes one rule of distribution upon another."[48] That is, members of the community exchange individual security, the price of which is the unequal distribution of scarce valuables. Some relinquish their share of these valuables in order to procure an equal share of the collective safety.

Group solidarity, then, based on the exchange of women, represents the "most immediate way to integrate opposition between the self and others," since the transfer of a valuable good makes two separate and opposed individuals into partners.[49] Social relations, then, take place between men, the only real actors, *by means of* women, or through the mediation of women, who are, in Lévi-Strauss's words, "merely the occasion of this real relationship.[50] The exchange of women in primitive societies does not involve profit in Western terms; it is a total and reciprocal transaction that has the function of creating solidarity. Lévi-Strauss argues that the prohibition against incest is less to prevent marriage with mother or sister than to require that they be given to other men. This is the "supreme rule of the gift."[51] Its role is to establish a community by establishing kin.

The exchange of women as a means for transforming strangers into affines or relatives by marriage prominently carries with it several of the specific dualities present in the exchange of commodities: the separation of exchange from use, quantity from quality, interaction with nature from social interaction, the opposition of participants in the transaction, and the problematic social synthesis. The other features of the exchange abstraction and abstract masculinity analyzed in the context of Lévi-Strauss's analysis of symbol systems are less directly present in his account of the exchange of women. One must remember, however, that language and the incest taboo are isomorphic for Lévi-Strauss: The one simply recapitulates the other.[52]

In the exchange of women the abstract and qualityless character of the commodity appears in Lévi-Strauss's insistence on the need to see women as signs with only two possible values: "same" or "other." He himself underlines the abstractness in this formulation when he adds that in some groups, the same women originally offered in exchange can be exchanged in return. "All that is necessary on either side is the sign of otherness, which is the outcome of a certain position in a structure and not of any innate characteristic. . . . [53] The exchange of women as described by Lévi-Strauss, then, is characterized by an absence of qualities and differentiation of exchange objects only according to quantity—quantity of other women to be exchanged in return, or cows, or cash. The qualitylessness gives them their reality in exchange.

The separation of exchange from use is present in the form of the incest taboo. Here, too, as in the exchange of commodities, the separation of exchange from use results in a separation of mind from action, where the use to which the women will be put is present in the minds and not the actions of the participants. Their minds are focused on the private; their actions are social. The result of this separation is the theoretical weight Lévi-Strauss gives to mind and to abstract and quantitative differences, coupled with his treatment of the activities of mind as profoundly different entities than those of the body.

The separation of nature from society is present, since the woman's change in status is purely social. Yet here, the exchange of women begins to differ from commodity exchange. Lévi-Strauss holds that the exchange of women marks the boundary between nature and culture, and mediates between the two terms. Rather than take place on only one side of the dualities, it brings them together. There is a second difference in the exchange of women from one lineage to the other. Unlike the exchange of commodities, it transforms all participants in the transaction. The buyer or seller of a commodity remains buyer or seller after the purchase/sale, but after a woman is exchanged, those who were strangers are now affines, and the woman herself becomes part of another lineage, a married woman, an adult. Every participant occupies a different place afterward. Dualism still reverberates through the transaction, but it is a more complex and contradictory dualism, which transforms not just the social status of the object in question but all other oppositions as well. Yet they remain as oppositions within the social synthesis created by the exchange of women.

The duality contained in the woman herself as both same and other is replicated in the opposition and duality of the separate men exchanging her, although there the opposition is embodied in the dual forms of men and not contained in a simple body. Each recognizes the other as an other who is not yet kin. Each move made by the one must be countered by the other for the exchange to succeed. The needs, feelings, and thoughts involved on both sides are polarized on the basis of whose they are. Not what they think but whose feeling or need will prevail is what shapes the relationship. That is, exchange requires solipsism between the participants. It is a relation between strangers. Lévi-Strauss includes this aspect of the exchange abstraction, too, in his theory. In the societies he describes, he argues, "either a man is a kinsman, actually, or by fiction, or he is a person to whom you have no reciprocal obligations and whom you treat as a potential enemy."[54]

This polar relation represents for Lévi-Strauss a characteristic inherent in any social relation. It represents a "universal situation" in which one is either part of a community formed by reciprocal obligations or else one is an enemy.[55] The fact that when strangers meet, enmity is presumed indicates that, for Lévi-Strauss, communities arise out of what can only be described as a Hobbesian need for security in a hostile world, a need for security so great that the individual will sacrifice his "naturally polygamous tendencies" in return for it.

Hobbes too has given an account of the organization of civil society by means of a covenant setting up a sovereign not subject to the laws of the community. In Hobbes's system, the scarce product is "power," and every man seeks ever more power over others. The war of each against all in the state of nature is changed by the covenant that institutes commonwealth from a situation in which there was equal insecurity of life and possessions to a situation where there was equal insecurity and equal subordination to the market.[56] While initially this may seem an extreme reading of Lévi-Strauss, one should recall his stress on the ways the incest taboo gives rise to alliance. And one should place him in the tradition of anthropological alliance theorists. One of the earliest and most important of these stated the situation in very Hobbesian terms:

> Among tribes of low culture there is but one means known of keeping up permanent alliance, and that means is inter-marriage. Exogamy, enabling a growing tribe to keep itself compact by constant unions between its spreading clans, enables it to overmatch any number of small intermarrying groups, isolated and helpless. Again and again in the world's history, *savage tribes must have had plainly before their minds the simple practical alternative between marrying-out and being killed out.* Even far in culture, the political value of inter-marriage remains.[57]

For Lévi-Strauss, as for Hobbes, community must be artificially yet necessarily always created through the imposition of human will on a natural order. More specifically, community is created through a social contract whereby terms are set for the exchange of valued commodities. Scarce goods, too, make their appearance. Due to the natural polygamous tendencies of men, the community created through the exchange of women is characterized by a scarcity of women, just as the community created through the exchange of commodities is characterized by the scarcity of commodities relative to demand. Men compete for women on equal terms, just as buyers compete with each other for commodities in market. This, Lévi-Strauss maintains, is true even when only a few men are allowed to possess most of the women.[58] Moreover, the men associate with each other for their mutual profit. Lévi-Strauss contends that the individual always "receives more than he gives" and "gives more than he receives."[59] In sum, Lévi-Strauss is arguing that all human groups are composed of the isolated individuals familiar to us from the social-contract theories of the seventeenth and eighteenth centuries. They associate with each other voluntarily, less for gain than for collective security.[60]

Thus, in positing exchange and mutual fear as the explanation for community Lévi-Strauss is suggesting that community, whatever form it takes, illustrates "the various modalities of one primitive need, the need for security."[61] On his account, and given the differences between the exchange of women and the exchange of commodities, it appears that the fragility of the social synthesis follows less from the exchange abstraction itself than from the operation of abstract masculinity. The social synthesis is made poorer by the fact that community is not an end in itself, but arises as a by-product of the search for security in a world seen as populated by hostile others. It is weakened as well by the fact that the integration of the perceived opposition of the self and other takes only indirect forms.

The hostile and combative dualism at the heart of this masculinist world view allows the creation of community with another only through the mediation of things. The Hegelian death struggle between self and other is prevented from occurring by the exchange of recognition carried in a person or object transferred between the two. The relations they construct, then, are only indirect. Lévi-Strauss's claim that this represents an "elemental" and "universal" condition betrays the abstract masculinity of his theory.[62] From a feminist standpoint, in which the self is understood as relationally defined, as constituted by a complex web of interactions with others, it seems perverse to deny a real connection with others and to argue that community can be constituted only indirectly, that men relate only through the mediation of things, that social relations are intentionally created by the act of passing things (most significantly, words and women) back and forth. Lévi-Strauss's work raises the question why even primitive men (at least as understood by Western anthropologists) have to (1) use women as mediators of their relations and (2) socially construct "others" who then must be socially transformed into kin by making the women of one's own clan "other."

The strangeness of all this is only a little compounded by the counterfactual on which the whole theory of the exchange of women rests: Women are not fully human. Why would reasoning, sign-producing beings, possessed of their own needs and desires, consent to becoming rather than possessing valuable objects? To becoming rather than producing signs?[63]

If we begin from the realities of women's lives, it is hard to imagine that women are not humans, but are the means by which humans (men) communicate and establish a social synthesis. On the basis of a division of labor analysis, one can see that the reality is the reverse. Women are not, as Lévi-Strauss would have it, the creation of an intentional act of the male mind, the invention of a symbol by means of which to construct society and to distinguish it from nature. Women are the literal and material producers of men, who in turn like to imagine that the situation is the reverse.

Lévi-Strauss's Marxism

The ridiculousness of Lévi-Strauss's claims to be making a contribution to Marxist theory should now be apparent, although this explanation flies in the face of Lévi-Strauss's own claims, as well as those of a number of commentators. Lévi-Strauss argues that he does not intend to question the primacy of the "infrastructure" or base and that he does not mean to give priority to superstructures, despite the attention he devotes to them. Moreover, he does "not at all mean to suggest that ideological transformations give rise to social ones. Only the reverse is in fact true. Men's conception of the relations between nature and culture is a function of modifications of their own social relations."[64]

Despite the fact that he does not mean to, Lévi-Strauss parts company with Marx on a number of fundamental grounds. First, he holds that production-based analysis applies only to historical (read Western) societies, and argues that others are based instead on blood ties and better understood through myth. He even seems to regret the technical progress Marx held essential to the possibility of communism. Second, he argues that "praxis" and "practice" are different and must be connected by the mediation of the conceptual framework. This not only runs counter to Marx's contention that theory and practice imply each other, but also leads Lévi-Strauss to transform the "mediation" into the primacy of the intellect in opposition to the primacy Marx gave to concrete human practice. This marks the third difference between Lévi-Strauss and Marx.

Lévi-Strauss contends that "all social life, however elementary, presupposes an intellectual activity in man of which the formal properties cannot, accordingly, be a reflection of the concrete organization of society."[65] Intellectual activity does not reflect the social organization of society; rather, it emanates from the intellect, the human mind ever the same and located outside history. Indeed, Lévi-Strauss has been characterized as "the very incarnation of the structuralist faith in the permanency of human nature and the unity of reason."[66] Marx, in contrast, had a historical concept of nature and a materialist concept of history. For Marx, human beings are at once social, historical, and natural beings. Because Lévi-Strauss rejects this view in favor of a permanent human nature, his materialism boils down to a positivist faith that humanity will eventually be understood as a series of chemico-biological processes.[67] Fourth, Lévi-Strauss's account of kinship as marking the boundary between nature and culture, as a solution to the opposition of self and other, indicates his assumption that human beings are not intrinsically social, but must intentionally construct a society. Marx explicitly rejected this assumption.

Finally, Lévi-Strauss parts company with Marx at the level of method. While he has been credited with employing Marx's method, his own descriptions of anthropology and linguistics make it abundantly clear that his method has far more in common with contemporary positivism than with Marxism.[68] Lévi-Strauss, unlike Marx, accepts the dichotomy of natural from social science. He remarks that "for centuries, the humanities and the social sciences have resigned themselves to contemplating the world of the natural and exact sciences as a kind of paradise which they will never enter."[69] Linguistics, however, is crossing the "borderline" into the natural sciences and is studying language in a "manner which permits it to serve as an object of truly scientific analysis."[70] Moreover, he contends that science requires value neutrality in order to be objective, another very "un-Marxist" contention.

The study of anthropology can only be scientific, he claims, if one "abstains from making judgments" that compare the objectives societies have chosen.[71] The anthropologist faces the dilemma of either contributing to the improvement of his own community, in which case he must condemn social conditions similar to those he is fighting against, wherever they exist, and "in which case he relinquishes his objectivity and impartiality. Conversely, the detachment to which he is constrained by moral scrupulousness and scientific accuracy prevents him criticizing his own society, since he is refraining from judging any one society in order to acquire knowledge of them all." The "thirst for universal understanding," he argues, "involves renouncing all possibility of reform."[72] He attempts to draw back from this dilemma by two means: (1) arguing that all societies contain a residue of evil, and that moderation should be used in considering customs remote from the West; and (2) advocating a Buddhist-inspired contemplation of "that tenuous arch linking us to the inaccessible," in "grasping . . . the essense of what it was and continues to be, below the threshold of thought and over and above society."[73] The only means he seems to see of escaping from positivism, then, takes the form of an escape into nonmeaning, and a glorification of the "scent that can be smelt at the heart of a lily [which] is more imbued with learning than all our books."[74]

Lévi-Strauss's thought, then, represents a contradictory amalgam that is at once deeply phallocratic, abstract, antimaterialist, ahistorical, and even mystical. Such a theory poses deep problems for both Marxists and feminists. And the implications of such a theory go far beyond the work of Lévi-Strauss himself and those who have used his work. Lévi-Strauss, after all, based his work on the dualist linguistic theories of Saussure, was a part of the structuralist tradition, and in turn influenced the development of poststructural "deconstructionism."[75] If the ancestry of contemporary deconstructionism is such, then despite the very real feminist commitments of many deconstructionists, one must ask about the effects theories such as Lévi-Strauss's have had on the understanding of symbol systems. How can such a theory be of use to feminist Marxists? One can only expect that those who have taken his theory as a base for their own, or have incorporated his theory into their own, will encounter a number of difficulties in putting forward a materialist account of women's oppression.

NOTES

1. See esp. Gayle Rubin, "The Traffic in Women: Notes on the 'Political Economy' of Sex," in *Toward an Anthropology of Women,* ed. R. Reiter (New York: Monthly Review, 1975); Simone de Beauvoir, *The Second Sex,* trans. H. M. Parshley (New York: Knopf, 1953); and Juliet Mitchell, *Psychoanalysis and Feminism* (New York: Pantheon, 1974).

2. Octavio Paz, *Claude Lévi-Strauss: An Introduction,* trans. J. S. Bernstein and Maxine Bernstein (Ithaca: Cornell University Press, 1970), pp. 133, 63, 5 respectively.

3. Respectively, Paul Ricoeur, cited in Paz, *Claude Lévi-Strauss,* p. 129; Rousseau's influence is mentioned by Edmund Leach, *Claude Lévi-Strauss* (New York: Viking, 1970), p. 35; and Thomas Shalvey, *Claude Lévi-Strauss: Social Psychotherapy and the Collective Unconscious* (Amherst, Mass.: University of Massachusetts Press, 1979), p. 59. Marshall Sahlins credits him with Hobbesianism in "The Spirit of the Gift," in *Stone Age Economics* (Chicago: Aldine-Atherton, 1972); Shalvey, p. 61, credits him as trying to synthesize Freud, Rousseau, and Marx and also devotes a chapter to Lévi-Strauss as socio-biologist.

4. Lévi-Strauss, *Tristes Tropiques,* trans. John and Doreen Weightman (New York: Atheneum, 1974), p. 315.

5. The quotations come from ibid., pp. 409, 407 respectively. They occur in the course of a more lengthy and very interesting argument that Islam is a barracks religion but also that it resembles Western society. "If one were looking for a barracks room religion, Islam would seem to be the ideal solution: strict observance of rules (prayers five times a day, each prayer necessitating fifty-genuflexions); detailed inspections and meticulous cleanliness (ritual ablutions); masculine promiscuity both in spiritual matters and in the carrying out of the organic functions; and no women" (p. 403). Buddhism, in contrast, is for Lévi-Strauss a female religion. As he discusses the temples of the Burmese frontier, he notes that the sculpture seems to be outside time and space, the sculptors perhaps in possession of "some machine for abolishing time." If any art has a right to be called eternal this is surely it. "It is akin to the pyramids and to our domestic architecture; the human shapes engraved in the pink, closegrained stone could step down and mingle with the society of the living. No statuary gives a deeper feeling of peace and familiarity than this with its chastely immodest women and its maternal sensuality which delights in contrasting mother-mistress with sequestered girls, both of which are in opposition to the sequestered mistresses of non-Buddhist India: it expresses a placid femininity which seems to have been freed from the battle of the sexes, a femininity which is also suggested by the temple priests whose

shaven heads make them indistinguishable from the nuns, with whom they form a kind of third sex, half parasitical and half captive.

"If Buddhism like Islam, has tried to control the excesses of primitive cults, it has done so by means of the unifying reassurance implicit in the promise of a return to the maternal breast; by this approach, it has reintegrated eroticism within itself after divesting it of frenzy and anguish. Islam on the contrary has developed according to a masculine orientation. By shutting women away it denies access to the maternal breasts: man has turned the female world into a closer entity. No doubt, by this means he too hopes to attain serenity; but he makes it depend on a principle of exclusion: women are excluded from social life and infidels from the spiritual community. Buddhism, on the other hand, conceives of its serenity as a form of fusion: with women, with mankind in general, and in an asexual representation of the divinity" (p. 407). This characterization seems very much influenced by Rousseau—the return to the modern-day noble savage by way of Buddhism. Note the traditional regional and sexual dichotomies: active/passive; West/East; and the characterization of the latter as female, placid, indistinguishable, and attempting fusion.

6. These two claims occur respectively in Claude Lévi-Strauss, *The Savage Mind* (Chicago: University of Chicago Press, 1966), p. 130; and idem, *Structural Anthropology* (New York: Anchor, 1967), pp. 336–37.

7. Paz, *Claude Lévi-Strauss*, pp. 50–51. He goes on to note that the texture of the screen is death—the need to distinguish between nature and culture contains "the echo and the obsession of knowing ourselves to be mortal" (p. 51).

8. Susan Griffin, *Woman and Nature* (New York: Harper & Row), p. 6.

9. Leach, *Claude Lévi-Strauss*, p. 32.

10. Lévi-Strauss, *Tristes Tropiques*, p. 413.

11. Lévi-Strauss, *Structural Anthropology*, p. 70.

12. Lévi-Strauss, *The Savage Mind*, pp. 9–10. See also Paz, *Claude Lévi-Strauss*, p. 133.

13. Lévi-Strauss, *The Savage Mind*, pp. 106, 75, 159.

14. Ibid., p. 217.

15. Ibid., pp. 75 ff. See also Leach, *Claude Lévi-Strauss*, p. 37.

16. Lévi-Strauss, *The Savage Mind*, p. 269. This represents a very interesting argument in favor of Sohn-Rethel's thesis that abstract thought required the previous introduction of exchange. There is also an interesting sexual overlay, since more than one theorist has argued that the inventions of the neolithic period—animal husbandry, pottery, weaving, preparation and conservation of food—were women's inventions, while modern science has been argued to spring from men's rather than women's experience. See Evelyn Fox Keller, "Gender and Science," and Sandra Harding, "The Gender-Politics Structuring the Scientific World View," in *Discovering Reality: Feminist Perspectives on Metaphysics, Methodology, and the Philosophy of Science*, ed. Sandra Harding and Merrill Provence Hintikka (Dordrecht: Reidel Publishing, 1981). See also Paz, *Claude Lévi-Strauss*, p. 117.

17. See Paz, *Claude Lévi-Strauss*, pp. 116, 133.

18. Leach, *Claude Lévi-Strauss*, p. 121.

19. Ibid., pp. 34, 41, 21.

20. Lévi-Strauss, *Structural Anthropology*, p. 32. He notes some difficulties, but hopes that it will be possible (pp. 37 ff).

21. The explicitness of this statement is Paz's. *Claude Lévi-Strauss*, p. 18.

22. Lévi-Strauss, *Structural Anthropology*, p. 60.

23. Ibid., pp. 60–61.

24. Lévi-Strauss, *The Savage Mind*, p. 123.

25. Ibid., p. 128. Put another way, natural species and manufactured objects are two mediating sets "which man employs to overcome the opposition between nature and culture and think of them as a whole" (p. 127). Cooking, too, for Lévi-Strauss is an activity that both separates and unites nature and culture, but discussion of this activity is not essential to my argument here. See Paz, *Claude Lévi-Strauss*, pp. 50 ff, for an account of the significance of the shared forms.

26. Paz, *Claude Lévi-Strauss*, p. 132, makes a part of this case. He, however, writes as an admirer of Lévi-Strauss. In addition, he argues—wrongly, I believe— that the products of culture are not for Lévi-Strauss essentially different from natural products. This, however, takes as given and correct Lévi-Strauss's dismissal of the concrete in favor of the formal.

27. Lévi-Strauss, *The Savage Mind*, p. 264.

28. See Leach, *Claude Lévi-Strauss*, p. 62, for the description.

29. Lévi-Strauss, *The Savage Mind*, p. 248. This latter phrase occurs as a part of Lévi-Strauss's argument against Sartre, an argument that one may finally understand all of life as a function of inert matter. The argument bears a certain and interesting resemblance to Stalin's deification of the "productive forces" in his *Historical and Dialectical Materialism*. The suggestion of transcendental objectivism occurs in Paz, *Claude Lévi-Strauss*, p. 129 ff.

30. Lévi-Strauss, *Tristes Tropiques*, p. 414.

31. See the discussion in Jean Piaget, *Structuralism*, trans. Chaninah Marchler (New York: Harper & Row, 1970), pp. 106–7, 112.

32. Lévi-Strauss, *The Savage Mind*, p. 254. This argument occurs in his largely well taken critique of Sartre.

33. Ibid., pp. 255, 257.

34. See Paz, *Claude Lévi-Strauss*, p. 133.

35. Ibid., p. 39. Italics in original.

36. Ibid., p. 132.

37. Ibid. I should make clear that my use of Paz's appreciation of Lévi-Strauss runs counter to his own intentions. He enthusiastically describes Lévi-Strauss's work as Marxism corrected by Buddhism. Of the last chapter of *Tristes Tropiques*, he says that there Lévi-Strauss's thought achieves "a density and transparency which might make us think of statuettes of rock crystal if it were not for the fact that it is animated by a pulsation which does not recall so much mineral immobility as the vibration of light waves" (p. 135).

38. Shalvey, *Claude Lévi-Strauss*, p. 62, in what appears to be a quotation of Lévi-Strauss without a citation.

39. Paz, *Claude Lévi-Strauss*, p. 136. While I confess that I do not find the latter contention so clearly present in the meditations at the end of *Tristes Tropiques*, the overall plausibility of Paz's sensitive reading is supported by Lévi-Strauss's argument that the "great deterministic laws" of the physical universe are "colonizing us on behalf of a silent world of which we have become the agents" (p. 391).

40. The exchange of women has a very interesting place in Lévi-Strauss's theory, since he notes that the exchange of women, unlike the exchange of words, is always "substantive" in part because unlike the illusory status of words as pure signs, women cannot become simply signs without value (see *The Savage Mind*, p. 106, and *Structural Anthropology*, p. 60). The real materiality of women's lives is reflected in Lévi-Strauss's treatment of the connection between marriage rules and eating prohibitions. The connection is not causal, of course, but metaphorical. And the source of the connection is the union of the sexes and the union of eater and eaten because both effect a "conjunction by complementarity," better described as the conjunction of opposites—e.g., the passive food is eaten by the active eater, etc. This leads Lévi-Strauss to take note of the familiar equation of males with "devourer" and female with "devoured or consumed." Interestingly enough, Lévi-Strauss recognizes the significance of the *vagina dentata* in mythology as direct rather than inverted coding (*The Savage Mind*, p. 106).

41. Claude Lévi-Strauss, *The Elementary Structures of Kinship*, trans. James Harle Bell, John Richard von Sturmer and Rodney Needham, eds. (Boston: Beacon Press, 1969), p. 233.

42. Ibid., p. 480.

43. Ibid., pp. 12–20, 30, 32. See also Paz, *Claude Lévi-Strauss*, p. 19.

44. Lévi-Strauss, *Kinship*, p. 490. See also his note in *Tristes Tropiques* (p. 317) that a society reduced to simplest expression is merely individual human beings. Lévi-Strauss notes that men have presented several solutions to the problem of the creation and maintenance of a community. Exogamy is one solution, and language itself is another. But Lévi-Strauss argues that words cannot serve very long the same role as the exchange of women. Words become common property and lose their value, impoverishing perception in the modern world (*Kinship*, pp. 496, 490). This view is no doubt one of the reasons he turns to myth to discover real meaning.

45. Lévi-Strauss, *Kinship*, pp. 37–38.

46. Ibid., p. 42.

47. Ibid., p. 39.

48. Ibid., p. 44.

49. Ibid., p. 84.

50. Ibid., p. 116.

51. Ibid., p. 481.

52. There are some problems with the isomorphisms, however, since if it is the case that the symbols produced by men turn on them and make use of men without their knowing it—myths speaking with each other, nature speaking with herself—then it might also be the case that Lévi-Strauss has not quite seen that the women exchanged as signs would form the real society, and make use of their exchangers for that purpose. But see note 40 above on the special status of women as material beings in the theory. See also Lévi-Strauss's recognition of the problem of seeing the exchange of words and women as isomorphic. The only way to resolve the contradiction created by the fact that certain terms have value both for the speaker and the listener "is in the exchange of complementary values to which all social existence is reduced" (*Structural Anthropology*, p. 61).

53. Lévi-Strauss, *Kinship*, p. 114.

54. Ibid., p. 482, quoted from E. E. Evans-Pritchard, *The Nuer* (New York: Oxford University Press, 1940), p. 183. See also Lévi-Strauss, *Tristes Tropiques*, p. 315, however, where Lévi-Strauss suggests that the providing of collective security is part of the "fundamental nature of social and political organization."

55. In the community, "one lays down one's arms, renounces magic, and gives everything away, from casual hospitality to one's daughter or one's property." (Quoted from M. Mauss, "Essai Sur le Don: Forme et Raison de l'Echange dans les Societies archaiques," *Annee Sociologique*, 1 (1925): 138, quoted in Lévi-Strauss, *Kinship*, p. 483.

56. See C. B. MacPherson, *The Political Theory of Possessive Individualism* (New York: Oxford University Press, 1962), pp. 84, 269; and Lévi-Strauss, *Kinship*, p. 54. I am not alone in seeing Lévi-Strauss as working from a Hobbesian model. See also Sahlins, "Spirit of the Gift."

57. Edward B. Tylor, "On a Method of Investigating the Development of Institutions; Applied to Laws of Marriage and Descent," *Journal of the Royal Anthropological Institute of Great Britain and Ireland* 18, (1888): 267. I am indebted to Kathleen Weston for locating this passage for me. (Her italics.)

58. See Lévi-Strauss, *Kinship*, pp. 39, 45, 37. Also see Sahlins, "Spirit of the Gift," on scarcity (pp. 1–39), in the original affluent societies: hunting and gathering groups.

59. Lévi-Strauss, *Kinship*, p. 30.

60. How ironic that a self-professed disciple of Rousseau should recapitulate the theory of the man Rousseau argues so strongly against!

61. Lévi-Strauss, *Kinship*, p. 868.

62. Ibid., p. 84.

63. One might attempt to say women did not consent but were forced. But this cannot get Lévi-Strauss off the hook, since he has argued that all power "originates in consent and is bounded by it" (*Tristes Tropiques*, p. 314). All feminists who have written about Lévi-Strauss, and Lévi-Strauss himself, have tried to argue that he was not maintaining that women were not human. Yet given his stress on the transaction of the exchange of women as a relation between men, and given the fact that only once in *The Elementary Structures of Kinship*, and in a single sentence, does he make the statement that women might be human, these arguments are unpersuasive. Consider the weight of his general case as I have laid it out in these pages. And consider such statements as the following: "Women are the most precious possession . . . above all because women are *not primarily* a sign of social value, but a *natural* stimulant; and the stimulant of the only instinct the satisfaction of which can be deferred, and consequently the only one for which, in the fact of exchange, and through the awareness of reciprocity, the transformation from the stimulant to the sign can take place" (*Kinship*, pp. 62–63).

One must balance statements such as this against his single statement that women are indeed human: "But woman could never become just a sign and nothing more, since even in a man's world she is still a person, and since in so far as she is defined as a sign she must be recognized as a generator of signs" (ibid., p. 496). Can one even say that there is a certain regretful tone about this statement? Would it not be simpler if "woman" (not women in all their empirical diversity but "woman" in all her mysterious splendor, one suspects) were simply a natural stimulant that could be transformed into signs?

64. Lévi-Strauss, *The Savage Mind*, pp. 130, 117. See also Lévi-Strauss, *Structural Anthropology*, pp. 330 ff.

65. Piaget, *Structuralism*, p. 107, quoting Lévi-Strauss, *Totemism* (Boston: Beacon Press, 1963), p. 96.

66. Piaget, *Structuralism*, p. 106.

67. Paz, *Claude Lévi-Strauss*, makes several similar points, but takes this not as a series of fundamentally important departures from Marx, but only as meaning that one would have to "stretch the term 'Marxist'" to cover Lévi-Strauss (pp. 113 ff).

68. Shalvey, *Claude Lévi-Strauss*, for example, holds that Lévi-Strauss employs dialectical materialism as a basis for his account of Bororo village structure since he argues that (1) the apparent structure is not the real one, (2) that understanding consists in reducing one type of reality to another and (3) that the hidden structure is always the diametrical opposite of the visible structure (p. 92). Shalvey also credits Lévi-Strauss with employing Marxist notions of praxis as the core of all the economic practices of society (p. 85). The account he gives of the Marxian notion of praxis, however, makes it clear that he had not understood Marx. Paz, who sees the strategy described above as more closely related to the influence of Freud, is more accurate.

69. Lévi-Strauss, *Structural Anthropology*, p. 69.

70. Ibid., p. 56.

71. Lévi-Strauss, *Tristes Tropiques*, p. 385. For a more complete account of the Marxian meaning of objectivity, see my "Objectivity and Revolution: The Unity of Observation and Outrage in Marxist Theory" (*mimeo*).

72. Lévi-Strauss, *Tristes Tropiques*, p. 386.

73. Ibid., p. 414.

74. Ibid.

75. See Fredric Jameson's discussion of the tradition in *The Prison-House of Language* (Princeton, N.J.: Princeton University Press, 1972).

nine

Gayle Rubin: The Abstract Determinism of the Kinship System

The discovery of sisterhood represented a necessary but not sufficient condition for the development of a materialist feminist analysis. Gayle Rubin's influential essay, "The Traffic in Women: Notes on the 'Political Economy' of Sex," generated a great deal of excitement both before and after its formal publication. It has been credited as being a kind of "watermark" for a Marxist feminist methodology, an essay that represented the beginning of a "much richer, more integrated analytical approach."[1] This essay has been one of the most widely and favorably cited the contemporary feminist movement has yet produced. Yet it is marred by the use of categories that locate it at the epistemological level defined by exchange, and suffers from some of the effects of abstract masculinity. Because of the importance feminists collectively have given to this essay, its problems should be regarded as collective ones, difficulties which arise from the fact that it was written and has been used in the context of a society itself deeply marked by the exchange abstraction. Thus, the problems to which I point here should be viewed as more general problems of feminist theory.

Rubin takes Lévi-Strauss and Freud as dual points of departure in pursuit of the project Engels "abandoned when he located the subordination of women in a development within the mode of production."[2] She pro-

poses to take over his method to identify the "relationships by which a female becomes an oppressed woman."[3]

Rubin recognizes the inadequacy of Marxism to account for the genesis
of the oppression of women; she rejects both those who subsume questions of women's oppression under the heading of the "woman question"
and those who point to the relationship between housework and the reproduction of labor to suggest that women's situation is an artifact of capitalism.[4] To explain women's usefulness to capitalism is one thing, she argues, but to argue that utility explains the genesis of oppression is
another. She chooses Lévi-Strauss and Freud because she sees in their
work the possibility of understanding a "systematic social apparatus
which takes up females as raw materials and fashions domesticated
women as products."[5] Her project as she describes it is to "isolate sex and
gender from 'mode of production,'" in order to counter those who tend to
see sex oppression as an outgrowth of economic forces, or, as she has put
it, to suggest that feminist theory should look for the "ultimate locus of
women's oppression within the traffic in women, rather than within the
traffic in merchandise."[6]

Rubin recognizes some of the dangers of the project she proposes. She
notes that the effort to borrow from structuralism and psychoanalysis in
order to carry on Engels's enterprise may lead to "a certain clash of epistemologies," that a "somewhat tortuous argument" is needed to integrate
them into feminist theory, and recognizes that her borrowing may have
brought in the sexism of the traditions, particularly since she has characterized both psychoanalysis and structural anthropology as "the most sophisticated ideologies of sexism around."[7] Unfortunately, Rubin's reliance on these theorists has indeed distorted her work. In an ironic echo
of Lévi-Strauss's contention that signs speak through and use human beings for their own ends, one might even say that Rubin, in attempting to
use his theory, has instead been used by it.

Specifically, her use of his account of the exchange of women leads her
to accept several of the specific dualities present in commodity exchange.
Thus she tacitly endorses the account of reality that grows from the practical separation of exchange from use, of quantity from quality, of interaction with nature from social interaction. She does not question the fundamental opposition of participants in exchange and as a result can provide
no alternative vision of a nonproblematic social synthesis.

In addition, like Lévi-Strauss, Rubin gives pride of place to the abstract
instead of the concrete and devalues material life activity in favor of the
production of symbols. The value she puts on the abstract as opposed to
the concrete leads her to reduce the material sexual division of labor to a
"taboo," to evaporate concrete social relations into systems of kinship understood as symbol systems, and finally to banish human activity alto-

gether as kinship systems assume the role of the "productive forces" of sex and gender. (This last move is curiously reminiscent of Stalin's doctrine of the primacy of the productive forces.) The concrete activity of real human beings is replaced by the operation of self-moving symbol systems. It is a curious confirmation of Lévi-Strauss's argument that the exchange of signs and the exchange of women recapitulate each other.

The result of the centrality of abstract symbol systems in Rubin's work is (1) acceptance of a gulf between nature and culture, and a stress on the primacy of the social, (2) the location of the oppression of women in the realm of ideology (taboo, convention) rather than in material life activity as structured by the division of labor. (3) Finally, Rubin, in adopting so many features of Lévi-Strauss's system of thought is implicated in several of his counterfactual claims, most specifically, that society is artificial, that women are signs, and that sex and gender are altogether distinct from each other.

Thus, despite Rubin's appropriately jaundiced view of Lévi-Strauss and his project, and despite her efforts to argue explicitly for recognizing sex/gender systems not as products of the human mind but as products of historical human activity, her effort to borrow his account of the exchange of women undermines her stated purpose. I do not mean to suggest that Rubin would endorse all the positions taken by Lévi-Strauss. Indeed, she explicitly rejects his idealism and is appropriately shocked by his treatment of women as words that are misused if not exchanged.[8] The real issues are the extent to which feminists can borrow from phallocratic ideologies without their own analyses suffering in consequence, and the extent to which feminist theory can take place without being relocated onto the ground provided by a specifically feminist epistemology.

Rubin's Reading of Lévi-Strauss

Rubin notes that anthropologists have long considered kinship to mark the discontinuity between semihuman hominids and human beings.[9] She proposes to adopt Lévi-Strauss's account of kinship, an account that rests on both the nature of the gift in primitive societies and the incest taboo. The two of them together, she argues, lead to the exchange of women. Unlike Lévi-Strauss, she does not choose to understand the exchange of women as definitional of culture, nor as a system in and of itself. Instead, she proposes to treat the kinship system as "an imposition of social ends upon a part of the natural world," and thereby define it as production in what she considers to be a Marxian sense: as a "transformation of objects . . . to and by a subjective purpose."[10]

Rubin chooses to modify Lévi-Strauss on several points in order to translate his theory of the exchange of women into a theory of the production of gender. First, she leaves out of her summary of his theory the "deep polygamous tendency" that Lévi-Strauss held responsible for creating the scarcity, and thereby the exchange of women.[11] Thus, her account of the exchange of women is detached from the force that set it in motion.

Second, she attempts to read Lévi-Strauss in too feminist a way, a reading that cannot be supported on the basis of her own account of his work. She credits him with positing a gendered human subject, and reinterprets kinship systems as not simply the exchange of women but as the exchange of "sexual access, genealogical statuses, lineage names and ancestors, rights and *people*—men, women, and children—in concrete systems of social relationships."[12] This is clearly contrary to Lévi-Strauss's intent but not a problem given her own purposes. It does, however, run counter to her argument that since it is the women who are being transacted, it is the men who are the partners in the social relation. And she quotes Lévi-Strauss to that effect.[13]

Here defense of women as not simply objects in the transaction only compounds the difficulties: To hold that objects in the primitive world are imbued with "highly personal" qualities indicates that she has accepted Lévi-Strauss's formula:

$$\frac{\text{women}}{\text{men}} \quad = \quad \frac{\text{words}}{\text{savage}}$$

Her acceptance of this formula, however, undermines her outrage at his contention that it is women's dual status as sign producers as well as signs, which explains why relations between women and men have preserved an "affective richness" and "mystery."[14] The imbuing of objects with personal qualities is what he is describing here, a position she has already endorsed. The source of the problem is the difficulty of using a theory that treats women as symbols and objects to analyze and expose systematic domination.

Third, because she wants to treat kinship as production, Rubin attempts to read Lévi-Strauss literally rather than metaphorically. Thus, she argues that "it is not difficult to find ethnographic and historical examples of trafficking in women," and proceeds to cite a number of instances.[15] It is worth remembering that Lévi-Strauss formulated his theory of the exchange of women out of his interest in the nature of symbol systems, most particularly his interest in formulating the laws governing the operation of the primitive mind. Rather than treat them as concrete social relations, Lévi-Strauss held that kinship systems were constructed by the mind at the level of unconscious thought.[16] Thus, each of these moves threatens to pose problems for Rubin.

The effort to treat kinship systems as a form of production is central to Rubin's effort, and this is where I center my attention. This is the means by which her theory is marred by association with Lévi-Strauss's symbol systems. Her explicit strategy is to carry on the series of transformations begun by Lévi-Strauss, from the construction of kinship systems by the exchange of women to the construction of gender by the kinship system. In fact, however, in the end her theory moves in the reverse direction—back to the system she has ignored, the construction of symbol systems by the human unconscious. Let us follow this progression (regression?) by means of which production becomes exchange and theory moves to the epistemological level of exchange, which in turn becomes exchange of women, which becomes the kinship system, which in turn becomes a symbol system, and in which, finally, as in Lévi-Strauss's work, the signs themselves seem to speak through persons.

Capitalist Production from the Perspective of the Exchange Abstraction

Rubin sees Marx's analysis of capitalist production as locating the key to the operation of the working class in the "traffic in merchandise." Her summary of the production and extraction of surplus value in capitalism is marked by an extraordinarily consistent focus on exchange. As a result, the material process of production involving interaction with nature, concentration on concrete qualities of real objects, and cooperation with others, vanishes. Instead, it is "the *exchange* between capital and labor which produces surplus value."[17] And the surplus value belonging to the capitalist no longer inheres in concrete products, but is represented by the purely quantitative difference between the amounts of goods necessary to reproduce labor power and the amounts of goods the labor force can produce.[18]

Even when she addresses production itself, her stress is always on the raw materials, factors of production, and the product, never on the lengthy process by which the one becomes the other. The accumulation of capital is described, then, as if from the perspective of the capitalist, whose world is constituted by a series of transactions, by buying and selling, and for whom the process of production is best conceptualized under the simple heading of "transformation."[19] The process of production, then, becomes "the system by which elements of the natural world are transformed into objects of human consumption."[20] Diverse and many-qualitied human activity in cooperation with others and interchange with nature has been replaced by an abstract "system."

Capital itself is redefined as something that "*reproduces* and augments *itself* by extracting unpaid labor, or surplus value, from labor and into itself."[21] This is a curiously disembodied and self-moving capital, obviously not close kin to the purchaser of labor power striding pridefully toward his factory, or "Moneybags" with whom Marx debates economic theory in the pages of *Capital*.[22] In Marx's analysis, capitalist production took place by means of the actions of specific individuals located in time and space. The capital Rubin describes is better understood as "abstract movement through abstract (homogeneous, continuous, and empty) space and time of abstract substances materially real but bare of sensequalities, which thereby suffer no material change and which allow for none but quantitative differentiation (differentiation in abstract, nondimensional quantity)."[23] This capital is not Marx's capital, but our old friend "Exchange" attempting to pass itself off as capital.

That capital should appear as abstract movement of abstract substances is not, of course, unique to Rubin's account. One can find important resemblances between this capital and the "productive forces" of economic determinism. They, like it, seem to need no human help to "select [social] structures according to their capacity to promote development," or even make "demands" and set requirements that humans must meet. For example, "the new productive forces require that the workers in production shall be better educated and more intelligent than the downtrodden and ignorant serfs, that they be able to understand machinery and operate it properly. *Therefore,* the capitalists prefer to deal with wage workers who are free of the bonds of serfdom. . . . "[24]

While one would have to force her analysis too far to claim that Rubin recapitulates economic determinist accounts of the operation of the productive forces, her summary of Marx comes uncomfortably close to doing so. This, then, is the reading of the Marxian account of production that structures Rubin's account of the operation of the kinship system. That the epistemological level of exchange and not production deeply structures Rubin's analysis of Marx as well as her understanding of kinship is underlined by the fact that when she calls for a Marxian analysis of sex/gender systems, she suggests that it should follow the lines of Marx's discussion of the evolution of money and commodities and does not mention his discussion of production.[25]

We have, then, completed the first transition that undermines the value of Rubin's theory: the inadvertent redefinition of production as exchange. Thus, even before she explicitly discusses the exchange of women, Rubin's work is marred by the presence of the exchange abstraction, with the concomitant attention to exchange rather than use, quantity rather than quality, and the opposition of nature to culture. (The transformation of objects by subjective purposes [production] will become in her discussion of the kinship system, the "seizing of control" of biology.) Her eventual destination is prefigured by her vision of a self-moving and disembodied capital which seemingly extracts surplus value without either the complex and many-qualitied processes of production or the intervention of human agents.

The Kinship System and the Production of Gender

Sex is the raw material the kinship system turns out as gender, females the raw material to be made women. But here we run up against a snag in the analogy between the kinship system and the productive forces. Production requires real changes in concrete objects in accord with human purposes and therefore involves both the natural and social worlds; kinship is purely a social phenomenon. This is of course one of the reasons Rubin finds it theoretically attractive, since it enables her to argue against those who would locate the oppression of women in their biological inferiority rather than their socially constructed oppression. This exclusively social character marks the next step, the transformation of exchange of women into kinship. The logic by which humans become the instruments of the signs they originally produced moves forward by means of the definition of a kinship system as a "system of categories and statuses which often contradict actual genetic relationships," an "invention." Thus, the production done by the system, the producing of gendered beings, is carried on by the operation of the categories of kinship.

Rubin's own discussion of the Nuer custom of "woman marriage" illustrates the purely social nature of kinship, as well as the fact that production of gendered beings is accomplished through the movement of categories. Among the Nuer, Rubin states, "a woman can be married to another woman, and be husband to the wife and father of her children, despite the fact that she is not the inseminator."[26] Her physical being, particular qualities as an individual, talents, and so forth, remain the same of course. Only her social classification has changed. Just as the concrete, quality-laden process of production vanished from Rubin's account of capital's self-expansion, so too women's concrete life activities vanish from the operation of the kinship system. All that matters is their abstract classification most fundamentally as either "same" or "different." All that is necessary for exchange is the sign of otherness. The possibility for persons to occupy statuses that do not reflect genetic relationships serves to underline the abstract and qualityless character of the symbols that constitute the kinship system.

Marx, of course, had encountered theories such as this. He described them as accounts of production "characteristic of philosophical consciousness," "for whom the movement of the categories appears as the real act of production." The system of categories is a "product of a thinking head," and "the real subject retains its autonomous existence outside the head just as before."[27]

Prob #2

We have, then, completed another step in the ascent into abstraction: the transformation of the kinship system into a symbol system. Only the final move remains to be made: the setting of the signs in motion. Rubin's reference to Lévi-Strauss's account of symbol systems as a "chess game" is stunningly apt.[28] We shall see that concrete human actors become instead chess pieces moved about the board by the inexorable forces of kinship. The chess pieces are, moreover, unconscious of the real character of their actions, since the requirements the kinship systems lay down for human beings are met by the oedipal phase of psychic development. "Kinship systems," Rubin states, "require a division of the sexes. The oedipal phase divides the sexes."[29] The kinship system, then (operating analogously to the productive forces of economic determinists), recruits the oedipal phase to its aid in transforming biologically sexed beings into gendered ones.

The final move has been made. One can perhaps begin to see that the category of kinship performs the same role in Rubin's theory as myth performed for Lévi-Strauss. For him, myth provides the lever needed to escape from history; for her, it is kinship. His escape from history rests in part on his positing of a permanent and universal structure inherent in the human mind; hers rests on the fact that she sees the exchange of women as operating across culture and history.[30] For him, myth must be understood as a "paralanguage" whose true meaning is unconscious; for her, the oedipal phase fulfills this role. He concludes that the originators of the myths do not know its meaning, that myths communicate with each other by means of men and without men knowing it; persons not only vanish but become instruments of that which they themselves produced. She seems to conclude that kinship systems, those human inventions, those socially constructed systems of categories, produce gendered human beings through the "mechanism" of the oedipal phase. For her, too, persons have become the passive instruments of the symbols they themselves produced. The death of subjectivity inherent in Lévi-Strauss's contention that myths speak to each other through the medium of men and without men knowing it here takes the form of the kinship system operating to produce gendered beings, without their full awareness.

Rubin's theory, then, begins its ascent into abstraction by giving centrality to the category of exchange. When coupled with the influence of Lévi-Strauss, the ascent becomes a flight. The myths that loom large over the terrain of Lévi-Strauss's theory are here replaced by an abstract and self-moving capital and a kinship system that serves not only as a mechanism for producing gendered beings but as a machine for the suppression of time and space and materiality.

Rubin's re-creation of Lévi-Strauss's system makes it impossible for her to give an account of women's oppression located in daily life activity, and instead requires that she locate its source in the purely social and even intellectual realm of ideology—in taboo, convention, and cultural tradition. Her use of the taboo on sameness is ambiguous. Whereas Lévi-Strauss indicated that it arose from the neurological structure of the human mind, Rubin gives no direct indication of the source for such a taboo. The oedipal phase is of course a good candidate. Rubin's location of the oppression of women in the realm of ideology is not something that must be "read out" of her text in the same way as her ascent into abstractness. She explicitly located "the entire domain of sex, sexuality, and sex oppression" in what Marx termed the historical and moral element in the determination of the value of labor power.[31] Marx was referring to the ways in which class struggle could affect the wages actually received by the worker, by raising or lowering the amount of labor time considered socially necessary. Rubin translates this as capitalism's "cultural heritage" of gender, thus seeming to locate this historical and moral element outside the structured relations of capital and labor altogether. But the question that remains is how sex oppression is structural rather than dependent on the specific state of the "battle of the sexes."

Rather than locate the oppression of women in the different activities performed by women and men, and the different consequences these have for roles in social organization, Rubin, following Lévi-Strauss, translates the division of labor by sex into a "'taboo': a taboo against the sameness of men and women," a taboo that itself creates difference.[32] The taboo is essential to the exchange of women, since they can only be exchanged on the basis of the sign of difference, and thus, "if Lévi-Strauss is correct in seeing the exchange of women as a fundamental principle of kinship, the subordination of women can be seen as a product of the relationships by which sex and gender are organized and produced."[33] Thus, and quite consistently with her intention, the oppression of women is located altogether in society rather than in biology. But Rubin's definition of society ends up locating the source of women's oppression in symbol systems rather than in the structure of material life activity, in systems of meaning rather than in systems of action.

As a result of her location of women's oppression in symbol systems, Rubin is led to posit a gulf between nature and culture, and thereby to implicate herself in the argument that society is artificial and the contention that sex is altogether different from gender. Thus, she seems to have adopted Lévi-Strauss's view that society is artificially constructed by means of a social contract memorialized in the kinship system. This is perhaps why she gives such prominence to "property" in the list of relations that characterize a kinship system. A kinship system, she states, "has its own relations of production, distribution, and exchange, which include certain 'property' forms in people."[34] Her inclusion of property as essential to the system is related to the stress she gives to exchange rather than production in her account of Marxian theory.

Property, after all, marks the separation the market makes of exchange from use.[35] One could read her to say that, given Mauss's and Lévi-Strauss's accounts of the exchange of women as the construction of community, the oppression of women results most centrally from the kind of problematic social synthesis that represents the only community possible on the model of exchange. The difficulty is that she never moves the discussion of the liberation of women beyond the suggestion that women might come to have "full rights to themselves."[36] "Rights" in oneself or to oneself limit one to a community constructed by property owners on the basis of mutual exclusivity of exchange and use, a community that is never anything but a relation between strangers whose creation of a social synthesis is only incidental to their intentional activity. And one must remember as well the fact that, as Mauss described the construction of the gift relation, it was an effort to circumvent the battle that might otherwise have occurred. The choice that led to exchange was that between exchange and war.

Thus, "rights" in themselves would free women to participate, like men, in the construction of a problematic and fragile social synthesis. It is difficult to determine whether this is in fact Rubin's vision of women's role in a more humane society, since her focus is so clearly on the oppression of women. The centrality of exchange in her thought, coupled with her several references to rights and her acceptance of the Mauss/Lévi-Strauss model of community, suggest that this will be so.[37] But real human beings, particularly women, are involved in and even constituted by social relations, and the notion of "rights" enters these relations (such as those between mothers and children) very late, if at all.[38]

Second, Rubin's treatment of sex as opposed to gender divides the two entirely: The one is entirely natural, the other entirely social; the one outside human control, the other subject to it. Kinship is the "seizing of control" of biology, and carries the connotation of making biology subject to human purpose. This overemphasis on the social and on the heterogeneity of society and nature is one source for Rubin's contention that "cultural evolution provides us with the opportunity to seize control of the means of sexuality, reproduction, and socialization, and to make conscious decisions to liberate human sexual life from the archaic relationships which deform it."[39] Given what she had said about the purely social location of women's oppression, and the central role she then seems to give to self-moving symbol systems, one wonders whether it is possible for humans to seize control.

Conclusion

I have attempted to demonstrate the ways feminist theorists can be led into abstraction by adopting theories built either on the categories central to the exchange abstraction or those which constitute abstract masculinity. A historical materialist feminism cannot be developed on the basis of the category of exchange. Nor can we build a materialist theory of women's oppression on the combative dualisms of abstract masculinity. Yet these categories have not only repeatedly proved attractive but have been the basis on which a number of feminist "classics" have been constructed. The high regard in which Rubin's essay "The Traffic in Women" is held indicates that large numbers of feminists hold similar views and have not seen the problems that can grow from taking exchange (whether of commodities, words, or women) as the most basic social relation. I have devoted so much critical attention to this essay in order to make clear the dangers these concepts pose for feminist theory, and to draw attention to their theoretical consequences.

An analysis that begins from the sexual division of labor—understood not as taboo but as the real, material activity of concrete human beings—could form the basis for an analysis of the real structures of women's oppression, an analysis that would not require that one sever biology from society, nature from culture, an analysis that would expose the ways women both participate in and oppose their own subordination. The elaboration of such an analysis cannot but be difficult. Women's lives, like men's, are structured by social relations that manifest the experience of the dominant gender and class. And feminists are not immune to the consequences of this fact.

NOTES

1. Rosalind Petchesky, "Dissolving the Hyphen: A Report on Marxist-Feminist Groups 1–5," in *Capitalist Patriarchy and the Case for Socialist Feminism,* ed. Zillah Eisenstein (New York: Monthly Review Press, 1978), p. 376.

2. Gayle Rubin, "The Traffic in Women," in *Toward an Anthropology of Women,* ed. R. Reiter (New York: Monthly Review Press, 1975), p. 169.

3. Ibid., pp. 169, 158.

4. Ibid., p. 160.

5. Ibid., p. 158.

6. Ibid., pp. 203, 175.

7. Ibid., pp. 159, 203, 208.

8. Ibid., pp. 204, 201.

9. Ibid., p. 170. One wonders why there must be a sharp discontinuity between humans and animals. Is this too an outgrowth of the masculinist project?

10. Ibid., pp. 176–77.

11. See my discussion above, Appendix 1, pp. 274 and n. 63.

12. Rubin, "Traffic," pp. 171, 177. See also p. 179.

13. Ibid., p. 174.

14. Ibid., p. 201.

15. Ibid., pp. 175–76.

16. Rubin's account of the operation of the kinship system and the oedipal phase seem to imply that she too holds the unconscious to be center. But perhaps this simply vitiates her own effort to read kinship systems literally.

17. Ibid., p. 161. (Italics mine.)

18. Ibid., p. 162. Her point, it is true, is to argue that housework is essential to reproducing the labor force. I have no problems with that, but I do have problems with the account of production that is not an account of production at all; rather, it is an account of the exchange of products. Cf. my discussion of production, pp. 116–126.

19. The term implies an instantaneous change, and indeed, from the perspective of the capitalist, it would be better if it were. See, for example, Marx's discussion of the impact of turnaround time on profit.

20. Rubin, "Traffic," p. 165.

21. Ibid., p. 161. (Italics mine.)

22. See, for example, Karl Marx, *Capital* (New York: International Publishers, 1967), 1:190 ff.

23. Alfred Sohn-Rethel, *Intellectual and Manual Labor* (New York: Macmillan, 1978), p. 53.

24. Italics mine. Joseph Stalin, "Dialectical and Historical Materialism," in Bruce Franklin, *The Essential Stalin* (Garden City, N.Y.: Doubleday, 1972), p. 325. The earlier quotation is from G. A. Cohen, *Marx's Theory of History: a Defence* (Princeton: Princeton University Press, 1978), p. 162. In fact, Rubin's account of production is perhaps more closely related to Althusser's definition of social practice itself as production—a "process of *transformation* of a determinate given raw material into a determinate *product*, a transformation effected by a determinate human labor, using determinate means (of 'production')." *For Marx*, trans. Ben Brewster (New York: Random House, 1970), p. 185. I have argued that Althusser has misunderstood Marx's account of production and that his understanding of the production of the concrete-in-thought runs directly counter to Marx's own statements. See Nancy C. M. Hartsock and Neil Smith, "On Althusser's Mis-reading of the 1857 Introduction," *Science and Society* 43, no 4 (Winter, 1978–80). Whether these practices are ideological, economic, political, or theoretical, for Althusser, their structure remains the same. Thus, Althusser describes the process of production of knowledge as involving three "generalities." Generality I is the precondition for scientific labor, the raw material to be transformed into knowledge. Generality II refers to the work done—although Althusser is unclear about whether this is simply the means of production or the labor process itself. Generality III is the knowledge produced through this process of transformation. The stress is on the distinction between Generality I and Generality III. Althusser's lack of clarity about the nature of Generality II marks his real lack of interest in the production process itself.

25. Rubin, "Traffic," p. 205.

26. Ibid., p. 169. See also p. 181.

27. Karl Marx, *Grundrisse*, trans. Martin Nicolaus (Middlesex, England: Penguin Books, 1973), pp. 100–102. Marx here is referring to Hegel.

28. Rubin, "Traffic," p. 171.

29. Ibid., pp. 124, 198. See also p. 199. I do not object to the statement that the oedipal phase divides the sexes. Indeed, this is congruent with my own analysis.

Rather, I object to the image of the cooperative oedipal phase racing to the rescue of the kinship system.

30. She draws back from claiming it is universal, but does hold that despite the fact that Lévi-Strauss's data base was non-modern, his description of the exchange of women is correct for modern society as well. In addition, she is attempting to formulate some basic generalities about the organization of human sexuality (ibid., pp. 170, 198, 83). Given the nature of her project, it is perhaps just as well that she wishes to isolate the sex/gender system from the mode of production (p. 198). One should also recognize the political reasons for doing so. When the article was written, it was necessary to respond to those who claimed that women's inferiority was "natural" and not social.

31. Ibid., p. 164.

32. Ibid., p. 178.

33. Ibid., p. 177. One wonders what she means by the organization of sex, as opposed to gender.

34. Ibid.

35. In addition, one should note that her formulation here clearly puts her in the camp of the dual systems theorists criticized by Iris Young in "Socialist Feminism and the Limits of Dual Systems Theory," *Socialist Review* 50–51 (Spring-Summer 1980).

36. Rubin, "Traffic," p. 177. See also her discussion of the strategy of separatism, which she sees as a claim by women of "rights in themselves" (p. 175).

37. If so, it would mean that, ironically, Rubin was back on the terrain she had attempted to avoid, a terrain defined by "the woman question" to which the solution is simply the provision of "democratic rights."

38. On the problematic and conflictual nature of "rights" as a means of organizing social relations, see Richard Flathman, "How Can We Possibly Justify Any Rights Whatsoever?" (mimeo, Department of Political Science, Johns Hopkins University, Baltimore, Md.)

39. Rubin, "Traffic," pp. 199–200. One wonders what the source for cultural evolution may be, as well as about whether there has been progress, since she has already said that Lévi-Strauss's exchange theories describe not only the primitive societies he was studying but Western society as well.

ten

Postmodernism and Political Change

Throughout the eighties, white North American feminist theorists were responding to arguments originating from radical women of color that feminist theory had to take more account of diversity among women.[1] Too much feminist theory was written from a perspective in which white middle-class women were seen as the norm and women of color were excluded. This had important effects on the theories white feminists developed. To give just one example, white feminist theory assumed a split between the private world of the family on the one hand and public life on the other. Yet Black feminists have pointed out that in the Black community there is often no private sphere protected from state intervention. Social workers, police, courts, and other state agencies all intervene on a scale that does not allow for a private familial world insulated from the state.[2] Feminist theory must take account of these structurally different situations. Note too, that given this example, it is not a matter of simply adding women of color and their situations to the list of things feminist theory is concerned about. The exclusion and inclusion of many different women will and must affect the concepts and theories themselves.

I believe that it was in part in response to these arguments that a number of feminist theorists found postmodernist theories attractive. Here were arguments about incommensurability, multiplicity, and the lack of definitive answers. These writings, many of them by radical intellectuals, ranged from literary criticism to the social sciences. The writers—Foucault, Derrida, Rorty, Lyotard, and others—argued against the faith in a universal reason we have inherited from Enlightenment European philosophy. They rejected stories that claimed to encompass all of human his-

205

The challenges by ♀ of color (♀ lesbians) in 1980s →adoption of pomo?

206   *Postmodernism and Political Change*

tory: As Lyotard put it, "Let us wage war on totality."[3] In its place, they proposed a social criticism that was ad hoc, contextual, plural, and limited.

Yet despite their own desire to avoid universal claims and despite their stated opposition to these claims, some universalistic assumptions have crept back into their work. Thus, postmodernist theorists, despite their efforts to avoid the problems of some forms of European modernism of the eighteenth and nineteenth centuries, manage at best to criticize these theories, without putting anything in their place. At worst, postmodernist theories can recapitulate the effects of Enlightenment theories that deny the right of some to participate in defining the terms of interaction. For those of us who want to understand the world systematically in order to change it, postmodern theories give little guidance. (I should note that I recognize that some postmodernist theorists are committed to ending injustice. But this commitment has not been not carried through in their theories.) Those of us who are not part of the ruling race, class, or gender, not a part of the minority that controls our world, need to know how it works. Why are we—in all our variousness—systematically excluded and marginalized?[4] What systematic changes would be required to create a more just society?

explanation of we – but before I read fn, I was thinking "what choo mean 'we,' white girl?"

The Enlightenment Tradition

Postmodernism is reacting against a particular body of thought that postmodernists argue is characterized by several important features. Most frequently, this body of thought is termed the "Enlightenment." The specifically modernist and Western tradition of political thought, a tradition that emerged in Western Europe over the past several hundred years, has been characterized by several distinctive epistemological features. First, the "god-trick" was pervasive: The tradition depended on the assumption that one can see everything from nowhere, that disembodied reason can produce accurate and "objective" accounts of the world.[5] Second, and related, the Enlightenment was marked by a faith in the neutrality of reasoned judgment, in scientific objectivity, in the progressive logic of reason in general and science in particular. Third, it claimed to assume human universality and homogeneity, based on the common capacity to reason. Differences were held to be fundamentally epiphenomenal. Thus, one could speak of human nature, truth, and other imperial universalities. Fourth, all this had the effect of allowing for transcendence through the omnipotence of reason. Through reason, the philosopher could escape the limits of the body, time, and space to contemplate the eternal problems related to man as knower. Finally, as a result of all this, Enlightenment political thought was characterized by a denial of the importance of power to knowledge and concomitantly a denial of the centrality of systematic domination in human societies. The subject/individual and power were held to be distinct.[6]

It is worth remembering that these fundamentally optimistic philosophies both grew out of and expressed the social relations of the expanding market/capitalist societies of Europe.[7] At the same time, many of the philosophers who were central to Western political thought also contributed to the development of ideologies that supported colonialism, the slave trade, the expansion of Western patriarchal relations, etc. One can recall J. S. Mill's statements about despotism's being a proper government for savages. Or Montesquieu's views about the effects of climate on human nature—to the detriment of those who lived in the tropics—and his use of the women of the harem as symbols of human depravity.

Thus, despite a stated adherence to universal principles, the epistemological and political thought of the Enlightenment in fact depended on the dualistic construction of a different world, a world onto which was projected an image of everything that ruling-class, European men wanted to believe they were not.

It must be remembered that this Eurocentric, masculinist, and capitalist world was constructed not only in theory but, more important, in fact through such practices as the Atlantic slave trade, the development of plantation agriculture in the New World, the introduction of markets and private property in Africa, the colonization of large parts of Asia, Latin America, and Africa, and the introduction of European forms of patriarchal and masculinist power. These were the means by which the domination of Europe, and later North America—the "rich North Atlantic democracies" as Richard Rorty has termed them—were institutionalized in fact as well as in thought. Inequality and domination were established in the name of universality and progress; ironically, power relations were institutionalized in and through a mode of thinking that denied any connections between knowledge and power or between the construction of subjectivity and power. The philosophical and historical creation of devalued Others was the necessary precondition, then, for the creation of the transcendent rational subject who could persuade himself that he existed outside time and space and power relations.

The Construction of the Colonized Other

In thinking about how to think about these issues, I found the work of Albert Memmi in *The Colonizer and the Colonized* very useful as a metaphor for understanding both our situation with regard to postmodernist theorists and the situation of some postmodernist theorists themselves: Those who have been marginalized enter the discussion from a position analogous to that which the colonized holds in relation to the colonizer. Most fundamentally, I want to suggest that the philosophical and historical creation of a devalued Other was the necessary precondition for the creation of the transcendental rational subject outside of time and space, the subject who is the speaker in Enlightenment philosophy. Simone de Beauvoir described the essence of this process in a quite different context: "Evil is necessary to Good, Matter to Idea, and Darkness to Light."[8] Although this transcendent subject is clearest in the work of bourgeois philosophers such as Kant, one can find echoes of this mode of thought in some of Marx's claims about the proletariat as the universal subject of history.[9]

Memmi described the bond that creates both the colonizer and the colonized as one that destroys both parties, although in different ways. As he drew the portrait of the colonized as described by the colonizer, the Other emerged as the image of everything the colonizer was not. Every negative quality was projected onto her/him. The colonized was said to be lazy, and the colonizer became practically lyrical about it. Moreover, the colonized was both wicked and backward, a being who was in some important ways not fully human.[10] As he described the image of the colonized, feminist readers of de Beauvoir's *Second Sex* cannot avoid a sense of familiarity. We recognize a great deal of this description.[11]

Memmi pointed to several conclusions drawn about this artificially created Other. First, the Other is always seen as "Not," as a lack, a void, as lacking in the valued qualities of the society, whatever those qualities may be.[12] Second, the humanity of the Other becomes "opaque." Memmi remarked ironically that the colonized had indeed to be very strange, if he remained so mysterious and opaque after years of living with the colonizer. Yet colonizers can frequently be heard making statements such as: "You never know what they think. Do they think? Or do they instead operate according to intuition?" (Feminist readers may be reminded of some of the arguments about whether women had souls, or whether they were capable of reason or of learning Latin.) Third, the Others are not seen as fellow individual members of the human community, but rather as part of a chaotic, disorganized, and anonymous collectivity. They carry, Memmi stated, "the mark of the plural."[13] In more colloquial terms, they all look alike. I want to stress once again that I am not claiming that women are a unitary group or that Western white women have the same experiences as women or men of color or as colonized peoples. Rather, I am pointing to a way of looking at the world that is characteristic of the dominant white, male, Eurocentric ruling class, a way of dividing up the world that puts an omnipotent subject at the center and constructs marginal Others as sets of negative qualities.

What is left of the Other after this effort to dehumanize her or him? She/he is pushed toward becoming an object. As an end, in the colonizer's supreme ambition, she/he should exist only as a function of the

arrogant perception

needs of the colonizer, that is, be transformed into a pure colonized, an object for himself or herself as well as for the colonizer.[14] The colonized ceases to be a subject of history and becomes only what the colonizer is not. After having shut the colonized out of history and having forbidden him all development, the colonizer asserts his fundamental immobility.[15] Confronted with this image in every institution and in every human contact, the colonized cannot be indifferent to this. The accusations in this picture worry the colonized even more because she/he both admires and fears the powerful colonizing accuser. We can expand our understanding of the way this process works by looking briefly at Edward Said's account of the European construction of the Orient. He made the political dimensions of this ideological move very clear: Said described the creation of the Orient as an outgrowth of a will to power. "Orientalism," he stated, "is a Western style for dominating, restructuring, and having authority over the Orient."[16]

Interestingly enough, in the construction of these power relations, the Orient is often feminized. There is, however, the creation—out of this same process of the opposite of the colonized, the opposite of the Oriental, the opposite of women—of a being who sees himself as located at the center and possessed of all qualities valued in his society (I use the masculine pronoun here purposely). Memmi described this process eloquently:

> The colonialist stresses those things that keep him separate rather than emphasizing that which might contribute to the foundation of a joint community. In those differences, the colonized is always degraded and the colonialist finds justification for rejecting his subjectivity. But perhaps the most important thing is that once the behavioral feature or historical or geographical factor which characterizes the colonialist and contrasts him with the colonized has been isolated, this gap must be kept from being filled. The colonialist removes the factor from history, time and therefore possible evolution. What is actually a sociological point becomes labeled as being biological, or preferably, metaphysical. It is attached to the colonized's basic nature. Immediately the colonial relationship between colonized and colonizer, founded on the essential outlook of the two protagonists, becomes a definitive category. It is what it is because they are what they are, and neither one nor the other will ever change.[17]

Said pointed to something very similar. He argued that "European culture gained in strength and identity by setting itself off against the Orient as a sort of surrogate and even underground self."[18] Orientalism is part of the European identity that defines "us" versus the non-Europeans. To go further, the studied object becomes another being with regard to whom the studying subject becomes transcendent. Why? Because, unlike the Oriental, the European observer is a true human being.[19]

The social relations that express and form a material base for these theoretical notions have been rejected on a world scale over the past several
decades. Decolonization struggles, movements of young people, women's
movements, racial liberation movements—all these represent the diverse
and disorderly Others beginning to demand to be heard and beginning to
chip away at the social and political power of the theorizer. These movements have two fundamental intellectual theoretical tasks—one of critique,
the other of construction. We who have not been allowed to be subjects of
history, who have not been allowed to make our history, are beginning to
reclaim our pasts and remake our futures on our own terms.

One of our first tasks is the construction of the subjectivities of the Others, subjectivities that will be both multiple and specific. Nationalism and
separatism are important features of this phase of construction. Bernice
Reagon (civil rights movement activist, feminist, singer with the band
Sweet Honey in the Rock, and social historian with the Smithsonian) described the process and its problems eloquently:

> [Sometimes] it gets too hard to stay out in that society all the time. And that's
> when you find a place, and you try to bar the door and check all the people
> who come in. You come together to see what you can do about shouldering
> up all of your energies so that you and your kind can survive. . . . That space
> should be a nurturing space where you sift out what people are saying about
> you and decide who you really are. And you take the time to try to construct
> within yourself and within your community who you would be if you were
> running society. . . . [This is] nurturing, but it is also nationalism. At a certain
> stage, nationalism is crucial to a people if you are ever going to impact as a
> group in your own interest.[20]

Somehow it seems highly suspicious that it is at the precise moment
when so many groups have been engaged in "nationalisms," which involve redefinitions of the marginalized Others, that suspicions emerge
about the nature of the "subject," about the possibilities for a general theory that can describe the world, about historical "progress." Why is it that
at the moment when so many of us who have been silenced begin to demand the right to name ourselves, to act as subjects rather than objects of
history, just then the concept of subjecthood becomes problematic? Just
when we are forming our own theories about the world, uncertainty
emerges about whether the world can be theorized. Just when we are
talking about the changes we want, ideas of progress and the possibility
of systematically and rationally organizing human society become dubi-
ous and suspect. Why is it only now that critiques are made of the will to
power inherent in the effort to create theory? I contend that these intellectual moves are no accident, but no conspiracy either. They represent the
transcendent voice of the Enlightenment attempting to come to grips with
the social and historical changes of the middle-to-late twentieth century.

However, the particular forms its efforts have taken indicate a failure of imagination and reflect the fact that dominant modes of thought remain imprisoned within Enlightenment paradigms and values. But these are simply questions. Let us look more closely at two efforts to describe the tasks we are told to engage in.

Richard Rorty's Conversational Alternative

Richard Rorty's contribution to postmodernist work deserves attention as a model for an account of what theorists might do. Fundamentally, Rorty argued against the epistemology of the Enlightenment—something he termed simply "Epistemology." (I read that as a statement that there always was only one way of knowing and to question that way of knowing is to question the project of knowing itself.) Rorty argued that the desire for a theory of knowledge was simply a desire for constraint. Moreover, it reflected an "overconfidence of theory." We had instead to "free ourselves from the notion that philosophy must center around the "discovery of a permanent framework of inquiry."[21]

Rather than view even normal science as the search for objective truth, he argued that we should see it as one discourse among others. One must reject a "tacit and self confident commitment to the search for objective truth on the subject in question." It was simply an error of systematic philosophy to think that such questions could be answered by some new transcendental discourse.[22] In addition, he argued against the notion of epistemology that assumes all contributions to a discourse are commensurable (one might substitute the notion of mutual intelligibility here). Rather, he argued for a recognition of cacophony and disorder. Epistemology told us that to be rational, that is, to be fully human, we must find agreement. But this assumes that such a common ground exists.[23] Rorty was confident that it does not. Thus, hermeneutics, his preferred mode of philosophizing, will redefine rationality as a willingness to abstain from epistemology, that is, to abstain from the idea that to be rational is to find the common set of terms into which all contributions should be translated if agreement is to become possible.[24] Hermeneutics is not to be a successor subject to epistemology; rather it represents the hope that the cultural space left by the demise of epistemology will not be filled.[25] Thus, it represents the abandonment of certain values—rationality, disinterestedness, of the possibility of floating free of educational and institutional patterns of the day.[26]

Moreover, we must give up the notion that there is a human essence; we must give up the idea of a search for the truth and simply try to redescribe ourselves yet again. This entails giving up the idea that any vocabulary has some privileged attachment to reality, and downgrading the acquisition of truth. That is, we must abandon the notion of correspondence to reality in the case of sentences as well as ideas. We must see sentences as "connected with other sentences rather than with the world."[27] Finally, Rorty argued that philosophers should give up the task of being constructive. Instead they should take up an oppositional reactive stance, should be skeptical about systematic philosophy.[28]

Rorty, then, was proposing an interesting but dangerous mix of ideas. He was attacking the transcendent knower who exists outside time and space, who has privileged access to true knowledge. Those of us who were marginalized, by our very acts of daring to speak, attacked the figure of this knower—whether we were conscious of it or not. Rorty, then, would seem to be involved in a project that is friendly to our own.

But to develop a better sense of whether the epistemological approach he advocated can be of use to us, let us examine the positive content of what he was suggesting. How would a hermeneutic approach work? Rorty proposed the notion of culture as conversation rather than as a structure erected upon foundations.[29] The conversation was to be about what he termed "edification"—"finding new, better, more interesting, more fruitful ways of speaking."[30] The point of doing philosophy, then, should be seen as continuing a conversation that is developing a program rather than discovering truth. We must avoid the self-deception that comes from believing that we know ourselves by knowing a set of objective facts and must avoid the notion that we are really different from "either inkwells or atoms."[31] Inquiry, then, should proceed on the ground that persons in conversation are simply those whose paths through life have fallen together, united by civility rather than by a common goal, much less by a common ground.[32]

Using an analogy to Kuhn's distinction between normal and revolutionary science, Rorty proposed a distinction between normal and "abnormal" discourse. Normal science is the practice of solving problems against the background of a consensus about what counts as a good explanation and about what it would take for a problem to be solved. Revolutionary science, in contrast, represents the introduction of a new paradigm indicating what is to count as a good explanation. By analogy, abnormal discourse is what happens when someone joins the conversation who is ignorant of these conventions—or who chooses to set them aside. The product could be nonsense or intellectual revolution.[33] One wonders how one could tell the difference in Rorty's system. Hermeneutics, then, is the study of these abnormal discourses through the creation of another abnormal discourse. As such it must be reactive and dread the possibility of being institutionalized. "Great edifying philosophers are reactive and offer satires, parodies and aphorisms. They know their work loses its point when the period they were reacting against is over. They are intentionally peripheral."[34]

Rorty argued that edifying philosophers should avoid having views, should "decry the notion of having a view while avoiding having a view about having views."[35] The proper image is one of edifying philosophers as conversational partners rather than as holding views on subjects of common concern. Moreover, the edifying philosopher wants to use the conversation to expand the community—that is, to see knowledge connected with solidarity rather than with power. One should, he argued, operate from an "ungroundable but vital sense of human solidarity," moral hope rather than a claim about what we may know of the world.[36]

This, then, is his critique of the transcendent subject of the Enlightenment and his alternative project for philosophy. Many postmodernists and many of the marginalized Others could agree with his critique. Yet, the alternative he proposed cannot fulfill the tasks we have in front of us. Indeed, despite its appearance of allowing space for many voices in the conversation, the effect of ideas like this is to smuggle back in the authority of the transcendental ego.

I have a number of problems with Rorty's argument. There are internal inconsistencies in his proposal—more interesting to me as a political philosopher than for my purposes here. My relevant objections to this methodology as something of value to minority discourses rest on several points. First, Rorty ignored power relations: We are not all in a position to participate as equals in a conversation. Many of us have not yet had a chance to name ourselves and our situations.[37] Second, Rorty set out to be reactive, unconstructive, and peripheral. But those of us who have been marginalized are all too familiar with the powerlessness that limits our options. Rorty was, in a sense, choosing to be marginal—a good thing for someone at the center but not for those at the margins, who have been forced to be reactive, unconstructive, and peripheral.

Third, and related, his substitution of "abnormal discourse" for Kuhn's concept of "revolutionary science" represents an important shift: It is a retreat from the idea that we are seeing historical agency and action. Fourth, Rorty chose to defend the values of the Enlightenment on the basis that they have produced good outcomes. Yet these values cannot be defended without dragging in again the omnipotent subject created by the Enlightenment.

Let us take up these objections in turn. Rorty invited us to join his conversation, but in a style reminiscent of the transcendent Enlightenment subject he inveighed against, he set the rules of the discussion in a way inappropriate to those of us who have been marginalized. Moreover, the notion of a conversation implies that we are all equally able to participate, that we are not marked by cultural and historically constructed differences. One is reminded of bell hooks's point about racism in feminist writing. "The force that allows white authors to make no reference to racial identity in their books about 'women' that are in actuality about white women is the same one that would compel any author writing exclusively on black women to refer explicitly to their racial identity." Hooks continued: "It is the dominant race that reserves for itself the luxury of dismissing racial identity while the oppressed race is made daily aware of their racial identity. It is the dominant race that can make it seem that their experience is representative."[38]

From being constructed as void, lack, forbidden to speak, we are now expected to join in equal conversation with someone who has just realized that philosophy has been overconfident. Rorty, with other postmodernists, had been the inheritor of the disembodied, transcendent voice of Reason. It was certainly a good thing for him to have abandoned the project of defining the world for everyone and instead to have proposed a conversation. But it will not work: Conversation implies the presence of subjects—contingent, historically limited subjects, to be sure—but subjects who can speak. But the silenced Others are just learning to speak, learning to name the world.

Let us turn to Rorty's second prescription for philosophy: that it should strive to be reactive and peripheral. Here, too, this is a good strategy for the inheritor of the voice of transcendental ego. Becoming marginal is an important and useful strategy for those of us who are privileged by race, class, gender, or heterosexuality. But for those of us who have been constituted as Other, it is important to insist as well on a vision of the world in which we are at the center rather than at the periphery. The "center" will obviously look different when occupied by women and men of color and white women than it does when occupied as now by white men of a certain class background. But as for being peripheral, we've done that for far too long. Let those who have put themselves at the center practice moving to the margins now.

Third, and related, Rorty proposed the idea of abnormal discourse as a modification of Thomas Kuhn's normal versus revolutionary science. Although he intended this to counter the hegemonic, normal, discourse of the suprahistorical subject, the substitution of "abnormal" for "revolutionary" is not innocent. Revolutionary science, or the more precise parallel, revolutionary discourse, would not necessarily remain peripheral but rather would transform normal discourse. This in fact is a much more appropriate formulation of our task. We should undertake the construction of revolutionary discourse that would not remain abnormal or peripheral but that would have the effect of transforming "normal" discourse.

Fourth, Rorty chose to defend the values of the Enlightenment and thus demonstrate his commitment to the project of the Enlightenment—that is, he brought in the project of the Enlightenment through the backdoor while claiming to get rid of it. These values have a homogenizing effect—

producing a homogeneous equality that fails to recognize the specificity of different communities. The overall result is that the Others constructed by the Enlightenment are once again silenced in the name of a rejection of the methods, if not the values, of the Enlightenment. To use the terms of Albert Memmi, Rorty can be perhaps described, not as the colonizer who consents, but as the citizen of the metropole who says: "But we gave them their independence. Why do they keep complaining about neocolonialism? Why do they keep bringing up questions of power?"

Foucault's Resistance and Refusal

Foucault represents another of the several figures of Memmi's landscape. I have so far spoken only of the colonizer and the colonized, and these are indeed the basic structural positions. But Memmi made an important distinction between the colonizer who accepts and the colonizer who refuses. If modernist theories, as a group, represent the views of the colonizer who accepts, postmodernist ideas can be understood as divided between two views: those who, like Richard Rorty, ignore the power relations and theorists such as Foucault, who, I would argue, represents Memmi's colonizer who refuses and thus exists in a painful ambiguity. The latter is, therefore, a figure who also fails to provide an epistemology that is usable for the task of revolutionizing, creating, and constructing.

Memmi stated that as a Jewish Tunisian he was in a position to know the colonizer as well as the colonized, and so "understood only too well (the difficulty of the colonizer who refuses) their inevitable ambiguity and the resulting isolation; more serious still, their inability to act."[39] He noted that it was difficult to escape from a concrete situation and to refuse its ideology while continuing to live in the midst of the concrete relations of a culture. The colonizer who attempts it is a traitor, but he is still not the colonized.[40] The political ineffectiveness of the Left colonizer comes from the nature of his position in the colony. Has one, Memmi asked, ever seen a serious political demand that did not rest on concrete support of people or money or force? The colonizer who refuses to become a part of his group of fellow citizens faces the difficult political question of who might he be.[41]

This lack of certainty and power infuses Foucault's work most profoundly in his methodological texts. He was clearly rejecting any form of discourse that could be characterized as totalizing: Reason, he argued, had to be seen as born from chaos, truth as simply an error hardened into unalterable form in the long process of history. He argued for a glance that dispersed and shattered the unity of man's being through which he sought to extend his sovereignty.[42] That is, Foucault appeared to endorse a rejection of modernity. Moreover, he engaged in social activism around prisons. His sympathies were obviously with those over whom power was exercised, and he suggested that many struggles could be seen as linked to a revolutionary working-class movement.

In addition, his empirical critiques in works such as *Discipline and Punish* powerfully unmask coercive power. Yet they do so by making use of the values of humanism that he claimed to be rejecting: That is, as Nancy Fraser pointed out, the project gets its political force from "the reader's familiarity with and commitment to modern ideals of autonomy, dignity, and human rights."[43] Moreover, Foucault explicitly attempted to limit the power of his critique by arguing that unmasking power could have only destabilizing rather than transformative effects.[44] But the sense of powerlessness and the isolation of the colonial intellectual resurfaces again and again. Thus, Foucault argued: "Humanity does not gradually progress from combat to combat until it arrives at universal reciprocity, where the rule of law finally replaces warfare; humanity installs each of its violences in a system of rules and thus proceeds from domination to domination."[45] Moreover, Foucault saw intellectuals as working only alongside rather than directly with those who struggle for power, working locally and regionally. Finally, in opposition to modernity, he called for a history that was parodic, dissociative, and satirical. These must be seen as positive steps that expressed Foucault's opposition to relations of the colonizer to the colonized. But what is the positive result?

Foucault was a complex thinker whose situation as a colonizer who resists imposes even more complexity and ambiguity on his ideas. I do not pretend to present a comprehensive account of his work here but rather to make just two arguments. First, despite his obvious sympathy for those who are subjugated in various ways, he wrote from the perspective of the dominator, "the self-proclaimed majority." Second and related, perhaps in part because power relations are less visible to those who are in a position to dominate others, systematically unequal relations of power ultimately vanish from Foucault's account of power—a strange and ironic charge to make against someone who was attempting to illuminate power relations.

Before I make these arguments I should insert some qualifications. It should be noted that Foucault himself might have recognized that he was in the position of the colonizer who resists. He recognized that some important features of the intellectual landscape had changed in the past decades. He noted that the most recent period had been characterized by a variety of dispersed and discontinuous offensives and an "insurrection of subjugated knowledges."[46] He added: "What has emerged is a sense of . . . the increasing vulnerability to criticism of things, institutions, practices, discourses. A certain fragility has been discovered in the very bedrock of existence . . . even . . . [those] aspects of it that are most familiar, most solid, and most intimately related to our bodies and to our everyday behavior."[47] At another point in the same essay, he referred to contemporary intellectuals as "fragile inheritors." Thus, one might argue that Foucault himself recognized the effects of decolonization and the revolt of many dominated groups. All this can only make my argument that he did not offer a theory of power adequate to the analysis of gender more difficult to support.

I will go even further and note that Foucault made a number of important contributions to our understanding of contemporary social relations. One can cite his accounts of the development of the confession as a means of producing power by requiring those who are to be dominated to take the initiative. One can note as well his substitution of domination/subjugation for the traditional problem of sovereignty/obedience. In addition, his development of the concept of disciplinary power, a power that possesses, in a sense, the same possibilities for expansion as capital itself, marks a major advance. One might continue to enumerate his contributions, but I will leave that to his disciples. Instead, what I want to argue here is that Foucault reproduced in his work the situation of the colonizer who resists and in so doing rendered his work inadequate and even irrelevant to the needs of the colonized or the dominated. So, let me return to the two central points I want to make.

Foucault's Perspective

Reading Foucault persuades me that Foucault's world is not mine but is instead a world in which I am made to feel profoundly alien. Indeed, when he argued that this was our world, I was reminded of a joke told about two U.S. comic book figures—the Lone Ranger and Tonto, "his faithful Indian companion" (and subordinate). As the story goes, the two are chased and then surrounded by hostile Indians. As the Lone Ranger comes to recognize their danger, he turns to Tonto and asks, "What do we do now?" To which Tonto replies, "What do you mean, 'we,' white boy?" Foucault's is a world in which things move, rather than people, a world in which subjects become obliterated or, rather, recreated as objects, a world in which passivity or refusal represent the only possible choices. Thus, Foucault was able to write that the Catholic institution of confession "detached itself" from religion and "emigrated" toward pedagogy,[48] or he could note that "hypotheses offer themselves."[49] Moreover, he argued that subjects not only ceased to be sovereign but also that external forces such as power were given access even to the body and thus were the forces that constitute the subject as a kind of effect.[50]

Edward Said has argued that one's concept of power is shaped by the reason why one wishes to think about power in the first place. He went on to set out several possibilities. First, you might imagine what you could do if you had power. Second, you might speculate about what you would imagine if you had power. Third, you might want to assess what power you would need to initiate a new order. Or, fourth, you might want to postulate a range of things outside any form of power we presently understand. Foucault, he argued correctly, was attracted by the first two. Thus Foucault's imagination of power was "with" rather than "against" power.[51] Said gave no "textual" evidence to support his assertions. But I believe there are a number of indications that Foucault was "with power," that is, understood the world from the perspective of the ruling group. First, from the perspective of the ruling group, other "knowledges" would appear to be illegitimate or "not allowed to function within official knowledge," as Foucault himself said of workers' knowledge.[52] They would appear to be, as Foucault variously categorized them, "insurrectionary," "disordered," "fragmentary," lacking "autonomous life."[53] To simply characterize the variety of "counterdiscourses" or "antisciences" as nonsystematic negates the fact that they rest on organized and indeed material bases.[54] Second, and related, Foucault called only for resistance and exposure of the system of power relations. Moreover, he was often vague about what exactly this meant. Thus, he argued only that one should "entertain the claims" of subjugated knowledges or bring them "into play."[55] Specifically, he argued that the task for intellectuals was less to become part of movements for fundamental change and more to struggle against the forms of power that could transform these movements into instruments of domination.

Perhaps this stress on resistance rather than transformation was due as well to Foucault's profound pessimism. Power appeared to him as ever-expanding and invading. It may even attempt to "annex" the counterdiscourses that have developed.[56] The dangers of going beyond resistance to power are nowhere more clearly stated than in Foucault's response to one interviewer who asked what might replace the present system. He responded that even to imagine another system was to extend our participation in the present system. Even more sinister, he added that perhaps this was what happened in the Soviet Union, thus suggesting that Stalinism might be the most likely outcome of efforts at social transformation.[57] Foucault's insistence on simply resisting power was carried even further in his arguments that one must avoid claims to scientific knowledge. In particular, one should not claim Marxism as a science because to do so would invest it with the harmful effects of the power of science in modern culture.[58] Foucault, then, despite his stated aims of producing an account of power that would enable and facilitate resistance and opposition, instead adopted the position of what he termed official knowledge with regard to the knowledge of the dominated, and he reinforced the relations of domination in our society by insisting that those of us who have been marginalized remain at the margins.

The Evanescence of Power

Despite Foucault's efforts to develop an account of power, and precisely because of his perspective as the colonizer who resists, systematic power relations ultimately vanish in his work. This is related to my first point: Domination, viewed from above, is more likely to appear as equality. Foucault had a great deal to say about what exactly he meant by power. Power must be understood in the first instance as the multiplicity of force relations immanent in the sphere in which they operate and which constitute their own organization; as the process that, through ceaseless struggles and confrontations, transforms, strengthens, or reverses them; or on the contrary, the disjunctions and contradictions that isolate them from one another; and lastly, as the strategies in which they take effect.[59]

(A very complicated definition!) He went on to argue that power was "permanent, repetitious, and self reproducing. It is not a thing acquired but rather exists in its exercise. Moreover power relations are not separate from other relations but are contained within them." At the same time (and perhaps contradictorily), power relations are both intentional and subjective, although Foucault was careful to point out that there was no headquarters that sets the direction.[60] His account of power is perhaps unique in that he argued that wherever there was power, there was resistance.

Much of what Foucault had to say about power stresses the systemic nature of power and its presence in multiple social relations. At the same time, however, his stress on heterogeneity and the specificity of each situation led him to lose track of social structures and instead to focus on how individuals experience and exercise power.[61] Individuals, he argued, circulate among the threads of power. They "are always in the position of simultaneously undergoing and exercising this power." Individuals were not to be seen as an atom that power strikes, but rather the fact that certain bodies and discourses were constituted as individuals, or subjects, was to be understood as an effect of power. Thus, power must not be seen as either a single individual dominating others or as one group or class dominating others.[62]

With this move, Foucault made it very difficult to locate domination, including domination in gender relations. He claimed that individuals were constituted by power relations, but he argued against their constitution by relations such as the domination of one group by another. That is, his account makes room only for abstract individuals, not women, men, or colonized peoples.

Foucault took yet another step toward making power disappear when he proposed the image of a net as a way to understand power. For example, he argued that the nineteenth-century family had to be understood as a "network of pleasures and powers linked together at multiple points," a formulation that fails to take account of the important power differentials within the family or the legal history of "couverture."[63] The image of the net ironically allows (even facilitates) his obfuscation of power relations at the same time as he was claiming to elucidate them. Thus, he argued that power was exercised generally through a "net-like organization" and that individuals "circulate between its threads."[64] Domination is not a part of this image; rather, the image of a network in which we all participate carries implications of equality and agency rather than the systematic domination of the many by the few.

Moreover, at times Foucault seemed to suggest that not only were we equals but that those of us at the bottom were in some sense responsible for our situations: Power, he argued, came from below. There is no binary opposition between rulers and ruled, but rather manifold relations of force that take shape in the machinery of production or in families and so forth, and then become the basis for "wide ranging effects of cleavage that run through the social body as a whole."[65] Certainly in the analysis of power, Foucault argued that rather than begin from the center or the top—sovereignty—one should conduct an ascending analysis of power, starting from the "infinitesimal mechanisms," each of which has its own history. One can then see how these have been transformed into more global forms of domination. It is certainly true that dominated groups participate in their own domination. But rather than stop with the fact of participation, we would learn a great deal more by focusing on the means by which this participation is exacted.[66] Foucault's argument for an ascending analysis of power could lead us to engage in yet another version of blaming the victim.

Finally, Foucault asserted that power must be understood as "capillary," that it must be analyzed at its extremities.[67] He gave the example of locating power not in sovereignty but in local material institutions, such as torture and imprisonment. But the image of capillary power is one that points to the conclusion that power is everywhere. After all, in physical terms, where do we not have capillaries? Indeed, Foucault frequently used language that argued that power "pervades the entire social body," or was "omnipresent."[68] Thus, all of social life comes to be a network of power relations—relations that should be analyzed not at the level of large-scale social structures but rather at very local, individual levels. Moreover, Foucault noted important resemblances between such diverse things as schools and prisons, or the development of sexuality in the family and the institutions of "perversion." The whole thing comes to look very homogeneous. Power is everywhere, thus ultimately nowhere.

In the end, Foucault appeared to endorse a one-sided wholesale rejection of modernity and to do so without a conception of what was to replace it. Indeed, some have argued persuasively that because Foucault refused both the ground of foundationalism and the "ungrounded hope" endorsed by liberals such as Rorty, he stood on no ground at all and thus failed to give any reasons for resistance. Foucault suggested that if our resistance succeeded, we would simply be changing one discursive identity for another and in the process create new oppressions.[69]

The "majority" and those like Foucault who adopt the perspective of the "majority," or the powerful, can probably perform the greatest possible political service by resisting and by refusing the overconfidence of the past. But the message we get from them is either that we should abandon the project of modernity and substitute a conversation (as Richard Rorty suggested) or that we should simply take up a posture of resistance as the only strategy open to us. But if we are not to abandon the project of creating a more just society, neither of these options will work for us.

Toward Liberatory Theories

Those of us who have been marginalized by the voice of universalizing theory need to do something other than ignore power relations, as Rorty did, or resist them, as figures such as Foucault and Lyotard have suggested. We need to transform them, and to do so, we need a revised and reconstructed theory (indebted to Marx, among others) with several important features.

First, rather than getting rid of subjectivity or notions of the subject, as Foucault did, and substituting his notion of the individual as an effect of power relations, we need to engage in the historical, political, and theoretical process of constituting ourselves as subjects as well as objects of history. We need to recognize that we can be the makers of history as well as the objects of those who have made history. Our nonbeing and invisibility was the condition for the taken-for-granted ability of one small segment of the population to speak for all; our various efforts to constitute ourselves as subjects (through struggles for colonial independence, racial and sexual liberation struggles, and so on) were fundamental to creating the preconditions for the current questioning of universalist claims.

In this task, the work of Antonio Gramsci can be very helpful. He suggested that we should reform the concept of the individual to see individuals as "series of active relationships, a process in which individuality, though perhaps the most important, is not the only element to be taken into account." Instead, one must see each of us as an "ensemble" of social relationships. "To create one's personality means to acquire consciousness of them and to modify one's personality means to modify the ensemble of these relations."[70]

We need to sort out who we really are. Put differently, we need to dissolve the false "we" I have been using into its real multiplicity and variety and out of this concrete multiplicity build an account of the world as seen from the margins, an account that can expose falseness of the view from above. The point is to develop an account of the world that treats our perspectives not as subjugated, insurrectionary, or disruptive knowledges but as potentially constitutive of a different world.

It may be objected that I am calling for the construction of another totalizing and falsely universal discourse. But that is to be imprisoned by the alternatives imposed by Enlightenment thought and postmodernism: Either one must adopt the perspective of the transcendental and disembodied voice of "reason" or one must abandon the goal of accurate and systematic knowledge of the world. Other possibilities exist and must be (perhaps can only be) developed by hitherto marginalized voices. Moreover, our history of marginalization will work against creating a totalizing discourse. This is not to argue that oppression creates "better" people: On the contrary, the experience of domination and marginalization leaves many scars. Rather, it is to note that marginalized groups are less likely to mistake themselves for the universal "man." We are well aware that we are not the universal man who can assume his experience of the world is the experience of all. But we still need to name and describe our diverse experiences. What are our commonalities? What are our differences? How can we transform our imposed Otherness into a self-defined specificity?[71]

Second, we must do our work on an epistemological base that indicates that knowledge is possible—not just conversation or a discourse on how it is that power relations work. Conversation as a goal is fine; discussing how power works in oppressive societies is important. But if we are to construct a more just society, we need to be assured that some systematic knowledge about our world and ourselves is possible. Those (simply) critical of modernity can call into question whether we ever really knew the world, and a good case can be made that "they" at least did not. They are in fact right that they have not known the world as it is rather than as they wished and needed it to be; they created their world not only in their own image but in the image of their fantasies. To create a world that expresses our own various and diverse images, we need to understand how it works.

Third, we need a theory of power that recognizes that our practical daily activity contains an understanding of the world—subjugated perhaps, but present. Here I am reaffirming Gramsci's argument that everyone is an intellectual and that each of us has an epistemology contained in our practical activity. The point, then, for "minority" theories is to "read out" the epistemologies in our various practices. We must not give up the claim that material life (class position in Marxist theory) not only structures but also sets limits on understandings of social relations and that, in systems of domination, the vision available to the rulers will be both partial and distorted.

Fourth, our understanding of power needs to recognize the difficulty of creating alternatives. The ruling class, race, and gender actively structure the material-social relations in which all parties are forced to participate; their vision, therefore, cannot be dismissed as simply false or misguided. In consequence, oppressed groups must struggle for their own understandings.

Fifth, as an engaged vision, the understanding of the oppressed exposes the relations among people as inhuman and thus contains a call to political action. That is, the critique is not one that leads to a turning away from engagement but rather one that is a call for change and participation in altering power relations.

The critical steps are, first, using what we know about our lives as a basis for critique of the dominant culture and, second, creating alternatives. When the various "minority" experiences have been described and when the significance of these experiences as a ground for critique of the dominant institutions and ideologies of society is better recognized, we will have at least some of the tools to begin to construct an account of the world sensitive to the realities of race and gender as well as class. To paraphrase Marx, the point is to change the world, not simply to redescribe ourselves or reinterpret the world yet again.

NOTES

1. This essay draws on "Foucault on Power: A Theory for Women?" in Linda Nicholson, ed., *Feminism/Postmodernism* (New York: Routledge, 1991); "Postmodernism and Political Change: Issues for Feminist Theory," in *Cultural Critique*, no. 14 (Winter 1989–1990); and "Rethinking Modernism: Minority vs. Majority Theories," *Cultural Critique*, no. 7 (Fall 1987). My thanks to Robin Dennis for her work in reorganizing the essays.

2. Aida Hurtado, "Relating to Privilege: Seduction and Rejection in the Subordination of White Women and Women of Color," *Signs: Journal of Women in Culture and Society* 14, 4 (Summer 1989), 833–855.

3. Jean-François Lyotard, *The Post-Modern Condition: A Report on Knowledge* (Minneapolis: University of Minnesota Press, 1984), p. 81.

4. My language requires that I insert qualification and clarification: I will be using a we/they language. But although it is clear that "they" represent the ruling race, class, and gender, the "we" is artificially constructed by the totalizing, Eurocentric, masculine discourse of the Enlightenment. I do not mean to suggest that white Western women share the material situation of the colonized peoples, but

rather to argue that we share similar positions in the ideology of the Enlightenment.

5. I owe the phrase "god-trick" to Donna Haraway, "Situated Knowledges: The Science Question in Feminism and the Privilege of Partial Perspective," *Feminist Studies* 14, 3 (Fall 1988), 575–599.

6. This is a case made about Enlightenment epistemology. Clearly there were other worldviews extant, but this is the one that seems to have come down to us as the dominant one and the one against which postmodernists argue.

7. See Chantal Mouffe, "Radical Democracy: Modern or Postmodern," trans. Paul Holdenraver, in Andrew Ross, ed., *Universal Abandon: The Politics of Postmodernism* (Minneapolis: University of Minnesota Press, 1988), pp. 31–45. See also the critique of the ways assumptions express the epistemology of the commodity in chapter 5 of Hartsock, *Money, Sex, and Power: Toward a Feminist Historical Materialism* (Boston: Northeastern University Press, 1984), pp. 95–114.

8. Simone de Beauvoir, *The Second Sex*, trans. H. M. Parshley (New York: Knopf, 1953), p. 72.

9. I should note that although I see some Enlightenment assumptions in Marx, I view his thought as a whole as fundamentally opposed to the Enlightenment assumptions postmodernists argue against, and thus in some ways on the side of postmodernist anti-Enlightenment theories.

10. Albert Memmi, *The Colonizer and the Colonized* (Boston: Beacon Press, 1967), p. 82.

11. For example, compare de Beauvoir's statement that "at the moment when man asserts himself as subject and free being, the idea of the other arises" (de Beauvoir, *Second Sex*, p. 73).

12. Memmi, *The Colonizer and the Colonized*, pp. 71–72.

13. Ibid., p. 85.

14. Ibid., p. 86.

15. Ibid., pp. 92, 95, 113.

16. Edward Said, *Orientalism* (New York: Vintage Press, 1978), p. 3.

17. Memmi, *The Colonizer and the Colonized*, pp. 71–72.

18. Said, *Orientalism*, pp. 3–8.

19. Ibid., pp. 97, 108. See also the reference to the tyrannical observer.

20. Bernice Reagon, "Coalition Politics: Turning the Century," in Barbara Smith, ed., *Home Girls* (New York: Kitchen Table Women of Color Press, 1983), p. 359.

21. Richard Rorty, *Philosophy and the Mirror of Nature* (Princeton: Princeton University Press, 1979), pp. 315, 381, 380.

22. Ibid., pp. 382, 383.

23. Ibid., p. 316.

24. Ibid., p. 318.

25. Ibid., p. 315.

26. Ibid., p. 331.

27. Ibid., pp. 357, 358, 361, 363, 372.

28. Ibid., p. 366.

29. Ibid., p. 319.

30. Ibid., p. 373.

31. Ibid.

32. Ibid., p. 318.

33. Ibid., pp. 320–321.

34. Ibid., pp. 353, 369.

35. Ibid., p. 371.

36. Richard Rorty, *Consequences of Pragmatism* (Minneapolis: University of Minnesota Press, 1982), p. 208.

37. In terms of conversation, virtually all the research on gender and conversation indicate that the playing field is not at all level. Men interrupt women more than the other way around, and they take up a great deal more conversational space.

38. bell hooks, *Ain't I a Woman* (Boston: South End Press, 1982), p. 138.

39. Memmi, *The Colonizer and the Colonized*, pp. xiv-xv.

40. Ibid., pp. 20–21.

41. Ibid., p. 41.

42. Michel Foucault, *The Archaeology of Knowledge* (Harper & Row, 1972), pp. 139–164.

43. Nancy Fraser, "Foucault's Body Language: A Post-Humanist Political Rhetoric?" *Salmagundi* 61 (Fall 1983), 59.

44. Charles Taylor, "Foucault on Freedom and Truth," *Political Theory* 12 (May 1984), 175–176.

45. Michel Foucault, *Language, Counter-Memory, Practice: Selected Essays and Interviews*, ed. Donald Bouchard (Ithaca, N.Y.: Cornell University Press, 1977), p. 151.

46. Michel Foucault, *Power/Knowledge* (New York: Pantheon, 1980), pp. 79, 81.

47. Ibid., p. 80.

48. Michel Foucault, *The History of Sexuality: An Introduction* (New York: Pantheon, 1978), p. 68.

49. Foucault, *Power/Knowledge*, p. 91.

50. Foucault, *The History of Sexuality*, pp. 142–143.

51. Edward Said, "Foucault and the Imagination of Power," in David Hoy, ed., *Foucault: A Critical Reader* (New York: Pantheon, 1986), p. 151.

52. Foucault, *Language, Counter-Memory, Practice*, p. 219.

53. Foucault, *Power/Knowledge*, pp. 81, 85–86.

54. Said, "Foucault and the Imagination of Power," p. 154.

55. Foucault, *Power/Knowledge*, pp. 83–85.

56. Ibid., p. 88.

57. Foucault, *Language, Counter-Memory, Practice*, p. 230.

58. Foucault, *Power/Knowledge*, pp. 84–85.

59. Foucault, *The History of Sexuality*, pp. 92–93.

60. Foucault, *Power/Knowledge*, p. 97.

61. Ibid., p. 98.

62. Ibid.

63. Foucault, *The History of Sexuality*, p. 45.

64. Foucault, *Power/Knowledge*, p. 98.

65. Foucault, *The History of Sexuality*, p. 94.

66. And here, of course, much of Gramsci's work on the construction and maintenance of hegemony is essential.

67. Foucault, *Power/Knowledge*, p. 95.

68. Foucault, *The History of Sexuality*, pp. 92–93.

69. Gad Horowitz, "The Foucaultian Impasse: No Sex, No Self, No Revolution," *Political Theory* 16, 1 (February 1987), 63–64.

70. Antonio Gramsci, *Selections from the Prison Notebooks*, ed. and trans. Quintin Hoare and Geoffrey Nowell Smith (New York: International Publishers, 1971), p. 352.

71. See, for example, Shane Phelan, *Getting Specific* (Minneapolis: University of Minnesota Press, 1994); and Chapter 4 herein, "Difference and Domination."

eleven

The Feminist
Standpoint Revisited

I first wrote a draft of the feminist standpoint essay ("The Feminist Standpoint," reprinted here as Chapter 6), then subtitled "Developing the Ground for a Specifically Feminist Historical Materialism," in December 1978 as a commentary on a paper Sandra Harding presented at the American Philosophy Association annual meeting. I continued to rewrite it until the summer of 1981, when it assumed a form close to its published version. In the years since I wrote the essay, among the many arguments in feminist theory, there have been those centered on standpoint theory, as opposed to postmodernism and critiques of standpoint theory on postmodernist grounds. I am of course not the only person to have made standpoint-type arguments, and a number of people who have commented on my essay have characterized others as standpoint theorists as well.[1] As the debate has widened, it has become possible to find discussions of standpoint theory as a general category of feminist analysis with no names attached.[2] And in these cases, the account of standpoint theory is sometimes fanciful. On more than one occasion I found myself wondering what possible sources the author could be referring to. This poses a problem for me in dealing with responses and critiques of standpoint theory. When no authors (or more frequently, authors with no page references) are cited, it is difficult to determine the textual basis for the critique. In addition, I have been surprised by the fact that my work is often compared with that of others engaged in somewhat different or even radically different projects.[3] Thus, it seemed best to respond only to the critiques that refer explicitly to my work, as opposed to "standpoint epistemologies" in general. And rather than respond specifically to each critique, it seemed more useful to respond to several general criticisms made by (usually) more than one author.

My Project

Here, then, I want to examine some of the responses to my argument in order to (1) clarify the points I was trying to make, and (2) rewrite and update the argument to correct some of what I see as its important flaws. Ironically, many of the published critiques of my work seem to represent significant misreadings of the project. I was attempting to follow the lead of Marx and Lukacs. I wanted to translate the concept of the standpoint of the proletariat, by analogy, into feminist terms. Marx, in *Capital*, adopted a simple two-class model, in which everything exchanged at its value. And only a few pages before the end of Volume 3, he stated, "At last we come to the problem of class," which he would show to be more complicated and demanding of subtle treatment. The manuscript, however, breaks off without presenting such an analysis. But given the fruitfulness of Marx's strategy, I adopted by analogy a simple two-party opposition between feminists and masculinist representatives of patriarchy. Following Lukacs's essay, "Reification and the Standpoint of the Proletariat,"[4] I wanted to translate the notion of the standpoint of the proletariat (including its historic mission) into feminist terms. I wanted to reformulate his arguments in my essay, in the light of his corrective 1967 introduction to *History and Class Consciousness*, which makes some important self-critical points. In particular, there, Lukacs noted the importance of his failure to begin his analysis with labor rather than with the reified forms of commodities in capitalism, that is, to begin his analysis with human activity itself.

I was arguing that, like the lives of proletarians in Marxist theory, women's lives also contain possibilities for developing critiques of domination and visions of alternative social arrangements. By examining the institutionalized sexual division of labor, I argued that a feminist standpoint could be developed that would deepen the critique available from the standpoint of the proletariat and allow for a critique of patriarchal ideology and social relations that would provide a more complete account of the domination of women than Marx's critique of capitalism.

There were several contentions involved in my formulation of the idea of a feminist standpoint. Most important, I posited a series of levels of reality in which the deeper level both includes and explains the surface or appearance. I have come to understand that the notion of levels of reality is very unpopular and that surfaces are all that is credible now. But the surface and depth metaphor is not necessary to feminist standpoint projects, nor are the psychoanalytically based theories of Nancy Chodorow.

Still, I think that standpoint projects are important and useful for most oppressed groups.

The most important aspects of standpoint theory bear repeating here.

1. Material life (class position in Marxist theory) not only structures but also sets limits on understandings of social relations.

2. If material life is structured in fundamentally opposing ways for two different groups, one can expect that the understanding of each will represent an inversion of the other, and in systems of domination the understanding available to the ruling group will be both partial and perverse (by which I mean to suggest both strange and harmful).[5] I would add as a reformulation that there are a variety of inversions that "match" the variety of dominant and subordinate groups.

3. The vision of the ruling group can be expected to structure the material relations in which all people are forced to participate and therefore cannot be dismissed as simply false consciousness. Not only do we all have no choice but to participate in the market, but today we also hear and read incessantly about the virtues of the market to solve all problems and promote democracy.

4. In consequence, the vision available to an oppressed group must be struggled for and represents an achievement that requires both systematic analysis and the education that can only grow from political struggle to change those relations.

5. As an engaged vision, the potential understanding of the oppressed, the adoption of a standpoint, makes visible the inhumanity of relations among human beings and carries a historically liberatory role.[6] For Marx, the liberatory role of the proletariat was in part a function of their historical mission. I would like to substitute for that understanding bell hooks's phrase of yearning for a better and more just world.[7]

As I have thought through the criticisms and reassessed my own argument, I have been struck with a paradox. First, the critiques are enabled and supported by a failure to recognize the Marxist dimension of my work, with its emphasis on historically specific social relations among groups rather than individuals. Thus, a number of the critiques read my essay in ways that locate it within a liberal humanist tradition. At the same time, I believe that the flaws in my argument are directly attributable to my efforts to locate the argument within the Marxist tradition, efforts that took the specific form of an attempt to theorize women's position by analogy to that of the proletariat and that depended on a too-literal reading of Marx's own too-schematic two-class model of society. The debates around my essay, then, and debates about standpoint epistemologies more generally have suffered from, on the one hand, a reading of the argument uninformed by familiarity with Marxist traditions and, on the other, my too-rigid insistence on the applicability of the two-class model of society to the situation of women in advanced capitalism.

As I have reflected on both these and other discussions of standpoint theories over the years, I have come to believe that it is this intertwining of issues of politics with more traditional philosophical questions concerning truth and knowledge, along with their conflicting criteria for claims of epistemological validity, that has been responsible for much of the controversy. That is, standpoint theories must be recognized as essentially contested in much the same way that I have argued the concept of power was essentially contested: Arguments about how to understand power rested on differing epistemologies. These same issues being in play may account for the existence of so many (conflicting) interpretations of the meaning of feminist standpoint theories. Still, I prefer now to see this proliferation of interpretations as an indication that standpoint theories provoke a fertile terrain for feminist debates about power, politics, and epistemology.

Some Responses

Nancy Fraser and Linda Nicholson argue that I claim "to have identified a basic kind of human practice found in all societies which has cross-cultural explanatory power. . . . The practice in question is associated with a biological or quasi-biological need and is construed as functionally necessary to the reproduction of society. It is not the sort of thing, then, whose historical origins need to be investigated."[8] They go on to state that it is doubtful whether these categories have "any determinate cross cultural content." Therefore, constructing a "universalistic social theory" risks projecting the dominant views of the theorists' own society onto others. Teresa de Lauretis shares their assessment: My work is a statement that what affords "women" a "true" and nonperverse "viewpoint" is their cultural construction as mothers based on their bodily productivity.[9] In this reformulation my effort to form a feminist standpoint has instead become a women's viewpoint based on biological destiny.

Jane Flax argues that in my essay I claimed that we can uncover truths about the whole as it really is. And this would require an "Archimedean point" outside our current social arrangements. Moreover, the construction of a feminist standpoint "depends on unexamined and questionable assumptions, . . . including an optimism that people will act rationally on their 'interests,' and that reality has a structure that a more perfect reason can discover more perfectly." This, she argues, is an uncritical appropriation of Enlightenment ideas. Moreover, she adds, a feminist standpoint assumes that the oppressed are not damaged by their experience of domination. Finally, to argue for a feminist standpoint requires that women, unlike men, can be free from determination by their own participation in relations of domination and requires an "unmediated relation to truth and reality."[10]

Iris Young reads the essay as an argument that masculine personality causes institutions of domination and that masculine personality generated by women's mothering produces the oppression of women.[11] This claim sounds reminiscent of some of the early radical feminist claims. Young goes on to argue that I have made "transcultural generalities without empirical warrant" and suggests that the data is not yet in on what is common to all societies.[12] Moreover, she holds, turning to femininity as the source of values on the basis of which one can criticize patriarchal culture leads to essentialism, that is, an account that "theorizes women as a category with a set of essential attributes" and, moreover, finds those attributes in the same place as patriarchy—women's biology and the activity of mothering.

Susan Hekman argues that feminist standpoint arguments "entail the claim that women because of certain aspects of their makeup possess a privileged position which provides them with a unique perspective." There is a particular appeal, she argues, to "woman's unique association with nature."[13] Hekman goes on to identify several problems: First, I have reified the nature/culture dichotomy by basing my argument on women's special relation to nature to ground a feminist epistemology. Second, the argument overlooks the historical elements of what Hekman has renamed "the women's perspective," and it forgets that women are always found in specific and varied social contexts. And third, the project is one that can lead to a substitution of a new truth and a new orthodoxy for the old.[14]

Kathy Ferguson sets up a dichotomy between interpretive strategies and genealogical strategies. She wants to argue that interpretation can be either materialist or idealist, but since I am the only representative of the interpretive "tradition" cited, some of her points seem strained in application to my Marxist version of "interpretation." Thus, she argues that interpretation employs an ontology of discovery and a hermeneutics of suspicion and proposes to investigate the disguises that cover up and distort reality. As she puts it, the claim is, "Ye shall know the truth, and the truth shall set you free."[15] As I see it, the truth is more likely to get you jailed or disappeared in most parts of the world. Ferguson argues that interpretation tends to seek explanations that rest on a search for origins, seeks to articulate the basis from which things grow, and to find in original circumstances something that gives birth to what comes after.[16] Interpretation, Ferguson argues, relies on the "constitution of conceptual unities, such as the categories of woman or women."[17] (Note once again the presence of the singular.) In the process, she states quite correctly, interpretation tries to understand difference, but the logic of the search for

"women" elides difference.[18] Ferguson discusses the inclination of interpretation to encounter radical otherness in a posture of inclusion, and she
recognizes, unlike most other commentators, that this move is related to
the Marxist feminist insistence on the utility of Marx's oversimplification
of capitalism into a two-class model.[19]

Wendy Brown carries the critique even further in the same direction
and engages in dishonest scholarship when she argues against those who
are hostile to postmodernism's "political decay and intellectual disarray."
In order to put me into the same category as Allen Bloom, that of "reac-
tionary foundationalism," she invented phrases and put them in quotation marks, suggesting that these were my words, thus making me fit her
taxonomy. The speciousness of such a strategy should be apparent to anyone acquainted with my work and that of Bloom.[20]

As I read the criticisms of my essay, it does seem strange to be told that
I believe biological categories can have determinate cross-cultural readings of women's status when I am so indebted to a theory that stressed
historical specificity. In addition, assertions that a feminist standpoint
rests on an assumption that people will act rationally on their interests
and that "reason" can discover the structure of reality do not fit comfort-
ably with Marx's (1) insistence that reality is concealed by layers of ideology; (2) insistence that the concept of reason itself is implicated in the construction of capitalism; (3) views that reject entirely the possibility of an
unmediated relation to something called truth; and (4) insistence that human nature itself is socially constructed (and presumably socially constructed in different ways given differing social relations). In addition,
there is Ferguson's statement that I am searching for origins. Yet Marx,
rather than search for origins, began resolutely in the present with an
analysis of capitalism and its immediate precursors. The search for origins is more properly traced to Engels in his highly speculative *Origins of
the Family, Private Property, and the State*.

Teresa de Lauretis, although critical of my work, is herself engaged in a
project that is very similar. She states that the current stage of reconceptualization of feminist theory involves a reconceptualization of the subject
as multiply organized across variable axes of difference.[21] De Lauretis
proposes instead a point of view of an eccentric position outside the male
heterosexual monopoly on knowledge. That is, she proposes that what
Flax has argued is impossible. She claims that the subject of a feminist
consciousness is unlike the consciousness defined and constituted by
women's oppression. It is less pure, probably complicit with the oppressor, and multiply organized across positions along several axes of difference.[22] Several of these points are good ones, but my argument in the
feminist standpoint essay was definitely that we are not pure victims but
instead are forced to be complicit in the projects of dominant groups.

Interestingly, when she proposes an alternative formulation, it bears a good deal of resemblance to my own argument but is more closely related to the argument I put forward below as a revision of my feminist standpoint argument. De Lauritis argues that the constitution of "eccentric subjects" involves a shift in historical consciousness. This shift redefines the terms of both feminism and social reality from a "standpoint at once inside and outside their determinations."[23] I take her to be making a point similar to my own point about the doubled or multiple consciousness of oppressed groups. The figures she cites as instances of eccentric subjects—Marilyn Frye's lesbian, Gloria Anzaldua's new Mestiza—are subjects of an unusual knowledge. But this consciousness is not universal or coextensive with human thought. It is historically determined, yet is achieved in a process of struggle and interpretation, "a rewriting of self . . . in relation to a new understanding of community, of history, of culture."[24] This is very much what I had in mind when I argued that the adoption of a feminist standpoint allowed one to see that the taken-for-granted common sense of Western culture was instead a very harmful ideology, one that I labeled "abstract masculinity."

This sort of reading of my project is supported by Sandra Harding's discussion of standpoint epistemology, which she claims incorporates anti-Enlightenment tendencies. Feminist standpoint theorists, she argues, oppose the idea that "ahistorical principles of inquiry can insure ever more perfect representations of the world."[25] Moreover, as with de Lauretis's eccentric subjects, from the perspective of a feminist standpoint, some of the overlapping social structures become visible. The oppressed, she argues, are indeed damaged by their experience, but what is a disadvantage in terms of social experience can be an advantage in terms of knowledge.[26] Finally, Harding argues that standpoint theory does not require feminine essentialism but rather analyzes the essentialism that androcentrism attributes to women; nor does it assume that women are free of participation in racist, classist, or homophobic social relations.[27]

I have rehearsed the various responses to the essay at such great length because they are so varied. But I believe that the most fundamental problem with the responses I have cited (with the exception of Harding's) is that the Marxist dimension of my argument has been lost. The most common reading of the essay is one that sees me as a radical feminist and therefore an Enlightenment and essentialist theorist. And although there are a number of aspects to this charge, for my purposes, I think there are several central criticisms. First, there is the argument that my case is based on biology and reinscribes the split between nature and culture. Second, probably the most common, is the charge of essentialism, the making of cross-cultural claims, arguing that such a thing as "woman's" singular point of view exists. Related is the argument that I am putting forward a notion of a unitary subject, constituted solely by oppression, and innocent of complicity in a social system that contains various forms of oppression. Then, some critics point to political dangers of a gender-oppositional strategy—coming either from the Left, saying that this strategy might lead back to conservative views, or from the Right, saying that it can impose a new orthodoxy. I think many of these criticisms are inaccurate and occur because many feminists lack familiarity with Marxist theory, though that is certainly not true for all of them.

Let me turn to the criticisms and look back at the text of "The Feminist Standpoint." First, the issue of biology—that my case is biologically based because I use the term "sex" rather than "gender." In the essay I argue that it is important not to separate the effects of nature and nurture, or biology and culture. I take my guidance here from Marx's insistence in his *Manuscripts of 1844* that we are part of nature and social at the same time. Marx wanted to argue that even plants, animals, light, and so on theoretically constitute a part of human consciousness and a part of human life and activity.[28] Nature itself, for Marx, appears as a form of human work, since we duplicate ourselves actively, in reality, and come to contemplate the selves we have created in a world of our own making.[29]

David Harvey has usefully expanded on these claims and pointed out the ways in which Marx was involved in the Enlightenment project of the domination of nature. At the same time, he underlined the extent to which Marx refused the split between nature and culture and insisted that humans were at once social and natural.[30]

These arguments mark the context in which I claimed that although there is a bodily component to human existence, "its size and substantive content will remain unknown until at least the certainly changeable aspects of the sexual division of labor are altered."[31] I also stated that it is specifically Western culture that chooses to treat aspects of female physiology as boundary challenges. This strategy was an attempt as well to follow Donna Haraway's lead. As she works through materials in the natural sciences, she argues strongly that the nature/culture split must be refused. The natural sciences must be seen as culturally constructed and as cultural artifacts. Nature is not "out there" but is invented and reinvented by human societies as well as discovered. As Haraway puts it, "We both learn about and create nature and ourselves."[32] She uses the example of the human genome project to argue that "technoscience *is* cultural practice," and that genes are the result of works of cultural construction. Thus, nature and culture mutate into each other. "Nature and culture implode into each other."[33] This is not bad science, she is clear, but rather the only science we have. Science is culture, as she puts it—and one might say as well that nature is culture and that culture cannot be thought about apart from nature.[34] As Marx so clearly noted, there is no "nature" except perhaps on undiscovered Pacific atolls. My strategy of using the term "sex" rather than "gender" may not have worked, and in a sense it could not work, given the terms of debate at that time. The introduction of the term "gender" represented a political strategy to distinguish the social, and by implication changeable, from the natural, and by implication unchangeable. I can still think of no terminology that refuses the opposition between nature and culture in the context of contemporary U.S. feminist theory. But what I was attempting to do was to denaturalize nature (Haraway's phrase) and to refuse the split.

Second, it has been claimed that I made cross-cultural, universalizing claims to have discovered woman's viewpoint—or a women's viewpoint—and thereby have engaged in essentialism. There are four key mistakes in this charge, marked by the terms "cross-cultural," "discovered," "woman's" or "women's," and "viewpoint." Let me unpack them one by one.

First, the cross-cultural argument: I stated that I was limiting my efforts to "women's lives in Western class societies" and argued that examining the sexual division of labor could allow us to "begin, though not complete" the ground for a specifically feminist historical materialism.[35] I noted as well that my primary focus was on capitalism.[36] Still, there were problems in that different women's lives were not the same in the context of Western capitalism. The disparities have only grown as capitalism has become more global and has integrated women into the wage labor force in very different ways. It seems to me odd that a self-described effort to lay the groundwork for a feminist historical materialist approach, explicitly based on Marx's method, would be read as making a series of cross-cultural and ahistorical claims about women in general.

As to a unitary standpoint, I did not give proper attention to differences among women (about which more later). In this regard, I believe that in following Marx's strategy of simplifying capitalist society, I made exactly the sort of mistake for which I criticized his work in *Money, Sex, and Power*. That is, just as his focus on the relation between capitalist and worker occluded other relations (such as gender), so my focus on a simplified model of masculinist and feminist perspectives left out of the account other important social relations.

Second, there is the argument that interpretation as an approach is about the "discovery of truth." Although this locution may represent the epistemology of the Enlightenment, in which the mind could discover truth while being itself located nowhere, it is much more problematic as a description of Marx's method. For Marx, notions of a truth to be discovered by reason are extremely problematic in a world defined, structured, and even in a sense created by human activity, especially the activity of work. Moreover, given Marx's argument that humans create the natural world as well as themselves, the role of reason is made both more complex and peripheral by his argument about the role of ideological reversals in capitalism, in which what seem to be relations between people are instead cast as relations between things. Finally, rationalist ideas about the discovery of truth do not fit well with a methodology that redefines truth as "the reality and power of our ideas in action" and insists that the point is not to interpret the world but to change it.[37] All this makes questionable any statement that Marx or Marxists are involved in an effort to discover truth, especially through reason. It rewrites Marx as an Enlightenment thinker and ignores his own profound anti-Enlightenment commitments.

Third, there is the translation of feminist standpoints into woman's or women's viewpoints. This is one of the most common moves and reflects a deep misunderstanding of what I (or Lukacs) meant by standpoint. Lukacs was clear that the standpoint of the proletariat was not a claim about what individual workers might believe. Moreover, he was clear in his 1967 Introduction to *History and Class Consciousness* that he did not mean a consciousness to be imputed to those located in a specific social location (something that does mar his presentation in his essay on class consciousness). Rather, a standpoint is a technical theoretical device that can allow for the creation of better (more objective, more liberatory) accounts of the world. Thus, I make no claim about the actual consciousness of existing women, but rather I am arguing about the theoretical conditions of possibility for creating alternatives. In this, my enterprise shares a great deal with de Lauretis's work on eccentric subjects.

Donna Haraway got it exactly right when she wrote:

> A standpoint is not an empiricist appeal to or by "the oppressed" but a cognitive, psychological, and political tool for more adequate knowledge judged by the nonessentialist, historically contingent, situated standards of strong objectivity. Such a standpoint is the always fraught but necessary fruit of the *practice* of oppositional and differential consciousness. A feminist standpoint is a practical technology rooted in yearning, not an abstract philosophical foundation.[38]

Thus, to return to the five claims made in my essay on the feminist standpoint (now I think standpoints): (1) Material life structures and sets limits on the understanding of social relations. (2) If life is structured in opposing ways, one can expect similar oppositions in the visions of different groups. (3) The vision of the ruling group structures the material relations in which all parties are forced to participate and therefore cannot be dismissed as simply false. (Given this formulation, I would like to underline the extent to which Ferguson's claims that interpretation is involved in an effort to discover truth are problematic.) (4) The understanding available to the oppressed group must be struggled for and represents an achievement that requires both systematic analysis and the education that grows from political struggle to change social relations. (This point is one that seems to be the most consistently missed, and its presence in my argument certainly works to undermine those who claim that I am positing an innate and biologically based "viewpoint of women." This point is also the key to the reasons I used the term "feminist" rather than women.) (5) As an engaged understanding, a standpoint exposes the real relations among human beings as inhuman and carries a historically liberatory role.

Each of these features of a standpoint is important, but I think now I would want to stress most the fact that a standpoint is not generated unproblematically by simple existence in a particular social location. It is a product of systematic theoretical and practical work, and its achievement can never be predicted with any certainty. The adoption of a standpoint may require a theoretical migration. There are some positions from which a standpoint emerges easily; others from which a standpoint requires much more effort. Consider bell hooks's statement:

> Living as we did—on the edge—we developed a particular way of seeing reality. We looked both from the outside in and from the inside out. We focused our attention on the center as well as the margin . . . this sense of wholeness, impressed upon our consciousness by the structure of our daily lives, provided us an oppositional world view—a mode of seeing unknown to most of our oppressors, that sustained us, aided us in our struggle to transcend poverty and despair, strengthened our sense of self and our solidarity.[39]

Paula Moya presents a much more detailed account of this process, under the heading of a "realist theory of Chicana identity," a term I would be reluctant to endorse, since, for me, her analysis follows what I take to be the outlines of a standpoint epistemology. Thus, she argues for six claims that can serve to support claims of epistemological privilege. First, there is the claim that different social "facts" that "constitute an individual's social location are causally relevant for the experiences she will have." The second claim is that an "individual's experiences will influence, but not entirely determine, the formation of her cultural identity."[40] Thus, membership in a group, whether voluntary or involuntary, can be expected to have effects. Third, possibilities of both errors and changes over time must be allowed for. Moya, for example, reports that she only became "belatedly and unceremoniously" a Mexican-American as opposed to a "Spanish" girl from New Mexico when she moved to Texas. Fourth, she argues that some identities have "greater epistemic value than some others the same individual might claim."[41] The criterion used to determine this is the extent to which an account of identity can grasp

the interaction among the various determinants that constitute one's social location. Thus, Moya argues persuasively that for her, an identity as a
Chicana carries more epistemological validity. Fifth, she argues that one's
location within power relations, especially relations of domination, is central to determinations of epistemic validity and epistemic privilege.[42] Finally, "a realist theory of identity demands oppositional struggle as a necessary (although not sufficient) step toward the achievement of an
epistemically privileged position."[43]

Others have found the adoption of a standpoint much more difficult, a
process that requires a reunderstanding of the social structure within
which one is located. In these terms the work of Michelle Cliff is particularly instructive. She describes the difficulty she had, a light-skinned Ja-
maican woman with a Ph.D. dealing with the Italian Renaissance, in coming to approach herself as a subject, or, in my terms, adopting a
standpoint. She states, in "Notes on Speechlessness" that she had inter-
nalized the "message of anglocentrism, of white supremacy."[44] She notes
that, through participation in the feminist movement, she began to retrace
the African part of herself and to reclaim it. She is clear about the difficulty of the project. In an earlier book, she said that she wrote as someone
who was unable to "recapture the native language of Jamaica" and relied
on English, but she still wrote from a feminist consciousness, a consciousness of colonialism, and a knowledge of self-hatred.[45] As she began to
write in a way that put her own identity and experience at the center, she
noted that her writing style became a kind of shorthand. "Write quickly
before someone catches you. Before you catch yourself."[46] Her writing is
informed by and structured by her rage and marks very clearly the struggle—both political and personal—involved in taking up a position from
which the dominant order becomes visible with all its distortions.

Michelle Cliff's struggles are illustrative as well for the final charge lev-
eled against my original essay, that I am describing a "women's perspective" constituted by oppression and unaware of its complicity in the oppression of others. As is evident from my discussion of the achieved
character of a standpoint, a standpoint is constituted by more than oppression and cannot be reduced to identity politics as usually understood.
Fredric Jameson probably grasped it most clearly when he stated that the
experience of negative constraint and violence, the commodification of labor power, dialectically produces the positive content of its experience as
the self-consciousness of the commodity.[47] Once again, Michelle Cliff's
work is instructive. She looks back, to try to locate what happened.
"When did *we* (the light-skinned middle-class Jamaicans) take over for
them as oppressors?"[48] Cliff is clearly conscious about her complicity with
imperialism and racism. It is a central aspect of her ability to locate herself in a critical context.

[margin handwritten note: but what about you? honor? honor?]

Reformulations

But there are problems with my argument; in particular, it worked to subsume the "marked" categories of feminists (feminists of color) under the unmarked and therefore white feminist, and lesbian under the category of straight, just as women have been subsumed under the category "man." That is, in following Marx's procedure of reducing the world to a two-class, two-man model, I ended up with a problem similar to his own—that is, unable to see important axes of domination, even while recognizing their operation. Thus, Marx was clear that widows were part of the lower layer of the reserve army of the unemployed. At the same time, he lost track of women's labor in reproducing the working class. So whereas I too took note of some race and class differences in terms of the sexual division of labor, I made no theoretical space that would have accorded them proper significance.

In revisiting the argument I made for a feminist standpoint I want to both pluralize the idea and preserve its utility as an instrument of struggle against dominant groups. I believe that the task facing all theorists committed to social change is that of working to construct some theoretical bases for political solidarity. Such theoretical bases are no substitute for collective action and coalition building but are a necessary adjunct to them. In revising the notion of feminist standpoint theory, I gain encouragement from a number of similar efforts by others who argue for a specific view from below.[49]

The work of Fredric Jameson has been particularly useful in my rethinking of the nature of a standpoint. He states that "the presupposition is that, owing to its structural situation in the social order and to the specific forms of oppression and exploitation unique to that situation, each group lives the world in a phenomenologically specific way that allows it to see, or better still, that makes it unavoidable for that group to see and to know, features of the world that remain obscure, invisible, or merely occasional and secondary for other groups."[50] Jameson is clear that in each case, the issue is the condition of possibility of new thinking inherent in each social location. It is not a matter of the aptitude of individual workers and still less "the mystical properties of some collective proletarian 'world view.'"[51] Jameson stresses the prerequisites of Marxist analysis: the diagnoses of blocks and limits to knowledge as well as positive features such as the capacity to think in terms of process.

Jameson also takes up feminist standpoint theories to argue that the experience of women generates new and positive epistemological possibilities. (Stress should be placed on the idea of possibilities and potentials.) Standpoint theory, he argues, demands a "differentiation between the various negative experiences of constraint, between the *exploitation* suffered by workers and the *oppressions* suffered by women."[52] If one begins from a feminist project, one can argue that it is important to differentiate situations that can be characterized as those of constraint. Jameson takes particular note of the Central European Jewish experience, which he characterizes as one of fear that crosses class and gender lines. Other groups, he suggests, experience fear, but for this group it is constitutive.[53] Thus, he indicates that it is important to dissolve the concept of oppression into the "concrete situations from which it emerged" and to examine the various structured constraints lived by dominated groups. But in the process, each form of domination must be understood to produce its own specific epistemology, or view from below.[54]

We need a revised and reconstructed theory, indebted to Marx, among others, and containing several important features of standpoint theories, as opposed to postmodernism theories. First, rather than getting rid of subjectivity, oppressed groups need to engage in the historical, political, and theoretical process of constituting ourselves as subjects as well as objects of history. We need to sort out who we really are and in the process dissolve this false "we" into its real multiplicity and variety. Out of this concrete multiplicity, it should be possible to build an account of the social relations as seen from below. I am not suggesting that oppression creates "better" people; on the contrary, the experience of domination and marginalization leaves many scars. Rather it is to note that marginalized groups are less likely to mistake themselves for the universal "man." And to suggest that the experience of domination may provide the possibility of important new understandings of social life.

Second, it is important to do our thinking on an epistemological base that indicates that knowledge is possible—not just conversation or a discourse on how it is that power relations work to subject us. We will not have the confidence to act if we believe that we cannot know the world. This does not mean that we need to believe that we have absolute knowledge, but rather that we need to have "good enough" certitude.[55]

Third, we need an epistemology that recognizes that our practical daily activity contains an understanding of the world—subjugated perhaps, but present. Here I refer to Gramsci's argument that all men are intellectuals and that everyone has a working epistemology. The point, then, is to read out the epistemologies contained in our various practices. In addition, we must not give up the claim that material life not only structures but also sets limits on understandings of social relations and that in systems of domination, the vision available to the ruling groups will be partial and will reverse the real order of things.

Fourth, our epistemology needs to recognize the difficulty of creating alternatives. The ruling class, race, and gender actively structure the world in a way that forms the material-social relations in which all parties are forced to participate; their vision cannot be dismissed as simply false or misguided. Oppressed groups must struggle to attain their own, centered, understanding, recognizing that this will require both theorizing and the education that can come only from political struggle.

Fifth, the understanding of the oppressed exposes the real relations among people as inhumane: Thus there is a call to political action.

In light of these needs, Jameson's extension of standpoint arguments, and in the spirit of attempting to develop theoretical bases for coalitions, I propose to read a number of statements of the view from below, or the perspectives of subaltern groups. I believe that although the phenomenological specifics differ, there are a number of connections to be made and similarities to be seen in the epistemologies contained as possibilities in the experience of dominated groups. In particular, I want to suggest that white feminists should learn the possibilities of solidarity from U.S. feminists of color and postcolonial subjects.

There are several important issues on which a great deal more work needs to be done. First, there is the question of the status of "experience" and its interpretation, most important, the political consequences of treating experience in different ways. Second, in the particularly American (or perhaps Anglophone) context, much more needs to be learned about the construction of groups, which must be thought of not as aggregations of individuals but as groups formed by their oppression and marginalization, groups whose members share enough experience to have the possibility of coming to understand their situations in ways that can empower their oppositional movements. Third, I believe there is a great deal of work to be done to elaborate the connections between politics, epistemology, and claims of epistemic privilege and to develop new understandings of engaged and accountable knowledge.

To understand these perspectives and the knowledges they support, generate, and express, we must understand at least the outlines of the situations of oppression from which they emerge, or put more clearly, the existential problems to which the worldviews of the oppressed must respond. Most fundamentally, the dominated live in a world structured by others for their purposes—purposes that at the very least are not our own and that are in various degrees inimical to our development and even existence. This takes a variety of forms, both globally and locally. There is an implicit "assumption of 'the West' as the primary referent in theory and practice." At the very least, as Carlos Fuentes put it from the perspective of Mexico, "The North American world blinds us with its energy; we cannot see ourselves [because] we must see YOU."[56]

As a result of this definition, dominated groups experience a series of inversions, distortions, and erasures that can become epistemologically constitutive. "The presupposition is that, owing to its structural situation in the social order and to the specific forms of oppression" inherent in that situation, each group lives the world in a way that allows it to see, or rather "makes it unavoidable to see and to know, features of the world that remain obscure, invisible, or merely occasional and secondary for other groups."[57]

Let us look more specifically at a very powerful experience of inversion. One of the most frequently mentioned features of the consciousness of the dominated as they become conscious of both relations of domination and possibilities for change is a recognition of the "insanity" or "unreality" of the "normal." Thus, Michelle Cliff writes of light-skinned, middle-class Jamaicans: "We were colorists and we aspired to oppressor status. . . . We were convinced of white supremacy. If we failed, . . . our dark part had taken over: an inherited imbalance in which the doom of the Creole was sealed." She steps back to look at what she has written and states that this "may sound fabulous, or even mythic. It is. It is insane."[58] Or consider a U.S. Black woman who told her interviewer, "I have grown to womanhood in a world where the saner you are, the madder you are made to appear."[59]

Eduard Galeano, writing of the situation in Latin America, noted, "'Freedom' in my country is the name of a jail for political prisoners and 'democracy' forms part of the title of various regimes of terror; the word 'love' defines the relationship of a man with his automobile, and 'revolution' is understood to describe what a new detergent can do in your kitchen.[60] He added: "Why not recognize a certain creativity in the development of a technology of terror? Latin America is making inspired universal contributions to the development of methods of torture . . . and the sowing of fear."[61]

This sort of understanding of the inversions created for the oppressed leads to a reunderstanding of the dominant group. As this understanding changes, it is striking how similar the descriptions are. Thus, one can begin to ask questions and formulate descriptions that are vastly different. Thus, we find questions raised among feminist, third world, and postcolonial writers. "Besides possessing more money and arms is it that the 'First World' is qualitatively better in any way than our 'underdeveloped' countries? That the Anglos themselves aren't also an 'ethnic group,' one of the most violent and anti-social tribes on this planet?"[62] And there is also the observation by a student of Black radicalism that "there was the sense that something of a more profound obsession with property was askew in a civilization which could organize and celebrate—on a scale beyond previous human experience—the brutal degradations of life and the most acute violations of human destiny." He added that the suspicion was mounting that "a civilization maddened by its own perverse assumptions and contradictions is loose in the world."[63]

The result of this kind of experience for knowledge and epistemology is expressed in Gabriel Garcia Marquez's Nobel Prize address. He presented a rich statement that "our crucial problem has been a lack of conventional means to render our lives believable. This, my friends, is the crux of our solitude. . . . The interpretation of our reality through patterns not our own serves only to make us ever more unknown, ever less free, ever more solitary."[64] The result is that the dominated and marginalized are forced to recognize (unlike whites, males, and Europeans) that they inhabit multiple worlds. W. E. B. Du Bois described this situation from an African American perspective: "It is a peculiar sensation, this double consciousness, this sense of always looking at one's self through the eyes of others, of measuring one's soul by the tape of a world that looks on in amused contempt and pity."[65]

The significance of this experience for developing knowledge and experience has been described in a number of ways. I argued in my feminist standpoint essay that for (white) women in Western industrial society, the experience of life under patriarchy allows for the possibility of developing an understanding both of the falseness and partiality of the dominant view and a vision of reality that is deeper and more complex than that view. Others have made similar arguments about the nature of the knowledge available to the subjugated. Thus, Sangari writes that for "third world" people, the difficulty of arriving at fact through the "historical and political distortions that so powerfully shape and mediate it" leads them to assert a different level of factuality, "a plane on which the notion of knowledge as provisional and of truth as historically circumscribed is not only necessary for understanding but can in turn be made to work from positions of engagement within the local and contemporary." She argues that marvelous realism operates because "if the real is historically structured to make invisible the foreign locus of power, if the real may thus be other than what is generally visible, . . . then marvelous realism tackles the problem of truth at a level that reinvents a more comprehensive mode of referentiality."[66]

Gloria Anzaldua, writing out of the experience of a Chicana living on the Mexico-Texas border, describes a similar phenomenon in terms reminiscent of Sangari's discussion. She points not only to the experience of living in two realities and thus being forced to exist in the interface but also to "la facultad," the capacity to see in surface phenomena the meanings of deeper realities, to see the "deep structure below the surface." And she argues that "those who are pounced on the most have it the strongest—the females, the homosexuals of all races, the dark skinned, the outcast, the persecuted, the marginalized, the foreign." It is a survival tactic unknowingly cultivated by those caught between the worlds, but, she adds, "it is latent in all of us."[67]

The knowledges available to these multiple subjectivities have different qualities from that of the disembodied and singular subject of the Enlightenment. Moreover, despite the specificity of each view from below, several fundamental aspects are shared. Among these are the qualities of multiplicity, of being locatable in time and space and particular cultures, of being embodied in specific ways, and, finally, of operating as social and collective points of view, indeed, operating as standpoints. Although I cannot discuss these qualities in detail, I can lay out a few of their general outlines.

 These are knowledges located in a particular time and space—situated knowledges.[68] They are therefore partial, the knowledges of specific cultures and peoples. As an aspect of being situated, these knowledges represent a response to an expression of specific embodiment. The bodies of the dominated have been made to function as the marks of our oppression.

One can describe the shape of these knowledges by attending to the features of the social location occupied by dominated groups. Because of these features, these knowledges express a multiple and contradictory reality; they are not fixed but change, and they recognize that they change with the changing shape of the historical conjuncture and the balance of forces. They are both critical of and vulnerable to the dominant culture, both separated from and opposed to it and yet contained within it. Gloria Anzaldua's poem expresses these characteristics:

> To live in the Borderlands means
> you are at home, a stranger wherever you are
> the border disputes have been settled
> the volley of shots have shattered the truce
> you are wounded, lost in action
> fighting back, a survivor[69]

All these mark achievement through struggle, a series of ongoing attempts to keep from being made invisible, to keep from being destroyed by the dominant culture.

Even more than this, however, the development of situated knowledges can constitute alternatives: They open possibilities that may or may not be realized. To the extent that these knowledges become self-conscious about their assumptions, they make available new epistemological options. The struggles they represent and express, if made self-conscious, can go beyond efforts at survival in order to recognize the centrality of systematic power relations. They can become knowledges that are both accountable and engaged. As the knowledges of the dominated, they are "savvy to modes of denial," which include repression, forgetting, and disappearing.[70] Thus, while recognizing themselves as never fixed or fully achieved, they can claim to present a truer, or more adequate, account of reality. They can form what Jameson has termed a "principled relativism." As the knowledges that recognize themselves as the knowledges of the dominated and marginalized, these self-consciously situated knowledges must focus on changing contemporary power relationships and thus point beyond the present.

NOTES

I would like to thank Karen Stuhldreher, who worked as my research assistant, for her help in researching this paper. Also Kathi Weeks took time out from her dissertation work to think about the project and put together a list of the most important sources to be responded to.

1. The list usually includes Dorothy Smith, Mary O'Brien, Hilary Rose (and formerly also Elizabeth Fee and Jane Flax), and more recently theorists such as Alison Jaggar, Sandra Harding, and Patricia Hill Collins who have more complicated relationships to standpoint theory. Missing are writers such as Donna Haraway, Chela Sandoval, bell hooks, and Paula M. L. Moya, who I see as involved in versions of standpoint projects. There are also issues to be taken up about "feminist" as opposed to "women's" standpoints. On this point see Hartsock, "Standpoint Theories for the Next Century," *Women and Politics* 18, 3 (Fall 1997).

2. For example, Norma Alarcon, "The Theoretical Subject(s) of *This Bridge Called My Back*," in Gloria Anzaldua, ed., *Making Face/Making Soul* (San Francisco: Aunt Lute Foundation, 1990), discussed an unnamed group of "standpoint epistemologists." Later in the essay she cited Harding and Jaggar as standpoint theorists.

3. For example, my work is often compared to Dorothy Smith's, though I see her as less influenced by radical feminism than I have been. See Dorothy Smith, "A Sociology for Women," in Julia Sherman and Evelyn Beck, ed., *The Prism of Sex* (Madison: University of Wisconsin Press, 1977). But compare also Alison Jaggar, *Feminist Politics and Human Nature* (Totowa, N.J.: Rowman and Allenheld, 1983), and Sandra Harding, "The Instability of the Analytical Categories of Feminist Theory," *Signs: Journal of Women in Culture and Society* 11, 4 (Summer 1986). I was surprised, however, to discover that my work was also lumped together with that of Dorothy Dinnerstein and Mary Daly—the latter a radical feminist. On this point, see Susan Hekman, *Gender and Knowledge: Elements of a Postmodern Feminism* (Boston: Northeastern University Press, 1990), p. 126.

4. Georg Lukacs, *History and Class Consciousness* (Boston: Beacon, 1971). For more on my debts to Marx, see Part 2.

5. I did intend to privilege the perspective available as a possibility within women's lives, though not to argue for a ranking of oppressions such that the vision available to the most oppressed group provided the best account. (Katie King seems to read inversion in this way. See *Theory in Its Feminist Travels* [Bloomington: Indiana University Press, 1994], p. 62.)

6. These five points are my restatement with only a few changes of the formulation that appeared in *Money, Sex, and Power: Toward A Feminist Historical Material-*

ism (New York: Longman, 1983; Boston, Northeastern University Press, 1984), p. 232.

7. bell hooks, *Yearning* (Boston: South End Press, 1994). See also Donna Haraway, *Modest_Witness@Second_Millennium.FemaleMan©Meets_OncoMouse*™ (New York: Routledge, 1997), pp. 127–129, reminding me very much of this work.

8. Nancy Fraser and Linda Nicholson, "Social Criticism Without Philosophy," in Linda Nicholson, ed., *Feminism/Postmodernism* (New York: Routledge, 1990), p. 31.

9. Ibid., p. 121.

10. Jane Flax, *Thinking Fragments* (Berkeley: University of California Press, 1990), pp. 140–141.

11. Iris Young, *Throwing like a Girl and Other Essays in Feminist Philosophy and Social Theory* (Bloomington: Indiana University Press, 1990), p. 42.

12. Ibid., p. 51.

13. Hekman, *Gender and Knowledge,* p. 126. The use of the singular here recalls the patriarchal use of "woman," where the one could stand for all, since women did not qualify as "individuals."

14. Ibid., p. 128.

15. Ferguson, "Interpretation and Genealogy in Feminism," *Signs* 16 (Winter 1991), 326.

16. Ibid., p. 331.

17. Ibid., p. 322. Note too the presence of the singular, "woman."

18. Ibid., p. 323.

19. I owe this reading of Ferguson to Karen Stuhldreher.

20. See Wendy Brown, *States of Injury* (Princeton: Princeton University Press, 1995). For more serious accounts of my work, see *Women and Politics* 19, 3 (Fall 1997), a special issue titled "Politics and Feminist Standpoint Theories."

21. Teresa De Lauretis, "Eccentric Subjects: Feminist Theory and Historical Consciousness," *Feminist Studies* 16, 1 (Spring 1990), 116.

22. Ibid., p. 137.

23. Ibid., p. 139. In this passage she also switched language and discussed an eccentric point of view as if it were the same thing as a standpoint.

24. Ibid., p. 144.

25. Sandra Harding, "Feminism, Science, and the Anti-Enlightenment Critiques," in Linda Nicholson, ed., *Feminism/Postmodernism*. Note that Cornel West in the *Ethical Dimension of Marx's Thought* (New York: Monthly Review Press, 1991) makes a similar argument about Marxism.

26. Ibid., p. 98.

27. Ibid., p. 99.

28. Karl Marx, *Economic and Philosophic Manuscripts of 1844,* ed. Dirk Struik (New York: International Publishers, 1964), p. 112.

29. Ibid., p. 114. See also Ibid., p. 137, where Marx stated that the human essence of nature only existed for social man. On the issue of the relation of natural to human worlds, see the very interesting account by Alfred Schmidt, *The Concept of Nature in Marx,* trans. Ben Foukes (London: New Left Books, 1971).

30. David Harvey, *Justice, Nature, and the Geography of Difference* (New York: Blackwell, 1996), pp. 120–175.

31. Nancy Hartsock, *Money, Sex, and Power* (New York: Longman, 1983; Boston Northeastern University Press, 1984), p. 233.

32. Donna Haraway, *Simians, Cyborgs, and Women* (New York: Routledge, 1991), p. 42.

33. Haraway, *Modest_Witness*, p. 148.

34. Haraway, *Simians*, p. 230.

35. Hartsock, *Money, Sex, and Power*, pp. 234, 231 respectively.

36. Ibid., p. 234.

37. On the Marxist ideas about truth, see Leszek Kolakowski, "Karl Marx and the Classical Definition of Truth," in Kolakowski, *Toward a Marxist Humanism* (New York: Grove Press, 1968). See introduction to Part 2 herein.

38. Haraway, *Modest_Witness*, pp. 198–199. See esp. n. 32, pp. 304–305.

39. bell hooks, *From Margin to Center* (Boston: South End Press, 1984), p. ix.

40. "Postmodernism, 'Realism,' and the Politics of Identity," in M. Jacqui Alexander and Chandra Talpade Mohanty, eds., *Feminist Genealogies, Colonial Legacies, Democratic Futures* (New York: Routledge, 1997), p. 137.

41. Ibid., p. 138.

42. Ibid., p. 139.

43. Ibid., p. 141. For my purposes it is important that Moya recognize the Marxist roots of this claim. In addition, it is interesting to note that my own arguments are accessed only through Sandra Harding and Satya Mohanty.

44. Michelle Cliff, *The Land of Look Behind* (Ithaca, N.Y.: Firebrand Books, 1985), p. 13.

45. Ibid., p. 16.

46. Ibid.

47. Fredric Jameson, "History and Class Consciousness as an 'Unfinished Project,'" *Rethinking Marxism* 1, 1 (1988), 67.

48. Ibid., p. 62.

49. See, for example, work by Patricia Hill Collins on a Black feminist standpoint, Marilyn Frye, Teresa De Lauretis, Molefi Asante, Sandra Harding, Chela Sandoval, and Donna Haraway.

50. Jameson, "History and Class Consciousness," p. 65.

51. Ibid., p. 66.

52. Ibid., p. 70.

53. Ibid.

54. Ibid. He went on to state that it was a project that would sound like relativism, but termed it a principled relativism.

55. See, for example, Ludwig Wittgenstein, *On Certainty* (New York: Harper and Row, 1969), and *Remarks on the Foundations of Mathematics* (Cambridge: MIT Press. See also Ilya Prigogine, *The End of Certainty* (New York: The Free Press, 1996).

56. Carlos Fuentes, "How I Started to Write," in Rick Simonson and Scott Walker, eds., *Graywolf Annual Five: Multicultural Literacy* (St. Paul, M.N.: Graywolf Press, 1988), p. 85.

57. Jameson, "History and Class Consciousness," p. 65.

58. Michelle Cliff, "A Journey into Speech," *Graywolf Annual*, p. 78.

59. From Edward Gwaltney, *Dryongso*, cited in Patricia Hill Collins, "The Social Construction of Black Feminist Thought," *Signs* 14, 4 (1989), 748.

60. "In Defense of the Word: Leaving Buenos Aires," *Graywolf Annual* (June 1976), pp. 124–125.

61. Ibid., pp. 114–115. See also his remarks about the importance of the consumption of fantasy rather than commodities (p. 117).

62. Guillermo Gómez-Peña, "Documented/Undocumented," in *Graywolf Annual*, p. 132.

63. Cedric Robinson, *Black Marxism* (London: Zed Press, 1984), pp. 442 and 452 respectively.

64. Quoted in Eduard Galeano, *Century of the Wind* (New York: Pantheon, 1988), p. 262. Marquez's work makes important points about incommensurable realities. He argued that ordinary people who have read *One Hundred Years of Solitude* have found no surprise, because "I'm telling them nothing that hasn't happened in their own lives." (*The Fragrance of Guava*, p. 36, cited in Kumkum Sangari, "The Politics of the Possible," *Cultural Critique*, no. 7 (Fall 1987), 164.

65. W. E. B. Du Bois, *The Souls of Black Folk*, 2nd ed. (New York: Fawcett World Library, n.d.), p. 16, cited in Joyce Ladner, *Tomorrow's Tomorrow* (New York: Anchor Books, 1971), pp. 273–274.

66. Sangari, "The Politics of the Possible," pp. 161 and 163 respectively.

67. Gloria Anzaldua, *Borderlands* (San Francisco: Spinsters, Aunt Lute, 1987), pp. 37–39.

68. I have been very much influenced by Haraway's essay "Situated Knowledges," in *Simians, Cyborgs, and Women*.

69. Anzaldua, *Borderlands*, p. 14.

70. These are Donna Haraway's terms (in *Simians, Cyborgs, and Women*).

Afterword

I begin with a brief assessment of what I see as the current situation of feminist theory. In particular, I see a reenactment of the unproductive split Richard Bernstein examined in the early eighties—that split between objectivism and relativism. Bernstein laid it out in his 1983 book, *Beyond Objectivism and Relativism*: "There is an uneasiness that has spread throughout intellectual and cultural life. It affects almost every discipline and every aspect of our lives. This uneasiness is expressed by the opposition between objectivism and relativism, but there are a variety of other contrasts that indicate the same underlying anxiety: rationality versus irrationality, objectivity versus subjectivity."[1]

Does this sound familiar?

He defined the problem in philosophy as focused on the problem of determining the nature and scope of human rationality.[2] I part company with him on this definition of the problem, since for me the problem is much more a question of determining how to think about how power structures what we take to be human rationality. But it does seem to me that he was right that many discussions, although they might not seem to be concerned with this dichotomy, in fact were still structured within the "traditional extremes," and this does have some relevance for feminist theory today—or for current discussions of the nature of science.

Debates in feminist theory seem to be reenacting some of the splits and questions he addressed. As he put it, "There is a movement from confidence to skepticism about foundations, methods, and rational criteria of evaluation.[3] He went on to state that the problem was not just intellectual but concerned questions about human beings, "what we are, what we can know, what norms ought to bind us, what are the grounds for hope." These concerns seem to me to bear close relation to some of the issues both in feminist theory and the ongoing "culture wars."

Objectivism has been reincarnated as essentialism, defined by Bernstein as "the conviction that there is or must be some permanent, ahistorical matrix or framework to which we can ultimately appeal . . . the search for an Archimedean point."[4] Relativism is reincarnated as an apolitical nihilism, or endless play. The relativist "accuses the objectivist" of "mistaking what is at best historically or culturally stable for the eternal and permanent."[5] Bernstein diagnosed these positions as unhelpful for philosophy, and I want to suggest that in feminist theory they lead to the construction of straw figures and, indeed, straw debates.

In the field of feminist theory today, often a hint of a "better" analysis, or what Harding has called "strong objectivity," or any claim to more accurate or more useful knowledge is dismissed as "positivism."[6] Indeed one hears that one must recognize that there are differing points of view.

I believe that the reception of standpoint theories has been in many ways symptomatic of the return of objectivism/relativism as the choices and the concomitant return of liberal humanism as that which feminism loves to hate. In particular, the contributions of Marxian theories and the epistemological and political possibilities to which they call attention have dropped from sight.[7] Here, then, I want to make several points: (1) The reception of standpoint theories has demonstrated that the only epistemology recognized as "out there" is a kind of liberal humanism, or something like Rorty's Epistemology with a capital E. That is, for many feminist theorists, as for Rorty, if there is no Epistemology, there is no epistemology that might act as a ground or provide criteria for evaluating knowledge claims. (2) This particular problem is rooted particularly in American culture, where individualism maintains such an important hold on public discourse, and where notions of collectivity or collective subjects are rarely present. Ideas about class are particularly obscured in public debates; most often references to working-class experience are coded as racial experience, especially as African American. In such a situation, identity politics both can seem like the only solution to the problem of collective action and can lead directly back to individualism, since ultimately the only one I can completely identify with is me. (3) There are important theoretical and political tools that can be drawn from the Marxist tradition. And here I offer two cautionary points: First, Marx stands in an ambivalent relationship to Enlightenment epistemologies and ideas. In this, of course, feminist theory shares a similar ambivalence. Second, Marxist theories have made little space for any form of domination other than class domination; thus one has to be careful about what can be appropriated and what is "fatally flawed."[8]

This Afterword is an effort to explore some of the theoretical bases and supports for coalition. In general, I want to suggest that political theory can be useful for politics and policy by helping to reveal possible new coalitions and alliances. This function is particularly important for groups that have been dominated and marginalized and consequently whose culture and vision of the world have been systematically made invisible, as we are forced to examine our experience through the eyes of other, more dominant, groups. The axes of domination are several, and most groups are privileged along some and disadvantaged along others. In any effort at coalition or alliance, close attention must be given to the specific situations of each group as defined by the axes of gender, race, class, and sexuality.

Feminist theory must locate itself in terms of both victimhood and complicity. Attention to the specifics of each group's situation must recognize the fact that the subordination of different groups is often obtained and maintained by different mechanisms. As a result of these differences, one must expect the feminisms of different groups to emphasize the political issues that are most salient in that particular social location: White feminists' efforts to bring the concerns of the private sphere into public life, Black feminists' emphasis on economic issues, Latina feminists' attention to issues of language and the family, all illustrate the ways in which certain issues become unavoidable for some groups while remaining less salient for others.

This sort of argument leads to an emphasis on difference and heterogeneity, a stress on the multiple possibilities for understanding the world, and the importance of multiple points of view. These emphases are shared with many postmodernist theories, and thus may have held that these theories were important resources for those who are thinking about theoretical bases for coalitions. In particular, postmodernist/poststructuralist theories' stress on dissonance, incommensurability, depthlessness, and the need to move to the margin has led some feminist theorists to find them attractive resources. I am, however, among those who are less sanguine about these theories. Postmodernist theories, I have held, represent the situated knowledges of a particular social group—Euro-American, masculine, and racially as well as economically privileged.[9] For me, far from being a resource for the development of new and more inclusive social movements, postmodernist theories represent and express the voices of the powerful.[10] These theories do, however, express the destabilized voices of the powerful being forced to come to terms with the voices of the disenfranchised. This may seem an odd claim, since the abandonment of the imperial certainties of the Enlightenment would seem to put postmodernism on the side of liberation struggles. Postmodernist theories should be understood as a situated knowledge that reveals itself as "the felt absence of the will or the ability to change things as they are . . . the voice of epistemological despair."[11]

But alternative understandings are possible, and feminist theory faces tasks that require moving to a new terrain, one not defined simply by the Enlightenment and the theoretical reaction against it. Feminist theory must be understood not only as analysis but also as an instrument of struggle against dominant groups and empowerment for the dominated.

The task facing all theorists committed to social change is that of working to construct some theoretical bases for political solidarity; such theoretical bases are no substitute for collective action and coalition building but a necessary adjunct to it. I will argue that there are other models of incommensurability and difference, especially those coming out of the experiences of marginalized and oppressed groups, that open possibilities for both resistance and transformation.

In this project, recent work by feminists of color and postcolonial subjects can be particularly important. Yes, it is work that insists on specifics of views from precise social locations; yes, it stresses the importance of attention to heterogeneity, dissonance, worldviews that differ from those taken for granted by the dominant culture. At the same time, it is work that insists on purposes other than play; it is work that has concerns for justice at its core; it is work that refuses to turn away from politics. I believe these theories can serve to remind feminist theorists who have turned away from these concerns that it is important to remember where we came from and why we began to work for the empowerment of women. The world has changed greatly since we all began, and the challenges have changed as well.

Feminist theory is at once entrenched and marginalized in academia. On the one hand, feminist theorists have been drawn into disciplinary and interdisciplinary debates. On the other, many academic disciplines operate in large part as though feminist work was nonexistent. The academic battles center on cultural studies, the science wars, and the status of interdisciplinary work. The political battles have also changed: Whereas many have long spoken about the globalization of capitalism, the reality of this globalization is becoming more and more unavoidable as factories migrate from higher-wage to lower-wage economies and use the threat of migration to control their workforces. The recent stock market turmoil that moved back and forth from the United States to Asia and to Europe provides another reminder of the interlocking of the global economy. The political battles have to do with the survival chances of poor women and their children whether in the face of welfare "reform" in the United States or of the expansion of Nike factories in Vietnam. We must learn to use what power we have gained to work on both fronts.

NOTES

1. Richard Bernstein, *Beyond Objectivism and Relativism* (Philadelphia: University of Pennsylvania Press, 1985), p. 1.

2. Ibid., p. 2.

3. Ibid., p. 3.

4. Ibid., p. 8.

5. Ibid., p. 9.

6. I can cite my experience at a quarter-long seminar on feminist epistemology at the University of California Humanities Research Institute during the fall of 1995. Two incidents stand out for me: (1) When Sandra Harding was our guest for a day she was accused of being a positivist; and (2) in more than one discussion, but no more clearly than when the topic was queer theory (a coincidence, I think), two of the seminar participants argued that one should do away with the idea of criteria of better or worse and simply recognize that these theories were just "different." All I could think of to say in response was that Newt (Gingrich) was not just different but that his worldview was definitely worse that that of others.

7. For example, the only one in my advanced graduate class this semester who had read Marx was a Yugoslavian student who had studied with the Praxis group. And I had a couple of auditors who came for those sessions, since there was no place else on campus, they said, where they could learn about Marx. In addition, few bookstores in my city carry any Marx texts.

8. See Jane Flax's introduction to *Disputed Subjects* (New York: Routledge, 1993), pp. 12–13, for her assessment of Marx.

9. Nancy C. M. Hartsock, "Postmodernism and Political Change: Issues for Feminist Theory," *Cultural Critique,* no 14 (Winter 1989–1990). The term "situated knowledge" is Donna Haraway's; see "Situated Knowledges," in *Simians, Cyborgs, and Women* (New York: Routledge, 1991).

10. I want to make a distinction between postmodernist theories and postmodernism as a cultural condition. I have found Jameson's argument about postmodernism as the cultural logic of late capitalism very interesting and fruitful. We do face an ever-increasing commodification of social life: The question is how to understand and cope with it. I suggest that the ways this is understood and acted upon differs profoundly with social location. Katie King suggested to me that the example of telecommuting was an interesting example of this. On the one hand, for professionals, it offers a way to combine work and family and to contribute to the improvement of the environment by not driving to work; on the other hand, for those less skilled, it becomes another form of piecework. See King, *Theory in Its Feminist Travels* (Bloomington: Indiana University Press, 1994).

11. Kumkum Sangari, "The Politics of the Possible," *Cultural Critique,* no 7 (Fall 1987), 161. She made a case similar to my own when she argued that the tenuousness of knowledge in the West was a symptom and critique of the contemporary social and economic situation in the West.

Index

Aggregation, 91–92
Alienation, 45–48, 53, 89–90, 141, 145, 152
    objectivity and, 81–82, 95–96
Althusser, Louis, 79, 82, 168–169, 203(n24)
    dualisms of, 135, 142–147, 158–159, 169
    political commitments of, 134, 159
    Works
        Essays in Self-Criticism, The, 137, 143,
            147, 148, 156, 159
        Lenin and Philosophy, 147
        For Marx, 145, 147
        Reading Capital, 147, 149
Anarchism, 60
Anderson, Perry, 134, 160
Anthropology, 173–174, 185
Anzaldúa, Gloria, 243, 244
Appropriation, 38–39, 88
    experience and, 38–39, 98–99
    knowledge and, 98–100, 154–155
Awareness, 98, 99

Bataille, Georges, 121–123
Bay, Christian, 21
Benton, Ted, 160
Bernstein, Richard, 249
Beyond Objectivism and Relativism
        (Bernstein), 249
Black movement, 59–60
Bourgeoisie, ideology of, 145–148, 151
Brewster, Kingman, 5
Brown, Wendy, 232
Buddhism, 173, 186–187(n5)
Bunch, Charlotte, 6, 9, 11, 19, 168

Capital, 77–78
    abstraction of, 196–197, 199
Capitalism
    change and, 124–125
    consumption and, 24, 89, 156–157
    estranged labor and, 45–48, 53, 89–90
    family and, 22–23
    global, 76
    labor legislation and, 26

totality and, 91–93
    See also Economics; Production; Wor
Capital (Marx), 6, 78, 90, 112, 144, 148,
    150–152, 197
Carroll, Berenice, 17, 20–21, 50
Change, concept of, 17–18
Chicago politics, 3–5
Chicago Women's Liberation Union, 5
Chicana identity, 237–238
China, work and, 49, 51
Chodorow, Nancy, 116–117
CIO. See Congress of Industrial
        Organizations
Civil rights movement, 2–3, 58–59
Class issues
    academia and, 2
    difference and, 65–66
    downward mobility, 65, 72(n19)
    elitism and, 33–34, 40–41
    feminist analysis of, 39–40
    humanism and, 148–151
    ideology and, 145–148, 151
    race and, 4
    as social relation, 92, 150–151
    theory and, 135, 136
    women's movement and, 10, 65–66
    See also Working class
Cliff, Michelle, 238, 242
Coalitions, 41, 250–252
Collective identity, 58, 79–80
Collectives, 1, 52–54, 61
Collective writing, 11
Colletti, Lucio, 85–86
Colonization, 207–211, 215
    Other as object, 208–209
    resistance and, 215, 216
Colonizer and the Colonized, The
        (Memmi), 207
Commodities, 108–109, 120
    exchange of women and, 179–182
Communism, 90, 103(n30)
Communist Manifesto, The (Marx and
        Engels), 76

254

Communist Party (CPUSA), 73
Compartmentalization, 26–27
Conceptualization, 96
Concrete-in-thought, 154–158
Congress of Industrial Organizations (CIO), 73
Consciousness, 79, 88, 120, 145
Consciousness raising (CR), 18–19, 35, 60, 63
Consumption, 24, 89, 156–157
Contradiction, 138–140, 150
Conversation. *See* Discourse
Cooperatives, 52–54
CPUSA. *See* Communist Party
CR. *See* Consciousness raising
Creativity, 48–49, 51, 67–70, 72(n23)
Culture
   as conversation, 212
   as creation of human mind, 174, 235–236
   feminism as, 33
   nature as, 234–235

Daley Machine, 3–4
Death, 121–124, 160, 178, 199
de Beauvior, Simone, 123, 129(n18), 208
Derrida, Jacques, 76, 79, 82
Detroit, 73
Dialectical materialism, 142–143, 149
Dialectics, 76, 93–94, 140, 147
Difference, 56, 251
   civil rights movement and, 58–59
   class and, 65–66
   creativity and, 67–70, 72(n23)
   denial of, 58–59, 62–63
   as domination, 59–62, 64–67
   as empirical phenomenon, 57
   empowerment and, 63–64
   institutionalization of, 69
   organizations and, 66–67
   separatism and, 57, 61
   as socially constructed, 58, 60
   specificity and, 57–58, 62–64, 70
   strategies, 69–70
   taboo and, 200
   theories of, 168
   value of, 66
   See also Power
Discipline and Punish (Foucault), 216
Discourse, 161, 212–214

Domination
   difference as, 59–62, 64–67
   logic of, 57–58
   overdetermination and, 139
   power as, 20–21, 25–26, 49–50
   in women's movement, 56–57
   See also Powe
Dualism, 106, 108–110, 135, 142–147, 158–159
   discourse and, 161
   exchange abstraction and, 172, 175, 178
   Marx's, 145–146
   masculinity and, 118–119, 176–178, 183
   self and, 97–98, 118–120
   thought and, 173–174
   See also under Althusser, Louis
DuBois, W.E.B., 27, 243

Ebert, Teresa, 76
Economic and Philosophic Manuscripts of 1844, The (Marx), 5, 68, 141, 234
Economics
   power and, 16–17
   racism and, 24–25
   women's role, 22–25
   See also Capitalism; Production; Work
Economism (economic determinism), 138, 140, 155, 162, 197
Elementary Structures of Kinship, The (Lévi-Strauss), 178
Elitism, 33–34, 40–41, 60–61
Empiricism, 156
Engels, Friedrich, 108, 113, 143, 192, 193, 232
Enlightenment, 76–77, 206–207, 211, 233–234
   as homogeneous, 214–215
Epistemological break, 140–144
   ideology and, 145–147, 149–150, 156
Epistemology, 7–8, 80
   Enlightenment, 211
   human activity and, 108, 222–223, 240
   material life and, 108
   standpoint and, 106–108, 110, 233, 237–238, 250
Equality, 26, 59, 109, 124, 219–221
   discourse and, 213–214
Equal Rights Amendment (ERA), 29
ERA. *See* Equal Rights Amendment
Essays in Self-Criticism, The (Althusser), 137, 143, 147, 148, 156, 159
Essentialism, 142, 149, 231, 233, 235

Estrangement. *See* Alienation
Exchange, 108–110, 120, 126
    dualism and, 172, 175, 178
    production and, 110, 196–198
Exchange of women
    as artificial link, 178–179, 200
    commodities and, 179–182
    community and, 181–183, 201
    enmity and, 181–182
    incest taboo and, 179–181
    mediation and, 180–181, 188(n25)
    polygamy and, 179–180, 182
    use vs. exchange, 180–181
    See also Kinship system
Experience, 36–37, 241
    appropriation and, 38–39, 98–99

Family, capitalism and, 22–23
Female Man, The (Russ), 49
Feminism, 35–37, 75
    as culture, 33
Feminist theory, 4–5
    academia and, 167–168
    activism and, 7, 168–169
    audience for, 168
    class, analysis of, 39–40
    lesbian feminism and, 6, 10, 33–35, 65
    splits in, 249–250
    See also Process; Socialist feminism;
        Standpoint theory; Women's
        movement; individual theories
Ferguson, Kathy, 231–232
Flax, Jane, 1, 116, 230, 232
For Marx (Althusser), 145, 147
Foucault, Michel, 77, 78–79, 82, 160, 169, 170
    activism of, 215–216
    as colonizer, 216, 218
    modernity, opposition to, 215–216
    perspective of, 217–219
    power, view of, 219–221
    resistance and refusal in, 215–217, 218
Fraser, Nancy, 216, 230
French, Marilyn, 114
French Communist Party (PCF), 159
Freud, Sigmund, 118, 192, 193
Friedan, Betty, 24
Fuentes, Carol, 241
Furies, 6, 10, 65–67

Galeano, Eduard, 242
Garcia Marquez, Gabriel, 243

Gender, production of, 198–201
German Ideology (Marx), 6, 141, 142, 152
Gift, The (Mauss), 126
Gouldner, Alvin, 130(n34)
Gramsci, Antonio, 39, 79, 80, 104(n66),
        221–222, 240
Grundrisse (Marx), 144

Haraway, Donna, 75, 81–82, 234–235, 236
Harding, Sandra, 81, 227, 233, 250
Hartman, Heidi, 74
Harvey, David, 76, 81–82, 234
Hegel, Georg Wilhelm Friedrich, 118, 120,
        138, 140, 142, 153, 156
Hekman, Susan, 78, 79, 231
Hermeneutics, 211–212
Heterosexism, 34, 61
Hindess, Barry, 159, 161
Hirst, Paul, 159, 161
Historical and Dialectical Materialism
        (Stalin), 6, 73–74, 143
Historical context, 1
    human activity and, 88–89
    of humanism, 149–150
    of Marxism, 75–76
    mythic thought and, 176–177, 184, 199
    process and, 92–93
    of self, 36–37, 88–89
    standpoint theory and, 97–98, 124, 236
Historical materialism, 142–143, 149–150,
        156, 160
History and Class Consciousness (Lukacs),
        81, 228, 236
Hobbes, Thomas, 17, 25, 182
Homosocial birth images, 75–76
hooks, bell, 66, 213–214, 229, 237
Housework, 46, 124
    See also Work
Human activity
    abstraction of, 194, 199
    culture as creation of, 174, 235–236
    epistemology and, 108, 222–223, 240
    exchange and, 179
    history and, 88–89
    as ontology, 87–90, 97, 151
    as reality, 92, 108, 111
    as social, 88–89, 108
    work as, 47–48, 87–88
Humanism
    class basis of, 148–151
    empiricism of, 149

historicism and, 149–150
human essence and, 148–150
opposition to, 141–142
See also Theoretical antihumanism
Human mind, 173–174, 176, 187(n16), 195,
     235–236

Idealism, 160–161
Identity. *See* Self
Identity politics, 250
Ideology, 9–10
   of bourgeoisie, 145–148, 151
   epistemological break and, 145–147,
      149–150, 156
   science and, 144–148, 150–151, 158–159
   self and, 25–28
   unconsciousness of, 145
Imperialism, 34
Incest taboo, 179–181
Institute for Policy Studies (IPS), 6,
     11
Internals, 98–99
In the Tracks of Historical Materialism
     (Anderson), 134
IPS. *See* Institute for Policy Studies
Isomorphism, 173, 189(n52)

Jameson, Frederic, 75–76, 238, 239–241, 245,
     253(n10)
Johns Hopkins University, 13
Jouvenel, Bertrand de, 17

Kaplan, Abraham, 18
Kardiner, A., 21
King, Katie, 253(n10)
King, Martin Luther, 3
Kinship systems
   abstract masculinity and, 172, 201–202
   dualism and, 172–175, 178
   human mind and, 174, 176, 195, 235–236
   language and, 174–175
   myth and, 176–178
   otherness and, 180–181
   as productive forces, 193–196
   property and, 200–201
   social character of, 193, 198, 200
   as symbol system, 193, 198–200
   taboo and, 179–181, 200
   women as symbols in, 180, 189(n40),
      190–191(n63), 195
   See also Exchange of women

Knowledge
   appropriation and, 98–100, 154–155
   as discovery of externals, 86–87
   Marx's view of, 77, 80
   multiplicity and, 243–245
   object and, 153–155, 158
   as possible, 222, 240
   power and, 77–78
   privileged, 80
   as production, 152–159
   self-knowledge, 79, 86–87, 90, 99
   See also Theoretical practice; Theory
Kolakowski, Leszek, 139
Kollias, Karen, 9–10
Kuhn, Thomas, 212

Language, 96–97, 160–161, 174–175
   myth and, 176–178
Language of Social Research, The, 18
Lasswell, Harold, 18
Last instance, 137–138, 162
   contradiction and, 138–140
   epistemological break and, 140–144
   ideology and, 146
Lauretis, Teresa de, 134, 230, 232–233, 236
Lévi-Strauss, Claude, 169, 193
   as amorphous, 171–172
   dualisms of, 172, 175–176
   idealism and, 175–176
   isomorphism and, 173, 189(n52)
   Marxism and, 184–186
   mythic thought and, 176–178, 184, 199
   positivism of, 185–186
   Works
      Elementary Structures of Kinship,
         The, 178
      Tristes Tropiques, 177
Leadership, 20–22, 52, 60–61, 131(n40)
League of Revolutionary Black Workers, 73
Left, male, 20, 22, 32
   leadership and, 60–61
   Old Left, 73
   process and, 33, 41
LeGuin, Ursula, 57–58
Lenin, 138, 143, 156
Lenin and Philosophy (Althusser), 147
Lesbian Caucus, 33
Lesbian feminism, 6, 10, 33–35, 65
Linguistics, 185
   anthropology and, 173–174
   myth and, 176–178

Lorde, Audre, 67
Lukacs, George, 20, 35, 81–82, 91–92, 97,
     102(n17), 228, 236
Luxemburg, Rosa, 40
Lyotard, Jean-François, 206

Male supremacy, 17
Marx, Karl, 26
  on appropriation, 99
  on capital, 77–78
  on communism, 103(n30)
  dualism and, 145–146
  epistemological break and, 140–144
  estranged labor and, 46–48, 76
  humanity, view of, 55(n19), 67–68, 87,
     127(n5)
  knowledge, view of, 77, 80
  on mediation, 93–94
  money, view of, 16–17, 50
  nature, view of, 88, 127(n6), 151, 234–235
  on private property, 101
  on process, 76
  on thought, 154–155
  on work, 47–48
  Works
    Capital, 6, 78, 90, 112, 144, 148,
       150–152, 197
    Economic and Philosophic
       Manuscripts of 1844, The, 5, 68,
       141, 234
    German Ideology, 6, 141, 142, 152
    Grundrisse, 144
    "Theses on Feuerbach," 77, 142, 149
Marxism, 4–5
  categories, 77–78, 144, 169, 198
  defeats of, 134
  historical context of, 75–76
  Lévi-Strauss and, 184–186
  methodology of, 73, 75, 106, 184–185
  as revolutionary science, 87, 135, 136,
     147, 212–214
  simplification of, 138
  theory, role of in, 136
  two-class formula, 34, 228–230, 232,
     239
Masculinity, abstract
  death and, 121–124, 178
  discontinuity and, 121–123
  dualism and, 118–119, 176–178, 183
  kinship theory and, 172, 201–202
  self and, 118–120

  sexual division of labor and, 117–118
  Western social relations and, 119
Materialism and Empirio-Criticism (Lenin),
     143
Material life, 107–108, 229
  objectivity and, 95–96
  See also Class
Mauss, Marcel, 126, 201
Mediation, 93–94, 101, 157
  exchange of women and, 180–181,
     188(n25)
  objectivity as, 97–98
  standpoint and, 110
Memmi, Albert, 207–209, 215
Methodology, 19, 35–36
  class distinctions and, 39–40
  dialectics, 76
  Marxist, 73, 75, 106, 184–185
  of revolution, 90
Mikva, Abner, 3
Mill, J. S., 207
Mitchell, Juliet, 29
Mode of life, 39–40, 88
Monetary system, 16–17, 50
Money, Sex, and Power (Hartsock), 235
Montesquieu, 207
Motherhood, 115–116, 131(n37)
Moya, Paula, 237–238
Multiplicity, 7, 222, 232–233, 239–240
  knowledge and, 243–245
Myth, 176–178, 184, 199

Nationalism, 210
National Lawyer's Guild, 73
National Opinion Research Center, 4
National Organization for Women (NOW),
     12, 59
Nature, 81, 151
  as culture, 234–235
  human mind and, 174, 187(n16),
     235–236
  Marx's view of, 88, 127(n6), 151,
     234–235
  as metaphor, 177–178
  order and, 174, 178
  sexual division of labor and, 113–114, 119
Nicholson, Linda, 230
Nin, Anais, 26
"Notes on Speechlessness" (Cliff), 238
NOW. See National Organization for
     Women

Object, 89, 95, 150–151
  knowledge production and, 153–155, 158
  Other as, 208–209
  theoretical practice and, 153–155
Objectivism, 249–250
Objectivity, 81, 206
  alienation and, 81–82, 95–96
  detachment and, 86
  as existence of material world, 95–96
  as involvement, 96–97
  as mediation, 97–98
  objectification and, 95
  revolution and, 100–101
  social science and, 85–87
Object relations theory, 116
Obligation, 4, 16
Oedipal crisis, 116–117, 199, 200
Off Our Backs, 11
Old Left, 73
Olivia Records, 52
Ollman, Bertell, 76, 83(n16)
Ontology, human activity as, 87–90, 97, 151
Oppositional consciousness, 79
Organizations, 20–22, 28
  difference and, 66–67
  as models for society, 69–70
  public vs. private, 37–38
  strategies, 40–41
  structureless, 60, 62
  work and, 49–51
  See also Consciousness raising
Orient, 209
Origins of Family, Private Property, and the
  State (Engels), 232
Otherness, 58–59
  colonization and, 207–211
  Enlightenment and, 207
  exchange of women and, 180–181
  power and, 213
  See also Difference
Overdetermination, 137–140, 150

Parsons, Talcott, 16
Patriarchy. *See* Capitalism; Masculinity,
  abstract
Paz, Octavio, 188(nn 37, 39)
PCF. *See* French Communist Party
Philosophy
  as edification, 212–213
  as reactive, 213–214
  science vs., 142–143, 159

Piercy, Marge, 49
Plato, 119
Plekanov, Georgy Valentinovich, 143
Political change
  change, concept of, 17–18
  power and, 15–17, 49–51
  self and, 18–19, 28, 36–37
  social science and, 16–18
  standpoint theory and, 240–241
  See also Organizations; Power
Political practice, 153, 159–160
Politics
  poststructuralism and, 134–135
  science vs., 143–144
  theory vs., 135–136
Politics, Ideology, and Ordinary Language:
  The Political Thought of Black
  Community Leaders (Hartsock), 4
Pornography, 122
Positivism, 185–186, 250
Possession, 16–17, 25, 50, 99
Postmodernism, 253(n10)
Poststructuralism, 78, 137, 169–170
  politics and, 134–135
Power, 7
  capillary, 220
  collective work and, 52–53
  as domination, 20–21, 25–26,
    49–50
  economy and, 16–17
  as empowerment, 63–64, 67
  equality and, 219–221
  knowledge and, 77–78
  leadership and, 20–22
  macroprocesses of, 78–79
  otherness and, 213
  perspective and, 216–218
  political change and, 15–17,
    49–51
  as possession, 16–17, 25, 50, 99
  resistance to, 215–218
  responsibility and, 52
  standpoint and, 110
  work and, 49–54
  See also Difference; Domination
Power and Society (Lasswell and Kaplan),
  18
Practice, theory and, 33–34, 38–39, 137,
  158
Pragmaticism, 161
Praxis, 87–88, 102(n10), 184, 191(n68)

Process, 33, 37–38, 41, 60
  historical context of, 92–93
  Marx's view of, 76
  self and, 79, 92
Production
  of consciousness, 88, 120
  consumption and, 156–157
  contradiction and, 138–139
  exchange and, 110, 196–198
  of gender, 198–201
  kinship systems as form of, 193–196
  knowledge as, 152–159
  point of, 73–74
  standpoint of, 97–98, 101, 109–111
  surplus value and, 103(n32), 109–110,
      128–129(n15), 196–198
  theory as, 153–154
Property, 90, 98–99, 101
  kinship system and, 200–201
Psychoanalytic theory, 116–118,
      193

Quest: A Feminist Quarterly, 6, 9–12, 53

Racism, 2, 4
  dismissal of, 66, 213–214
  economics and, 24–25
  imperialism vs., 34
  strategies for, 64–65
Radical Lesbians, 6
Reading Capital (Althusser), 147,
      149
Reagon, Bernice, 210
Reality, 36, 77–78
  concrete-reality, 154–156
  dual levels of, 106, 108, 228, 232
  human activity as, 92, 108, 111
Reductionism, 149, 156, 158, 160
"Reification and the Standpoint of
      the Proletariat" (Lukacs), 81, 228
Relativism, 160–161, 249–250
Reproduction, 115–116, 122–123
Responsibility, 52
Rethinking Marxism, 82, 169
Revolution
  method and, 90
  objectivity and, 100–101
  science and, 87, 147, 212–214
Rich, Adrienne, 64, 116, 120
Robinson, Cedric, 242
Rorty, Richard, 170, 207, 211–215, 221, 250

Rubin, Gayle, 169–170
  view of surplus value, 196–198
  See also Kinship systems
Ruddick, Sara, 112
Russ, Joanna, 49
Russell, Bertrand, 16

Said, Edward, 209, 217–218
Sandoval, Chela, 79, 80
Sangari, Kumkum, 243
Science
  historical context of, 93
  ideology and, 144–148, 150–151,
      158–159
  immediacy and, 98
  Marxism as, 87, 147, 212–214
  normal vs. revolutionary, 212–214
  philosophy vs., 142–143, 159
  as self-contained, 155–156, 160
  truth and, 146, 147
  See also Methodology; Theoretical
      practice
SCLS. See Southern Christian Leadership
      Conference
Second Sex (de Beauvoir), 208
Self, 19–20
  collective identity, 58, 79–80
  compartmentalization and, 26–27
  dualism and, 97–98, 118–120
  female, 120
  historic context of, 36–37, 88–89
  ideology and, 25–28
  knowledge and, 86–87, 90, 99
  masculine, 118–120
  as oppositional, 118, 120
  organizations and, 20–22
  political change and, 18–19, 28, 36–37
  process and, 79, 92
  society and, 36–37, 47, 79, 88
  work and, 47–48
Separatism, 57, 59, 61–63, 69
Sexual division of labor, 111–113, 183,
      202
  change and, 114, 120
  death vs. life and, 121–124
  dualism and, 118–120
  individuation and, 116–117
  masculinity and, 117–118
  nature and, 113–114, 119
  reproduction and, 115–116, 122–123
  socialization and, 117

subsistence activity and, 113–115,
128(n14)
See also Work
Socialist feminism, 12
patriarchal socialism, influence on,
33–35, 37–38
tokenism and, 34–35
Socialist Feminist Conference, 12,
32
Socialization, 117
Social relations
autonomous spheres of, 153, 155–156
class and, 92, 150–151
masculinity and, 119
self and, 36–37, 47, 79, 88
theoretical antihumanism and, 150–151
theoretical practice and,
157–158
Social science
objectivity and, 85–87
political change, view of,
16–18
Southern Christian Leadership Conference
(SCLS), 3
Soviet Union, 139
Specificity
difference and, 57–58, 62–64, 70
standpoint and, 239–240
Stalin, Joseph, 6, 73–74, 143, 194
Standpoint theory
biological destiny and, 230–231, 233–234
change and, 110–111, 124–125
definitions, 107–108, 236
epistemology and, 106–108, 110, 233,
237–238
historical patterns and, 97–98, 124, 236
interpretation and, 231–232, 235–237
inversion and, 241–243
materialism of, 172
multiplicity and, 232–233, 239–240
political action and, 240–241
of production, 97–98, 101, 109–111, 228
specificity and, 239–240
subaltern groups and, 82, 241
subjectivity and, 79–80, 240
two-class formula and, 228–230, 232,
239
women's viewpoint and, 235–236, 238
Strategies, 9–10, 28–29
difference and, 69–70
organizations and, 40–41

racism and, 64–66
reformist, 58–59
Structuralism, 135, 160, 169, 184
Subjectivity, 78–79, 160, 178
death of, 160, 178, 199
eccentric, 232–233
Enlightenment and, 208
experience and, 98
individuality vs., 219–221
standpoint theory and, 79–80, 240
subversion of, 169
transcendence and, 208, 213–214
Subsistence, 113–115, 128(n14)
Surplus value, 103(n32), 109–110,
128–129(n15), 196–198
Symbol systems, 173
as location of women's oppression, 193,
198–201
See also Kinship systems

Theoretical antihumanism, 79, 141
See also Humanism
Theoretical practice, 152–153
concrete-in-thought vs. concrete reality,
154–158
consumption and, 156–157
generalities and, 153–154, 157
object and, 153–155
reductionism and, 149, 156, 158, 160
social relations and, 157–158
validity and, 155–156
See also Knowledge; Science; Theory
Theory
as aspect of class struggle, 135, 136
politics and, 135–136
practice and, 33–34, 38–39, 137, 158
as production, 153–154
See also Knowledge; Theoretical practice;
individual theories
"Theses on Feuerbach" (Marx), 77, 142, 149
Third World women, 34–35, 60
This Bridge Called My Back, 67
Thought
dualism and, 173–174
Marx on, 154–155
mythic, 176–178, 184, 199
Totality, 91–93, 146, 156–157
contradiction and, 138, 140
"Traffic in Women, Notes on the 'Political
Economy' of Sex, The" (Rubin),
192, 202

Transcendence, 208, 213–214
Tristes Tropiques (Lévi-Strauss), 177
Truth, 76–78, 235–236
    hermeneutic approach to, 211–212
    objectivity and, 86
    science and, 146, 147

"Unhappy Marriage of Marxism and
        Feminism, The" (Hartman), 74
Universalism, 206
University of Chicago, 3
University of Michigan, 5
Use-values, 113–114

Values, 86, 96
Vanguard party, 40

Washington, D.C., 6–7
Washington Statehood Party, 10
Webster's Third International Dictionary,
        18, 20–21, 50
Weeks, Kathi, 80
Wellesley Civil Rights group, 2–3
Wellesley College, 2–3
West, Cornel, 134
White supremacy, 24–25
WITCH. *See* Women's International
        Conspiracy from Hell
Woman on the Edge of Time (Piercy), 49, 69
Women of color. *See* Third World women
Women's International Conspiracy from
        Hell (WITCH), 5
Women's Liberation Movement,
        59

Women's movement
    consciousness raising, 18–19, 35, 60, 63
    socialist feminism and, 33
Women's Radical Action Project, 5
Women's Room, The (French), 114
Women's Union of Baltimore, 12
Work
    alternatives to estrangement, 48–49,
        51–52
    Chinese restructuring of, 49, 51
    collectives and cooperatives, 52–54
    creative, 48–49, 51
    definitions, 45
    as estranged labor, 45–48, 53,
        89–90
    feminist organizations and, 49–51
    housework, 46, 124
    as human activity, 47–48, 87–88
    leisure time and, 46
    mental vs. manual, 51, 61, 93–94, 112, 120
    point of production, 73–74
    power relations and, 49–54
    reification and, 82
    skills development, 53
    wages, 24–25
    See also Capitalism; Housework; Sexual
        division of labor
Working class
    standpoint of, 97–98, 101, 109–111, 228
    women's movement and, 65–66
    See also Class issues

Yale University, 5
Young, Iris, 106, 231

152

Charlotte Bunch
170
Susan Griffin
Pé nature